I0605703

WES ANDERSON

A RETROSPECTIVE

Published in 2025
by Gemini Gift Books
Part of Gemini Books Group

Based in Woodbridge and London

Marine House, Tide Mill Way,
Woodbridge, Suffolk IP12 1AP
United Kingdom

www.geminibooks.com

ISBN 978-1-78675-176-8

A CIP catalogue record for this book is available from the British Library.

Manufacturer's EU Representative: Eurolink Compliance Limited, 25 Herbert Place, Dublin, D02 AY86, Republic of Ireland. admin@eurolink-europe.ie

Printed in China

10 9 8 7 6 5 4 3 2 1

WES ANDERSON

A RETROSPECTIVE

CLARISSE LOUGHREY

CONTENTS

PROLOGUE

Wes Anderson is looking for home. His movies are each a perfect diorama, a collector's shelf of trinkets accumulated over a lifetime of travel, through places, music, movies, books and other people's lives. Everyone knows their markers: the fussy symmetry, the stilted manner of speech, wardrobes and possessions that seem to exist out of time. Every frame is immaculate, every emotion measured.

Yet, cut into one of Anderson's pristine stories, and out bleeds loss and confusion. Family in *The Royal Tenenbaums* and *Moonrise Kingdom* is a useless, broken term. Fascism and decay have descended on *The Grand Budapest Hotel* and *Isle of Dogs*. Grief in *The Darjeeling Limited* and *Asteroid City* is so hard to bear that it leaves the afflicted wondering at the very meaning of existence. A Wes Anderson movie is always bittersweet. To live in his world is to yearn for something more.

Anderson had what he'd describe as a relatively ordinary childhood. But he was deeply pained by the divorce of his parents at the age of eight.[1] And he felt, inexplicably, at odds with the universe. "I don't think I allowed myself to feel, or to acknowledge, how much I felt like I didn't fit in," he's said. "I think I had probably too much embarrassment about not fitting in to even let it be known to myself that this was the case."[2]

He'd never experienced much beyond his arid hometown of Houston, Texas,[3] so adulthood brought with it an intense curiosity. He's made movies set in France, India, Britain, Central Europe and the open seas. At first, he wanted to be a writer. He also wanted to be an architect.[4] His work sits somewhere in the middle, a cortège of beautiful words presented beneath a sturdy, finely trimmed portico.

The director is, as they always say, a true original. Director James L. Brooks, who produced his debut, *Bottle Rocket* (1996), once declared him in

Wes Anderson steers the Deep Search submarine, formerly the Jacqueline, on the set of *The Life Aquatic with Steve Zissou*. His filmography is one filled with adventures from all across the globe: Central Europe, France, India, Japan.

"possession of a real voice" – to him that was "always a marvel, an almost religious thing".[5] Brooks's early support meant *Bottle Rocket* was made under Columbia Pictures, and Anderson has since worked exclusively within the Hollywood mainstream.

Yet, his unwavering allegiance to his authorial voice, despite all the financial pressures of the modern industry, has had a distinct impact on the independent scene. Without Anderson, it's hard to believe the market for neatly framed comedies about eccentric, soul-sick protagonists, like Miranda July's *Me and You and Everyone We Know* or Taika Waititi's *Hunt for the Wilderpeople*, would have flourished as it did. He's become a shining beacon for the soulful writer-director, guiding tender, creative hands towards the distinct and self-determined. He's one of Hollywood's last auteur powerhouses and a rare household name.

There exists, now, such a thing as the Andersonian. It's seeped into fashion and interior design, via candy colours and monogrammed leather suitcases, and was parodied by a 2013 *Saturday Night Live* sketch, a horror homage titled, "The Midnight Coterie of Sinister Intruders".

At its most hollow, the Andersonian has been reduced to a marketable trend: the Instagram account "Accidentally Wes Anderson", in which users upload pleasantly symmetrical photographs from around the world, and, in a grotesque turn, AI recreations of popular movies such as *Star Wars* and *The Shining*, retooled in the director's style. In 2012, Slate released their "Wes Anderson Bingo", which allowed players to cross off his most famous trademarks, from "a slow-mo shot set to music" to a beret or a precocious child.

But the Andersonian is far more than mere aesthetic. He's an individual artist, but also the proud and conscientious student of vast cinematic, literary and cultural canons. Each story of his is really a bundle of ideas, influences crossed with influences, mixed in with incidents and characters from his own life.

The French Dispatch is both a tribute to his lifelong admiration of *The New Yorker* magazine and a document of his experiences as an expat in Paris, where he now lives part-time. *The Grand Budapest Hotel* is both a spiritual adaptation of the works of Viennese author Stefan Zweig and a character study of an old friend. He's deeply indebted to his directorial predecessors, among them Jean Renoir, Louis Malle, Federico Fellini, Akira Kurosawa, Satyajit Ray, Mike Nichols, Michael Powell and Emeric Pressburger.

His movies, too, represent the cumulative efforts of an entire nation of close collaborators. He's famous for his actors, who rotate roles like a Swiss cuckoo clock: Bill Murray, Owen Wilson, Jason Schwartzman, Angelica Huston, Willem Dafoe, Jeff Goldblum, Tilda Swinton and so on. Yet, those behind the camera remain just as familiar: co-writers Wilson, Schwartzman, Roman Coppola and Noah Baumbach; cinematographer Robert Yeoman; composers Mark Mothersbaugh and Alexandre Desplat; music supervisor Randall Poster; production designers Mark Friedberg and Adam Stockhausen; and costume designer Milena Canonero.

His sets are often compared to summer camps. There are no trailers for actors to burrow into, and rarely more than a handful of crew present at one time. Everyone sleeps and eats under the same roof. Anderson may have gathered seasoned legends like Gene Hackman and Tom Hanks, right alongside green recruits like *The Grand Budapest*'s Tony Revolori and *Moonrise*

ABOVE Wes Anderson, in bright yellow socks, perches on a camera dolly on the set of *Moonrise Kingdom*.
OPPOSITE (ABOVE) Anderson has a tête-à-tête with Bill Murray and Cate Blanchett, his *The Life Aquatic with Steve Zissou* stars.
OPPOSITE (BELOW) Jeff Goldblum, Anderson and a large, very dead bear on the set of *The Grand Budapest Hotel*.
NEXT SPREAD The director poses for the paparazzi at the 80th Venice International Film Festival in 2023, where he premiered his short *The Wonderful Story of Henry Sugar*.

Kingdom's Kara Hayward and Jared Gilman, but all of them learned to speak the same language, to live in what Angelica Huston has termed "Wes world".[6]

It's not a place everyone is so inclined to inhabit. For all the acclaim, Anderson may never quite shake his detractors, who rail against his preciousness as proof of emotional detachment, and claim his characters have no more life to them than puppets on a string. There's little he can do about that. But, to his admirers, the director's work has become a comfort and a refuge. "You know, the people who I meet who are the real die-hard fans of my movies, they're always kind of outsiders," the director has said. His work is full of them, too. Anxious souls fret over their place in the world.

Anderson makes fables, which rarely communicate directly with our modern world, but he is by no means an apolitical filmmaker. In the past, he's aligned his work with the elaborate analogy behind Frank Herbert's sci-fi epic *Dune*, "where the politics have been created for the story. It can deepen the fantasy of the movie if there are political layers to the society that you've invented."[7]

His characters seek the same control over their lives that Anderson commandeers over his frames, their inhabitants so intentionally and elegantly positioned that you're never unaware of the director's godlike touch. He shoots many takes, and rarely allows for improvisation – or, indeed, any deviation from his carefully chosen words. "On some level a director has to be a good general," Willem Dafoe said. "And he's a beautiful general. The troops love him and he's clear about what he has to do."

A turning point in the director's career arrived when he began to use animatics, storyboards cut to an audio track, as part of his first animated movie, *Fantastic Mr. Fox* (2009). All of a sudden, he could create a rough but complete rendition of his vision, every shot pre-determined before the cameras ever rolled. Every movie since has become, inch by inch, a fuller celebration of its own craft.

But even within all that control, exercised by both the director and his onscreen heroes, unruly emotion has a way of breaking through. It's here that an Anderson movie blooms into its fullest expression: when Steve Zissou, the washed-up oceanographer, finally confronts the marine creature that killed his best friend, and begins to cry; or when Richie Tenenbaum, the dejected son of a family of former prodigies, all trapped in arrested development, shaves off his hair and attempts suicide.

An Anderson character does everything in their power to keep up the facade, but it always proves impossible. Ultimately, all they can do is admit to themselves that they are deeply human and hopelessly lost. Home is out there, but it takes a lifetime's work to find it.

Wes Anderson attends a red-carpet event at the 2023 Venice International Film Festival for *The Wonderful Story of Henry Sugar*.

KHAKI SCOUTS
NORTH AMERICA

Schlotzsky's
Schlotzsky's

I
BANDE À PART

On *Bottle Rocket*

Wes Anderson's brothers were his first movie stars. Born in Houston, Texas, on 1 May 1969, Wesley Wales was one of three boys – the middle son, which psychoanalytical theory would suggest is destined to be left adrift. Mel Jr, the eldest Anderson, would become a physician, while Eric grew up to be an author and illustrator whose cartographic creations pepper both Wes's movies and their promotional materials.

Anderson developed an early interest in film, nurtured by regular trips to his local repertory cinema and by a series of Betamax tapes his family owned of Alfred Hitchcock's work.[8] The latter was a revelation. He'd never before seen a director's name blown up in a font so large.

Around the age of nine, Anderson decided to adapt a book he'd found in the library,[9] titled *The Skateboard Four*. It concerned a boy named Morgan, whose supremacy as the leader of his clique is threatened by the arrival of new blood. Mel and Eric starred. His father loaned him a Super 8 camera under contract, though he never asked for it back.[10]

The Skateboard Four was the first of Anderson's litany of social clubs and hierarchical organizations, in which men (and occasionally women) determine their self-worth through illusionary pecking orders. In Anderson's debut, *Bottle Rocket* (1996), Dignan (Owen Wilson) runs his gaggle of thieves like a well-intentioned cult.

He breaks his friend Anthony (Luke Wilson) out of a psychiatric hospital, unaware he was there on a voluntary basis, and immediately presents him with a 75-year plan for both their futures. They'll start with a practice heist, followed by a real one, before seeking mentorship under full-time landscaper and part-time ne'er-do-well Mr Henry (James Caan).

Dignan's idea of camaraderie has been siphoned entirely from the movies and comic books of his youth – stories about outlaws, mobsters and adventurers, men who act but rarely talk. *Bottle Rocket* itself came from

Dignan (Owen Wilson) and his crew, Anthony (Luke Wilson) and Bob (Robert Musgrave), in *Bottle Rocket* – the first of Wes Anderson's many, many clubs.

these sources, yet was born out of a diametrically opposite friendship, in which two men began to talk and never really stopped.

In 1987, Anderson enrolled at the University of Texas, Austin, to study philosophy.[11] He opted for a playwriting class, populated almost entirely by loud people with nothing much to say. So he sat, silent, in one corner. In another, equally reticent, was a guy with sharp baby blues and a crooked nose, usually buried behind a copy of *The New York Times*.[12] "I always thought, 'Who does this guy think he is, this anti-social guy sitting in the corner?'" Anderson said. "But I was doing the exact same thing."[13]

At the beginning of the next semester, Anderson was suddenly compelled to approach him, and ask what creative writing courses he should take. The young man introduced himself as Owen Wilson and the pair bonded almost immediately. Both were the middle of three sons, possessed the same sense of humour, and loved the same movies, by Terrence Malick, Robert Altman and Sam Peckinpah.

Eventually, they became roommates. Anderson and Wilson shared a flat with broken window cranks, meaning that several of their windows were stuck permanently half-open. No matter how desperately they implored their landlord, nothing was done. So, the friends came up with what they believed was an ingenious scheme: they'd fake a break-in and, when the cops arrived, blame the windows for their misfortune. The landlord took one look at the crime scene and declared it an inside job. Hostilities continued. At one point, Anderson and the landlord ended up locked in a violent struggle over a vintage 8 mm camera, set to be confiscated until they paid the rent they'd withheld.

A resolution was reached only when Anderson proposed he make a documentary about his adversary in order to settle his and Wilson's debts. The man was a German immigrant, who'd arrived via Colombia. He told a story about when he took in an abandoned python, discovered after an old tenant had hightailed and fled. He grew to love the snake, only for it to die in his arms. But the landlord didn't much like Anderson's documentary. "I don't think he was mad," the director reflected. "He just didn't think it was going to be helpful to him."[14]

Yet, the staged break-in sparked a grander, loftier idea. Anderson and Wilson would make a movie about the whole affair. At first, all they did was talk. They'd tell each other stories, about themselves or other people, and scribble ideas down onto scraps of paper. Anderson and Wilson dreamed of following in Francis Ford Coppola or Martin Scorsese's footsteps, to make a gritty crime saga with a James Dean-esque protagonist.[15] Maybe someone would get shot and die. But they weren't those kind of men, and they couldn't really tell that kind of story. Eventually, it grew less serious, a little stranger and sweeter instead.

In the meantime, they relocated to Dallas, so that Anderson could work for Wilson's older brother, Andrew, who produced corporate videos.[16] A coffee shop named Cosmic Cup became their new go-to spot to talk and write.[17] The men had become friendly with its owner, Dipak Pallana, and

They're not really criminals,
but everybody's got to have a dream.

BOTTLE ROCKET

ABOVE The theatrical poster for *Bottle Rocket*.
RIGHT Luke Wilson, who had something of a movie star look about him, plays Anthony, the romantic. Owen Wilson, meanwhile, stars as Dignan, the idealist.

The Bottle Rocket short is somewhat alien to the filmmaker Anderson would soon become.

his ex-Vegas showman father, Kumar. They were funny guys, who not only ended up in *Bottle Rocket*, but helped shape its sensibility. Dipak turns up as the unfazed bookstore employee targeted by Anthony and Dignan in their first "real" heist, while Kumar stars as the crew's designated safecracker, who botches his single responsibility.

Wilson first met Robert Musgrave at the Stoneleigh P bar, a haven for anti-establishment types. A West Virginia native, he'd drifted between passions – stand-up comedy, then blues – but couldn't make anything stick. The two played pool, which left Musgrave $40 poorer.[18] So, Wilson suggested he try out for a role.

They met him out in a parking lot,[19] and Musgrave fumbled all his lines. A friend of Wilson and Anderson's, who happened to be there, volunteered to step in and try out the scene while Musgrave watched. Anderson would later admit this may have been a little cruel. Yet, the psychological ploy worked: Musgrave begged for a second chance, triumphed, and made for such a natural getaway driver that they eventually renamed his character Bob, in his honour.

Anderson, while working for Andrew, had met a handful of industry types who were willing to invest in their movie. Wilson would play Dignan, the idealist, while his younger brother, Luke, who had something of a movie star look about him, would play Anthony, the romantic. And in May 1992, on a $4,000 budget, Anderson shot the first eight minutes of *Bottle Rocket*.

The Wilson patriarch had once been president of Dallas's public television station and had made the acquaintance of writer-director L. M. "Kit" Carson, who'd helped finesse Sam Shepard's script for Wim Wenders's 1984 road movie, *Paris, Texas*. Carson had been invited over to dinner with an eye to talking the Wilson boys out of a career in film. Evidently, he failed. Instead it was Carson and his wife, producer Cynthia Hargrave, who the *Bottle Rocket* boys first turned to.

What they'd written was a little messy, but there was something pure to it that Carson said was akin to "reading *The Catcher in the Rye* as written by Holden Caulfield".[20] He and Hargrave encouraged them to shoot a few more minutes, package up what they had into a short, and accompany them to the 1993 Sundance Film Festival. There, they were hustled into a writing lab, which was really an opportunity to network and (hopefully) raise enough money to complete the movie.

At 13 minutes, the *Bottle Rocket* short rattles through the first two heists of the full feature – the first we see, as Anthony and Dignan rob the former's family home, while the second, in which they target the local bookstore, is only talked about in its aftermath.

Anderson's camera scurries after his dual thieves in jittery, handheld tracking shots. The narrative opens with a short, conversational digression about *Starsky & Hutch* that would feel more comfortably at home in a Quentin Tarantino picture (his debut, *Reservoir Dogs*, released the year before, had already radically shifted people's perception of what independent films should look and sound like).

The *Bottle Rocket* short is somewhat alien to the filmmaker Anderson would soon become. He'd continue to be influenced by Coppola, Scorsese and Altman – and, in turn, the French New Wave movies of the sixties by François Truffaut, Éric Rohmer and Jean-Luc Godard that shaped their work. But, soon enough, he'd shed that loose, spontaneous quality. Innocence is maintained, however, thanks to the use of Vince Guaraldi's sprightly jazz score for the 1965 animated TV special *A Charlie Brown Christmas*. Anthony and Dignan think they walk and talk like one of Scorsese's or Tarantino's antiheroes, but it's like watching a child hobble around in their mother's heels, desperate to impress.

Perhaps it was a little too sincere for the moment. The short failed to grab attention at Sundance. Still, it made its rounds, and both the short and the fuller, feature script were passed by Carson to producer Barbara Boyle, who passed it on to producer Polly Platt, who passed it on to producer James L. Brooks. He was thrilled: "It had such a great selling point: You never saw any of these guys before."[21]

Brooks had founded Gracie Films, which produced *The Simpsons*, and co-created the sitcoms *Taxi* and *The Mary Tyler Moore Show*. He was a director, too, and had won three Oscars for *Terms of Endearment* (1983) and earned two nominations for *Broadcast News* (1987). He wanted to meet the *Bottle Rocket* crew and so flew to Dallas. At the time, Anderson, the three Wilsons and Musgrave all lived in a single apartment that Owen described as "a real hovel".[22] Brooks was mystified that, despite all of them inhabiting the same space, no one had actually thought to read the script aloud.[23]

He invited them to his hotel, where Anderson's 120 pages of script turned out, in reality, to be triple the expected length. It was something to do with the choice of font. As they toiled, reading out page after page, hell unspooled before them. The air conditioning malfunctioned.[24] The water pitchers ran dry. Voices turned raspy. Luke couldn't stop sweating. Clearly, the script needed work. But, as they all said their goodbyes outside, Anderson chased Brooks across the street.

"Are you going to make the movie?" he asked.[25] Brooks offered the diplomatic answer. There was no way to know at this stage. Anderson repeated the question. To that, all the producer could say was: "I don't know, man." Still, Brooks brought Anderson and Wilson to Hollywood, where they were given their own offices on the Sony Studios lot, with a secretary and golf carts to whip around in.[26] They were flown out first class. Wilson reckoned he could trade the ticket in for a seat in economy class and secretly pocket the difference. He was told by the airline that wouldn't be possible.

Their relative outsider status seemed to unsettle the L.A. set. Anderson, who still dressed like a student, possessed confidence without the expected vanity or showmanship. In a city of talk, he wasn't afraid to marinate a little in his thoughts before he launched into his sentences. Neither he nor Wilson had the impulse to take notes or offer much of a reaction to other people's opinions. "He knew the picture he wanted to make," Brooks said.

Still, changes needed to be made. Brooks wanted the romance beefed up. After Anthony and Dignan rob the bookstore, they flee to a local motel, where Anthony falls for a Paraguayan housekeeper named Inez (Lumi Cavazos). She doesn't speak English. He doesn't speak Spanish. They must instead pitch woo via a translator.

Anderson, who still dressed like a student, possessed confidence without the expected vanity or showmanship.

OPPOSITE (ABOVE) Luke Wilson, Owen Wilson, Kumar Pallana and Robert Musgrave all in yellow, with Wes Anderson in still-smart, more-drab colours.
OPPOSITE (BELOW) The Wilsons, Anderson, Musgrave and cinematographer Robert Yeoman.

CABELL'S
NO
PARKING

Anthony (Luke Wilson), while on the run, finds himself romantically distracted by Paraguayan housekeeper Inez (Lumi Cavazos).

Anderson and Wilson continued to tinker with their script until, finally, in November 1994, they were ready to shoot. Brooks, who then had a deal with Columbia Pictures, agreed to executive-produce the movie with the studio. It was relatively unheard of for a first-time director to make his debut with a major studio and a $5 million budget. Columbia didn't even demand Luke, Owen and Musgrave make way for Hollywood stars. Andrew would end up in the role of Bob's older brother, Futureman – named so because, as Dignan recounts in a deleted scene, "He looks like he's designed by scientists for future warfare."

Bottle Rocket did, however, require a major name for the role of Mr Henry. At first, Anderson and Wilson yearned for a director, someone like Oliver Stone or Peter Bogdanovich. Yet, it happened to be that they shared an agent with James Caan.[27] And he was an ideal fit, an actor whose solemn, downturned expressions and volatile machismo saw him associated with the moral underbelly onscreen, with roles in two *Godfather* movies, *Dick Tracy* and *Honeymoon in Vegas*. Offscreen, he'd even acquired a certain reputation for socializing with known mobsters.

Anderson and Wilson, naturally, were a little nervous about meeting the man, so Brooks reassured them: "Just try to find some common ground with him." That turned out to be karate. Five minutes after being introduced, Caan asked Wilson to strangle him. He'd been studying under a man named Takayuki Kubota, or Tak, who'd advised on several martial arts movies, and was eager to show off what he'd learned.

Tak had not only become a trainer, but a sort of spiritual advisor. Caan referred to him as his "master", though Wilson joked that he treated him

Bob (Robert Musgrave) and Mr Henry (James Caan) dine – everyone might idolise the latter, but does he really have the gang's best interests at heart?

more like a personal assistant. He has a brief cameo in the movie. *Bottle Rocket* was Caan's first gig after a stint in drug and alcohol rehab, and he was determined to prove that he could work without issue. When on set, he stuck to his trailer, where he ran lines or practiced his karate skills.

The entire 45-day shoot passed by without major incident. Anderson was what Brooks would call "a natural" behind the camera – a worrier in private, but a leader on set.[28] He knew precisely what shots he needed, to the point he could turn a little obstinate if any of the producers disagreed.

He worked off a large pin-up board, onto which he'd pinned the sprawling collage of his vision, where colours shifted in unison with his story. *Bottle Rocket* opens with neutrals, which explode into bright reds, yellows and greens once Anthony reaches the motel and his new love Inez. When Mr Henry officially enters the picture, those tones grow darker, richer and a little more seductive.

Anderson had sent cinematographer Robert Yeoman, whose work on Gus Van Sant's *Drugstore Cowboy* he'd enjoyed, a handwritten note asking him to read the script.[29] Yeoman liked what he saw, and in the months before shooting, the pair would hang out in the director's office to watch movies and share ideas.[30]

He was, however, unable to license Guaraldi's *A Charlie Brown Christmas* score. He'd written a letter to its creator, Charles Schulz, but it was blocked by the show's producer, Lee Mendelson, who, in a series of increasingly terse faxes, refused to allow Charlie Brown to be associated with any movie that contained curse words.[31] Composer and Devo frontman Mark

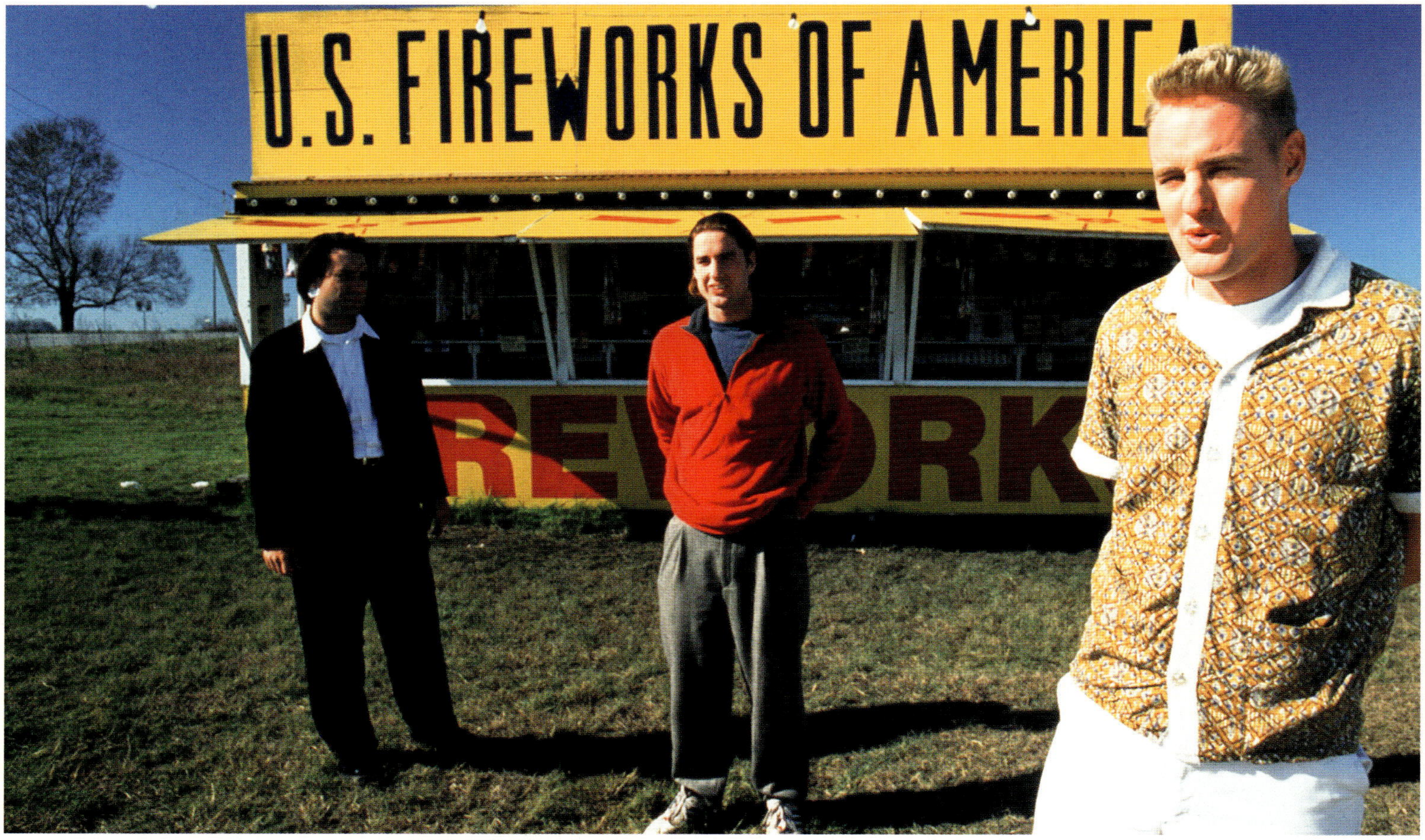
U.S. FIREWORKS OF AMERICA

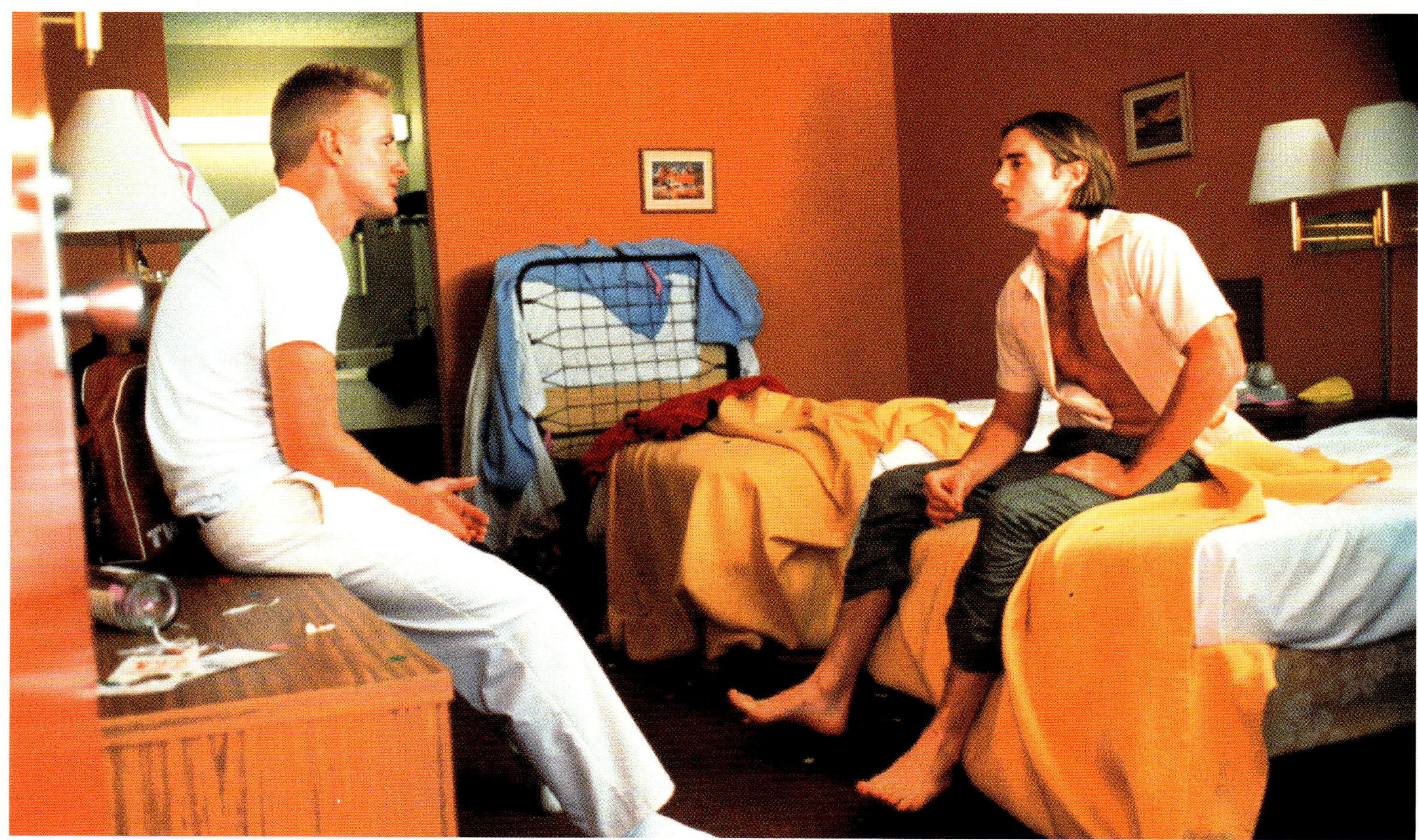

OPPOSITE (ABOVE) Luke Wilson, Owen Wilson and Robert Musgrave neatly spaced out for the camera. The Wilson brothers would become two of Anderson's closest early collaborators.
OPPOSITE (BELOW) Dignan (Owen Wilson) and Anthony (Luke Wilson) find their desires incompatible while on the lam, hiding out in a motel room.

Mothersbaugh stepped in instead, and crafted his own take on freewheeling, jazzy naïveté.

The studio felt good about *Bottle Rocket*. There was talk of a wide release at the height of summer, in the hope idle teenagers would turn it into a sleeper hit. Then, it was test screened for several hundred patrons of a Santa Monica AMC cinema. Anderson sat in the back row with the executives, and watched as a steady stream of hunched shoulders and bundled jackets shuffled out of the room.[32] He fled to the projection booth. By the end, little more than two-thirds of the audience remained.

It was one of the worst test screenings in the history of Columbia Pictures.[33] "I feel like I was never more confident in my life than when we made that film," Anderson said. "And never less confident than when we screened it."[34] Audience members turned in their reaction cards, among them declarations that the director's work "SUKD [*sic*]" and that it was a travesty they never got to see the lead actresses's breasts.

Anderson, however, remembers a single card, written by a woman who seemed to have a total understanding of what he'd set out to achieve. "I remember saying, 'This is our audience,'"[35] he said.

Still, it drove Anderson to despair. There were reshoots to be done and he could barely focus. One day, Wilson found him huddled over a desk, with his "head down like a kid in study hall."[36] He asked the director if he'd come up with anything new, only for Anderson to slide over a sheet of paper on which he'd simply written: "Bob Mapplethorpe. Potential Getaway Driver. Go." In the movie, it forms our first introduction to the character, spoken by Dignan in the snappy tone of someone utterly convinced they're the protagonist of a heist movie.

In reality, there was nothing Anderson could do to turn *Bottle Rocket* into the indifferent, sardonic, Gen-X comedy Columbia Pictures wanted. He was too gentle in his worldview, too intellectually curious about his characters. It bombed at the box office, opening in only 28 cinemas in the US.[37] More shockingly, it failed to get into any of the major festivals – not even Sundance, which had opened its doors for the original short. Brooks was furious.[38] So, too, thankfully, was *Los Angeles Times* critic Kenneth Turan, who decried the decision as near-criminal. Here, he wrote, was a gem of a movie with a "delicate deadpan sensibility".[39]

Other critics weren't so kind (Barry Walters, of *SFGate*, accused it of "radiating amateurishness with every shot"[40]), but its admirers turned quickly into ardent cheerleaders, and Anderson soon found himself an ally in none other than Martin Scorsese, the man whose work he'd first tried to emulate in those early, early drafts. He named it one of his favourite movies of the '90s.[41]

And, in the March 2000 issue of *Esquire*, he even offered Anderson up as his choice for who the next Scorsese might be. "The central idea of the film is so delicate, so human: a group of young guys think that their lives have to be filled with risk and danger in order to be real," he said of *Bottle Rocket*. "They don't know that it's okay simply to be who they are."[42]

It may lack the fussy symmetry that would come to define Anderson's work, but it still arrived on stylistic terra firma: the 90-degree whip pan, borrowed from Scorsese, makes an appearance, alongside a dialogue-free montage and the Futura font. All of these would soon become the director's staples. Anthony and Dignan, too, would find common ground with any of

Anderson's other privileged protagonists. While Anthony and Bob are the movie's explicit rich kids, there's never a sense that any of the *Bottle Rocket* boys have really faced much strife – and if they have, Anderson is sure to conceal it.

Still, comfort can sometimes deteriorate into ennui, and Anthony starts the movie having admitted himself into a psychiatric hospital for what he calls "exhaustion" (his kid sister, cynically, asks how that can be: "You haven't worked a day in your life, how could you be exhausted?").

But, as he explains to some sorority girl he meets: "One morning, over at Elizabeth's beach house, she asked me if I'd rather go water-skiing or lay out. And I realized that not only did I not want to answer that question, but I never wanted to answer another water-sports question, or see any of these people again for the rest of my life. Three days later, I was on my way to the desert and that was that."

Like many of Anderson's characters, Anthony and Dignan would rather write themselves into a fantasy, where their problems are entirely self-created, than stare into the void and have to answer the question of who they really are. At heart, they're no cads or criminals, but it's an easier life to pursue than that of the confused, directionless and afraid. Anthony tells Inez he's in love, though they've barely met, and begs her to run away with him. He can't quite understand that she has a job, friends and prior commitments, that people have a tendency to be tethered to where they are.

Is this romance? Or merely the acting out of it? Can Dignan really be considered a gangster if he thanks his victims for their cooperation, spins his gun around like a samurai sword, and dresses his crew in matching, sunshine yellow jumpsuits? These are men, after all, who are repeatedly forced to remind others that they're adults now, not children.

They're nothing more than the Skateboard Four with wallets and polo shirts, really – tender, little hearts desperate for respect, to feel bigger than a mere speck in the universe. In the end, Anthony ends up with Inez, and Dignan ends up in prison. It's not quite what they planned, but they'll make it work. Nothing about *Bottle Rocket*'s creation and release was quite as Anderson had planned, either, but he too made it work.

OPPOSITE Dignan (Owen Wilson) and Anthony (Luke Wilson) with their getaway driver Bob (Robert Musgrave). Musgrave proved such a perfect fit for the role that they named the character after him.

NEXT SPREAD Dignan at target practice, which is really his excuse to play at being the outlaw.

NORTH
ATLANTIC
OCEAN

2
SIC TRANSIT GLORIA

On *Rushmore*

Wes Anderson spent his youth enrolled in a Houston preparatory school named St. John's, an imposing post-war building of Austin limestone, seemingly designed to resemble a monastery. He was what you might refer to as a troubled child, wounded greatly by the divorce of his parents when he was eight years old. A teacher took pity on him. The young Anderson had taken an interest in the theatre, so was allowed to stage a new play every two weeks, on the condition that he'd remain committed to his schoolwork.[43]

He dabbled primarily in large-scale epics with titles like *The Five Maseratis* and *The Battle of the Alamo* and, at one point, attempted to stage an adaptation of *Star Wars* – "it was difficult to mount that with the limitation of an elementary school production," he later confessed.[44] His grades deteriorated regardless.

Convinced the collegiate system would still recognize some elusive, untapped potential within him, Anderson applied solely to Princeton, Dartmouth and Harvard universities. When they all rejected him, he made a panicked (albeit successful) bid to be accepted into the University of Texas.[45]

For years, the filmmaker had wanted to make what he considered a "school movie", akin to *Dead Poets Society* or Spike Lee's *School Daze*.[46] While his debut *Bottle Rocket*, by all traditional measures, was a failure on release, what fans it had acquired were borderline evangelists. Clearly, the movie had reached the right kind of people. Walt Disney Studios chairman Joe Roth made an offer to Anderson, determined he make his next project with the House of Mouse. That movie would be his "school movie", *Rushmore*. He was so fixated on the idea, in fact, that his girlfriend at the time dumped him and blamed the movie for their relationship's demise.[47]

Ambitious but troubled student Max Fischer (Jason Schwartzman) represents Russia at his school's Model United Nations.

Anderson by then had settled in Los Angeles, sharing a Spanish-style home with Luke and Owen Wilson. The latter had found his own success as an actor post-*Bottle Rocket*, with roles in *The Cable Guy*, James L. Brooks's *As Good as It Gets*, and Michael Bay's disaster epic *Armageddon*. But he was still a writer, and an Anderson collaborator, at heart. *Rushmore*'s script, like *Bottle Rocket*, represents their combined efforts. With a budget of only $10 million,[48] the movie posed no titanic risk, and Roth had made clear that he wanted an Anderson movie made on Anderson's terms.

Max Fischer, *Rushmore*'s juvenile hero, is not Anderson. He's consistently denied the interpretation.[49] He is, however, a romanticized ideal for wayward kids with outsized ambitions and limited material success. "I think if I had seen this movie when I was fifteen years old," Anderson said. "That would have been my movie. It would have changed me."[50]

He's introduced mid-reverie, setting down his broadsheet, taking a sip from his china cup and strolling up to the chalkboard to solve, without fuss, "probably the hardest geometry equation in the world". The entire class bursts into applause. He's then jostled awake.

Max is a Don Quixote of the educational set, enamoured by the chivalric idea of academic achievement – the only one in school who pairs his blue shirt with a navy blazer, his enamelled pins for punctuality and perfect attendance fastened to its lapel.

Anderson introduces Max's extensive catalogue of extracurricular activities – Stamp & Coin club, Lacrosse Team, the Max Fischer Players who stage his original plays etc. – in what would become the director's trademark brand of montage. There's a theatricality to how each frame is blocked, and Max looks often into the camera, as if we're the ones he's trying to prove his credentials to.

Yet, as Headmaster Nelson Guggenheim (Brian Cox) laments, "He's one of the worst students we've got." Having been placed on "sudden academic probation", Max seeks solace in a futile crush on first-grade teacher Rosemary Cross (Olivia Williams), who he tracks down after finding a quote scribbled inside a book by oceanographer Jacques Cousteau: "When one man, for whatever reason, has the opportunity to lead an extraordinary life, he has no right to keep it to himself." It leads him into a rivalry with a local steel magnate, Herman Blume (Bill Murray).

Anderson couldn't help but think of St. John's while he wrote, though his initial plan was to shoot in New England.[51] Production conducted an extensive search across the United States, Canada and the United Kingdom. But, when Anderson's mother sent him pictures of his old prep school, he could no longer deny the underlying truth of his story: Anderson may not have been Max Fischer, but *Rushmore* was St. John's.

A few alterations had to be made. Fake leaves were spray-painted in autumnal shades. Inspired by the fertile greens and gilded luxury of late-fifteenth and sixteenth-century painters Agnolo Bronzino and Hans Holbein the Elder,[52] Anderson convinced the school to allow him to redecorate one of its formal rooms, typically used by mothers for cheese-and-tea events.[53]

Max, eventually, is expelled, and sent to Grover Cleveland High School. The location used, Lamar High School, happens to be right across the street from St. John's. Anderson's father had gone there for a semester or so. Wilson was kicked out of his school, St. Mark's in Dallas, on the basis that he'd cheated at geometry. He, however, added a little "shabby nobility"

ABOVE Wes Anderson behind the camera, shooting *Rushmore*. It took around 50 days to complete the movie. **OPPOSITE** The theatrical poster for *Rushmore*.

to the story by suggesting he'd also refused to give up the identities of his collaborators.[54] They broke him, eventually. He named names and was still booted out. His parents were mortified – his father was on the board of trustees.

For the role of Max, Anderson had imagined "a fifteen-year-old Mick Jagger",[55] a jumble of bones with a keen intelligence behind the eyes. But, after a year of auditions, he'd become desperate. At one point, he toyed with the idea that Max would speak with a fake English accent, "which would actually be a real English accent because we'd be using an English actor. We were just coming up with really bizarre ideas."[56] There was a month left before filming was set to start. It seemed as if Anderson might have to throw the entire project out the window and start afresh.

Davia Nelson, who was overseeing casting for the movie in Northern California, was at a party held in honour of composer Carmine Coppola, father of legendary director Francis Ford Coppola.[57] She fell into conversation with Francis Ford's daughter, Sofia, a director herself, and mentioned she was working on a project about an idealistic teen infatuated with an older woman. "That sounds like my cousin," Sofia replied.[58]

Jason Schwartzman, the 17-year-old son of actress Talia Shire, and nephew of Francis Ford, had turned up to the event in a rented tuxedo, with top hat and cane. The previous summer, he'd both written and directed a play.

Three years earlier, he'd fallen in love with his live-in tutor, a swimmer on the UCLA team. He told her, "Look, I want you to know that I'm madly in love with you." She replied, "I don't think that's gonna work right now."[59] He was a musician, not an actor, the drummer for indie band Phantom Planet, whose song "California" became the theme for teen series *The O.C.*. But, when he read the script, something clicked: "I just remember thinking, 'This is everything that I think is funny, in one movie.'"[60]

He agreed to an audition, skipping school for the day and turning up in a blazer he'd embellished with a handmade *Rushmore* patch. The moment he met Anderson, his nerves seemed to dissipate. The director had on Converse One Star Sandals, while Schwartzman was wearing green New Balances with bright red reflectors. They complimented each other's choice of shoe. Then they talked about *Pinkerton*, the Weezer album.

Twenty or so minutes went by before Schwartzman even looked at his script. "I remember thinking and maybe even saying, 'I don't know if we should [do the scene] because this has gone so well,'" Schwartzman said. "'I don't want to. This is enough. You're so awesome. Let's not ruin it.'"[61] But he needn't have worried. Anderson had found his newest star, collaborator and friend.

Schwartzman didn't look like Jagger, but he did remind Anderson of Dustin Hoffman in *The Graduate* – that softer, more soulful look.[62] To pass as a 15-year-old, Schwartzman's chest was waxed. It took around two hours.

Max tells everyone his father is a neurosurgeon at St Joseph's Hospital. In reality, he's the son of a barber (Seymour Cassel, known for his work with John Cassavetes), at Rushmore by the grace of a scholarship. Blume's success, fuelled largely by resentment, gives Max hope that his grand facade may, one day, turn in positive results.

Anderson and Wilson wrote the role with Bill Murray in mind, having once hoped to cast him in *Bottle Rocket*.[63] They were fans. As a child,

Max Fischer (Jason Schwartzman) with the object of his romantic jealousy, local steel magnate Herman Blume (Bill Murray).

Anderson had dressed up as a Ghostbuster for Halloween.[64] But the actor was notoriously difficult to pin down, and most likely beyond what they could afford, so they'd dismissed the idea as wishful thinking.

Still, they sent Murray *Rushmore*'s script and a copy of *Bottle Rocket*. He read the script, but didn't watch the movie. His agents sent him another copy. Murray called Anderson up. The director asked whether he'd seen *Bottle Rocket*. He again hadn't, so Anderson sent him another copy. He ended up with four in total. He watched none.[65]

The script, however, intrigued him. "I figured the writing was so specific that whoever wrote it knew exactly what they were going to shoot," Murray said. "I never have a problem with guys who make a movie that misses as long as they make the movie they want to make."[66] His last two projects, however, *Larger than Life* (1996) and *The Man Who Knew Too Little* (1997), had disappointed critics and audiences alike. And, with *Rushmore*, he could better channel the profound, self-wounding melancholy that seemed to underpin even the broadest of his characters.

When Murray phoned him, they didn't talk much about the role. Instead, the actor started to describe to him the plot of Akira Kurosawa's *Red Beard*, about a doctor with mighty ambitions, who's disappointed to be sent out to a rural clinic. They spoke for roughly an hour about the movie.

Anderson hadn't seen it. He watched it afterwards, and still couldn't really understand why Murray had brought it up. At the end of the conversation, the actor concluded: "Yeah, I think I'll do... I'll do *Rushmore* with you, yeah."[67] He waived the fee Anderson offered, which was already

Max Fischer (Jason Schwartzman) with the object of his romantic affections, first-grade teacher Rosemary Cross (Olivia Williams).

lower than usual, and agreed to do the movie for the standard Screen Actors Guild day rate, a total of nine thousand dollars.[68]

The director, at first, was "a little terrified". He'd heard that Murray had a somewhat volatile personality (there was a story he'd heard about him throwing someone in a lake).[69] In *Rushmore*, Blume and Max lock horns over their mutual infatuation with Miss Cross.

Olivia Williams's only previous theatrical film credit was Kevin Costner's disastrous post-apocalyptic neo-Western *The Postman*, though she'd had extensive experience on stage, including with the Royal Shakespeare Company. Schwartzman came to her for advice when he had to write a paper on *Hamlet*.

As Wilson admitted, Miss Cross exists "on a pedestal", and isn't quite as fleshed out as Max or Blume.[70] But, in Williams's hands, we find a woman trying to navigate an old grief over the untimely death of her oceanographer husband (Wilson, though he appears only in photographs), now repeatedly forced to shoulder these men's lightly Freudian miseries.

Max's repeated attempts to woo her – he successfully petitions to have Latin restored to the curriculum, after she offhandedly expresses her admiration for the dead language, and attempts to convert part of the school's baseball field into an aquarium – turn into a full-blown conflict with Blume.

Schwartzman, too, was nervous about meeting Murray. "He's someone who I grew up watching," he said. "His movies meant so much to me and now all of a sudden I'm working alongside him. We have the same job now."[71]

Murray flew in to Houston the night before the shoot started, and the pair suffered through a disastrous rehearsal in Anderson's hotel room.

"He was terrible, just terrible," Murray said. "And I got very depressed and immediately afterwards went straight to the bar. I had to work with this guy who didn't have a clue."[72] Murray would whisper odd asides into Schwartzman's ear right before the camera rolled: "Just try to get this shot in one take, kid, I want to go play golf today." As Schwartzman noted, "It was kind of scary to hear that from a Ghostbuster."[73]

Max, in his territoriality over Miss Cross, can be quite cruel. He gets drunk and abuses her doctor friend, Peter (Luke Wilson). Each rejection is an unwanted reminder that he's still a child, despite his own delusions.

It culminates in a painfully awkward scene where Anderson tosses control away in favour of the havoc of a handheld camera, as she confronts him with the words: "Do you think we're gonna have sex?" He's taken aback: "That's kind of a cheap way to put it." She stands firm: "Not if you've ever fucked before, it isn't."

But there's something in Max that Blume can't help but admire, the confidence of a young person with his future stretched out tantalizingly in front of him, like the protagonists of *Bottle Rocket*. Max's home is next to the cemetery, and we find him in front of his mother's grave, marked like the tomb of a general with a quote from Thomas Gray's poem *Elegy Written in a Country Churchyard*: "The paths of glory lead but to the grave." She was the first to encourage him, the one who brought his play about the Watergate scandal to *Rushmore* and secured him a scholarship.

Death flits constantly around the edges of Anderson's movie. It lives in the place where Miss Cross sleeps, her husband's old childhood bedroom. He owned the Cousteau book that first drew Max to her – he'd gifted it to her when they were teenagers, and she handed it off to the school library once he was gone. "I guess we both have dead people in our families," Max notes, casually. What he means is that grief marks people. It becomes a part of their identity.

Blume seems struck by some prescience of his own death. He's older now, lost, and forced to examine his own legacy. When he moves on, will anyone live for him like Max and Miss Cross do for their lost ones? Perhaps that's why, when Max finally introduces his father (revealing him to be a barber, not a neurosurgeon), Blume's face softens and grows gentle. Here's someone who's been honest and vulnerable with him, who might actually care for him as a person.

Despite Anderson's nerves, he connected almost instantaneously with Murray. He admired his intelligence. Schwartzman warmed to him, too: "I realized, around halfway through, that he was just kind of softening me. It was all on purpose."[74] When Disney refused to pay for a helicopter shot, Murray wrote Anderson a cheque for around $25,000. The director changed his mind on the shot, but kept the cheque. It's probably still somewhere in his archives.[75]

Rushmore was shot in around 50 days, wrapping in late January 1998.[76] Anderson's brother Eric played the architect that Max hires for his

Murray flew in to Houston the night before the shoot started and the pair suffered through a disastrous rehearsal.

OPPOSITE Herman Blume (Bill Murray) with Max Fischer's bicycle, which he sabotages by running over with his car.

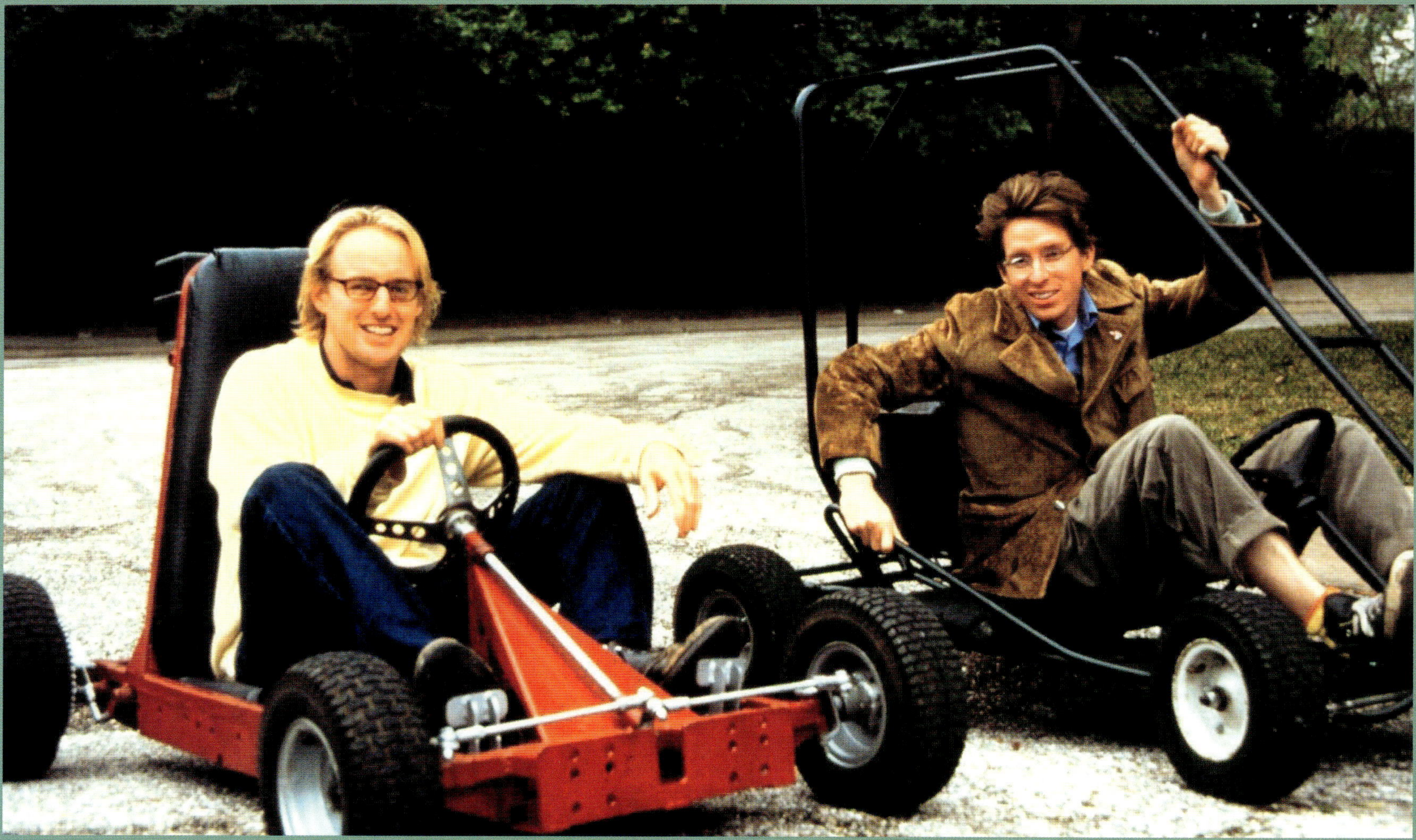

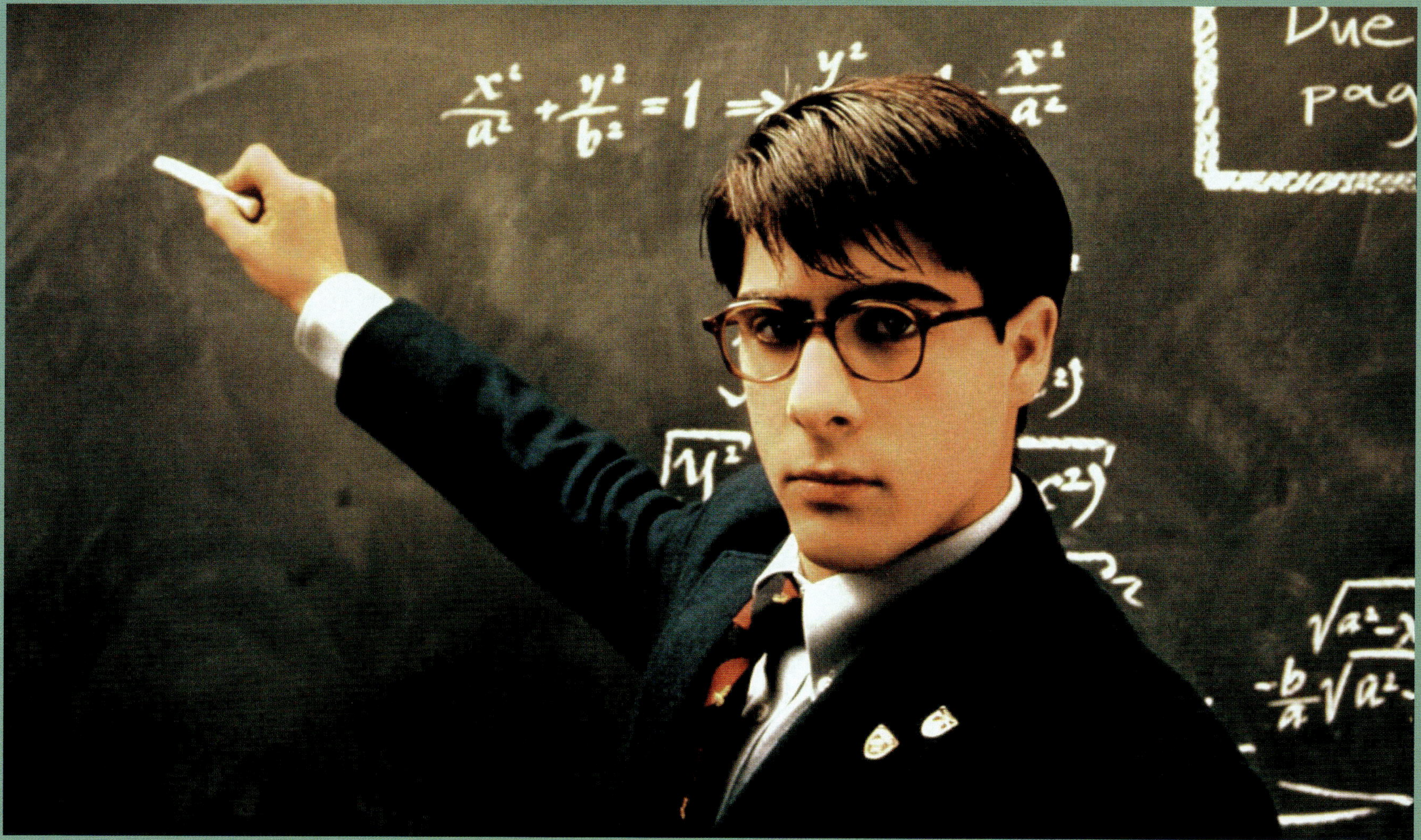

$\frac{x^2}{a^2}+\frac{y^2}{b^2}=1 \Rightarrow$
Due

OPPOSITE (ABOVE) Owen Wilson and Wes Anderson take a pair of go-karts for a joy ride.
OPPOSITE (BELOW) Max, in a reverie, solving "probably the hardest geometry equation in the world".
ABOVE Schwartzman with his onscreen dad, Seymour Cassel.

aquarium. He also shot the making-of documentary that appears on the Criterion Collection disc of the movie. Luke and Owen's brother, Andrew Wilson, took the role of Coach Beck.

Sarah Tanaka, who was enrolled at Rhode Island's Brown University at the time, was cast as Max's age-appropriate love interest, Margaret Yang. She works now as a physician. Anderson largely used the same crew that had worked on *Bottle Rocket*: cinematographer Robert Yeoman, composer Mark Mothersbaugh, production designer David Wasco, costume designer Karen Patch, and editor David Moritz.

Bottle Rocket's cast had consisted almost entirely of people Anderson already knew, meaning *Rushmore* presented his first real test as a leader. "I wanted it to be a group of people who would come together and become friends," the director said. "It's a movie that's sort of about friendship, and I wanted that kind of feeling on the set."[77] There were go-karts on set one day. Once Anderson called cut for the final time, he grabbed one of the vehicles for a joy ride around Houston's back streets. "It was probably the best time of my life," Schwartzman reflected.[78]

"We always thought of it as a fable," Anderson explained.[79] Its narrative is divided into chapters, marked by the passing months, each title appearing across a drawn-back curtain. It was an effect achieved in-camera, using a xenon projector, in homage to the luscious theatricality of *The Red Shoes* and *Black Narcissus*'s directors Michael Powell and Emeric Pressburger.

Rushmore, too, was the first Anderson movie to be shot in anamorphic widescreen – a way to add to that slightly unreal, storybook feel, since "you can stage the actors, many people in a frame, who are all in a close-up simultaneously."[80]

But, when *Rushmore* was finally test-screened for audiences, a horrible sense of déjà vu struck: the reactions were dismal, the worst that producer Barry Mendel had seen for one of his movies.[81] Thankfully, Roth stood by Anderson, and told him not to change a single frame. Instead, *Rushmore* played at a string of fall film festivals, and was scheduled for a limited run in December 1998 – Disney hoped they could drum up an Oscar nomination for Murray, though it failed to materialize.[82]

The movie was received far more favourably by critics than *Bottle Rocket* had been, though it was bound to be a little divisive. This would become a running theme. *Empire* magazine's Caroline Westbrook warned that "its quirkiness will irritate the hell out of some," yet, in the same breath, declared it "the year's best kept cinematic secret".

Anderson was a longtime fan of film critic Pauline Kael, who'd written extensively for *The New Yorker*, and had since retired. He was determined to show her his movie. Having ventured out to her home in the Berkshire Mountains, in western Massachusetts, the director escorted her to a local movie theatre and played her a print. She responded afterward, "I don't know what you've got here, Wes," and remarked that "Wes Anderson" was a terrible name for a director.

He was a little disappointed, but walked away from the encounter with two first editions of her books, graciously signed.[83] Francis Ford Coppola's primary reaction seemed to be annoyance – Anderson had featured a case of wine in the background that belonged to Far Niente, the chief rival to his own business in the Napa Valley.[84]

Rushmore ends, like *Bottle Rocket*, with a moment of false hope. Dignan might be in prison, but he's already planning his jailbreak. Max may have made peace with Blume and Miss Cross, and struck up a relationship with Margaret, but it's Max and Miss Cross alone, slow dancing, when the credits roll. Anderson had entered his cinematic maturity. But he was still the dreamer, same as ever.

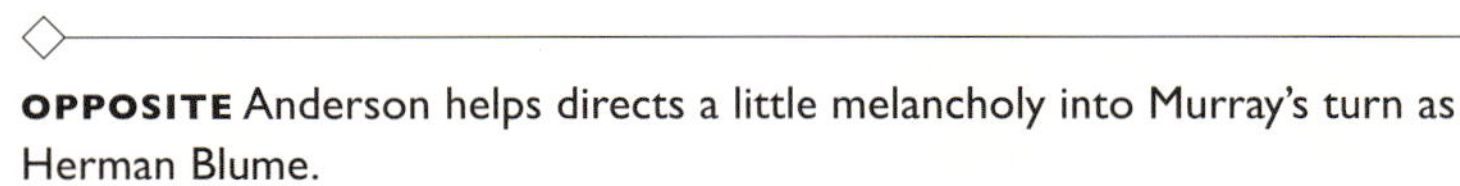

OPPOSITE Anderson helps directs a little melancholy into Murray's turn as Herman Blume.

NEXT SPREAD Max Fischer (Jason Schwartzman) finally makes peace with his impossible crush, Rosemary Cross (Olivia Williams).

3
LES ENFANTS TERRIBLES

On *The Royal Tenenbaums*

When Wes Anderson was eight years old, his parents separated. It was, to him, the most traumatic event of his young life. His mother, Texas Ann Burroughs, became an archaeologist, and would sometimes invite her three boys on digs – once to the site of a Karankawa Indian burial ground in Galveston.[85]

His father, Melver Leonard Anderson, worked in advertising and public relations. He had a jocular personality, but remained mild-mannered.[86] He was nothing, then, like Royal Tenenbaum (Gene Hackman), the catalyst of Anderson's third movie, a patriarch with a con man's soul, who cannonballs his way back into his family's life.

Royal has run out of cash and been kicked out of his temporary abode at the Lindbergh Palace Hotel. Worst of all, the woman he's still technically married to, Etheline (Anjelica Huston), has fallen in love with another man, her business manager Henry Sherman (Danny Glover). He lies to them all, and announces that he's been diagnosed with terminal cancer.

Royal fears that Henry, a good man, might actually heal the "two decades of betrayal, failure and disaster" that have befallen the Tenenbaums since his departure. Each of his children is a shipwreck, former prodigies trapped in intellectual, creative and emotional stasis.

Chas (Ben Stiller) still has a BB pellet embedded between his knuckles that his father fired during a childhood game (the hand in the movie is provided by Andrew Wilson, the pellet a relic from when he was accidentally shot by his brother Owen).[87] His wife recently perished in a plane crash.

Richie (Luke Wilson), a tennis player who turned pro at 17, grew up in an attic room dominated by trophies. He was Royal's favourite child, the only one he'd invite on his jaunts around the city. Following a nervous

The Tenenbaums household: Richie (Luke Wilson), Margot (Gwyneth Paltrow), Royal (Gene Hackman), Chas (Ben Stiller), his sons Ari (Grant Rosenmeyer) and Uzi (Jonah Meyerson), Buckley the beagle, Etheline (Anjelica Huston), Henry Sherman (Danny Glover) and Pagoda (Kumar Pallana).

breakdown, suffered mid-match, he abandoned his career for life aboard an ocean liner.

The incident coincided with the marriage of his adopted sister Margot (Gwyneth Paltrow) to neurologist Raleigh St Clair (Bill Murray). He's in love with her. Always has been. Margot was adopted into the family at the age of two. She is immensely secretive, an outsider in her own home, and an acclaimed playwright who hasn't completed a work in seven years. As of now, she spends six hours a day in the bathtub, watching television.

Anderson's friend and writing partner Owen Wilson, who also stars as the wannabe Tenenbaum, their neighbour Eli Cash, had always told him he should write about his parents' divorce.[88] Yet, his ideas always ended up so disconnected from his own circumstances. What he had, instead, were a handful of ideas laid out on scrap paper. He imagined, for example, the face of a woman, arriving somewhere for some reason, to the tune of Nico's "These Days". She'd wear a particular expression, a kind of wounded serenity.

It's become one of Anderson's signature scenes: Margot, in slow-motion, disembarks from the Green Line Bus to reunite with Richie. She's walking back into the private world they've maintained since they were children, running away from home to hide in the African Wing of the Public Archives. Paltrow, who has never particularly liked seeing herself onscreen, has said it's possibly the only moment of her career that she can stand to watch.[89]

The Royal Tenenbaums' opening narration is directly inspired by that delivered by Welles at the start of *The Magnificent Ambersons*, in which the history of both the town and the family are made plain.

Anderson had originally submitted treatments for *The Royal Tenenbaums*, *Bottle Rocket* and *Rushmore* as part of his applications to film school, long before he made his directorial debut. He failed to get into a single one.[90] But by 1999, Anderson was living in New York City, and his morose clan of cosmopolites came circling back into his mind.

Once again, he collaborated on a screenplay with Wilson, who was busy in Los Angeles with his newfound screen stardom. The distance made it difficult, but they worked as best they could.

The opening narration of *The Royal Tenenbaums* is directly inspired by one delivered by Orson Welles at the start of *The Magnificent Ambersons*, in which the history of both the town and the family are made plain. In Anderson's movie, the voice is that of Alec Baldwin. The movie's title card is the cover of a library book, stamped and checked out by the director's own hands, inviting[91] us to imagine that we're watching the adaptation of a novel that never existed. Scenes are divided into chapters.

For decades, all Anderson knew of New York existed in stories. It's a fantasy he wanted to preserve in *The Royal Tenenbaums*, even though he now called the city home. He'd even briefly contemplated shooting the entire movie on a soundstage, the Tenenbaum home embraced by a perpetual fall of artificial snow.

In the end, he chose to film on location in Harlem, the Bronx, Yonkers and New Jersey. But he fictionalized his own New York, with neighbourhoods like Mockingbird Heights, and a transport system that includes the Green Line Bus.

OPPOSITE (ABOVE) Acclaimed playwright and child prodigy Margot Tenenbaum (Irene Gorovaia).
OPPOSITE (BELOW) The same woman, years later (Gwyneth Paltrow). She hasn't completed a work in seven years.

While shooting one scene, he ushered Kumar Pallana – his old friend, here in the role of Royal's valet, Pagoda – to stand in front of the Statue of Liberty and block it from shot. It was too recognizable for Anderson's tastes. Hackman was bemused by the decision.

Like *Rushmore*, *The Royal Tenenbaums* takes place in an undefined era in which phone booths still line the pavement, suspended between the elegance of the interwar period and the graffiti-sprayed anarchy of Walter Hill's 1979 classic *The Warriors*. Two decades pass over the course of the story, yet nothing changes, much like the Tenenbaums themselves.

Anderson searched for months for the perfect residence to transform into the Tenenbaum home. It was his friend, music producer George Drakoulias, who suggested a place in Hamilton Heights, at 144th Street and Convent Avenue – a Flemish Revival mansion built in 1899, with a rounded turret that reminded Anderson of the house in *The Magnificent Ambersons*.[92]

A sign in the window revealed it had recently been foreclosed on, and bought up by new owners who were planning extensive renovations. Anderson and his crew swept in, spending six months transforming its rooms and completing many of the necessary structural repairs themselves.[93] The amount they paid in rental costs exceeded what the owners had originally spent on the property.

Its staircase was narrow, forcing Anderson's camera to adopt unexpected angles, while the roof was accessible only by ladder. Each day, the building seemed to lean a little more to the side.[94] A few rooms – the kitchen, Etheline's study and the ballroom – had to be sought elsewhere, at nearby locations.[95] But Anderson made it his design paradise.

David Wasco and Sandy Reynolds-Wasco, the husband-and-wife team of production designer and set decorator who'd already worked on *Bottle Rocket* and *Rushmore*, were instructed by Anderson to take inspiration from the vibrant, baroque frames of Federico Fellini's first colour film, *Juliet of the Spirits* (1965).[96]

Margot's room was decorated in a crimson, zebra-patterned wallpaper borrowed from the now-closed, but once-famous Italian eatery Gino, on Lexington Avenue between 60th and 61st street.[97] For Etheline's study, the expertise of both the local archaeology society and Anderson's mother was sought.[98] Eric Chase Anderson, his brother, painted the murals that cover Richie's bedroom walls and recount the history of the Tenenbaums, as well as his 17 portraits of Margot.

Each of the Tenenbaums gradually returns to this home, as if returning to the womb. Royal arrives with his faux-diagnosis, hospital equipment, and elevator operator posing as a doctor (*Rushmore*'s Seymour Cassel). Chas turns up, on high alert, having fled his house due to a lack of sprinklers – not that there are sprinklers on the Tenenbaum property, either. Margot skulks in, demanding some space away from her husband. Richie is coaxed back from his life at sea.

At first, Anderson and Wilson wanted to centre their movie on Richie's homecoming. And, while their attentions inevitably shifted towards Royal, as

ABOVE The theatrical poster for *The Royal Tenenbaums*.
OPPOSITE The Flemish Revival mansion used as the Tenenbaum residence, located at 144th Street and Convent Avenue in Hamilton Heights.

tends to occur in Richie's own life, the director still considers the youngest Tenenbaum sibling to be the movie's true hero.[99] He's the last of the family, notably, to leave the cemetery in its final scene.

Richie is the silent witness to this genealogy of pain, cursed by his father's admiration, and by his love for his adopted sister. Originally, Anderson had intended Richie and Margot to be related by blood, in deference to the tragically co-dependent siblings at the centre of Jean Cocteau's novel *Les enfants terribles*, adapted onto film in 1950 by Jean-Pierre Melville.

For decades, all Anderson knew of New York existed in these stories. It's a fantasy he wanted to preserve in *The Royal Tenenbaums*, even though he now called the city home.

Margot and Richie, like Cocteau's pair, seek absolution from within a secret world of their own making. A part of it you can touch. While Royal and his sham deathbed occupy Richie's old attic quarters, he invites Margot into the yellow camping tent set up in the ballroom, so they can whisper about their desires. The rest lives in unspoken sentences.

It's a space we're ever-so briefly invited into, in the scene where Margot steps off the bus to Nico's "These Days" in slow motion. The soft, wounded expression on both their faces seem to say, "It hurts to be near you. It hurts far more to be away from you."

They talk in the graveyard, after Eli, who's also in love with Margot, shares with her details of the letter he received from Richie in which he confesses his feelings. She tells him about it. Richie doesn't respond. A carton of cigarettes drops from her pocket to the ground. Margot has smoked in secrecy since the age of twelve, so this seems especially careless. It's her own way of inviting Richie in, of telling him she loves him back. Anderson eventually decided Margot would be adopted, which both suited the story and made it more plausible.

The part had been written especially for Luke Wilson, who Anderson believed possessed untapped potential. "There's a gentleness about him that comes across clearly," he explained. "He's someone who can be soft-spoken, good natured, really sweet-tempered. But there's a dangerous side to Luke. I've seen some things."[100]

Richie's suicide attempt is the first direct, however awful, expression of pain in the movie. Anderson borrowed the line "I'm going to kill myself tomorrow" from a Louis Malle movie about a terminally dissatisfied man, *Le Feu follet (1963)*.[101] It sounds nonsensical coming from Richie, who proceeds with the act there and then, yet, tomorrow neither he nor anyone in his family will wake up quite the same person. "I never understood any of us," Royal admits, defeatedly. His real sin is that he never tried.

No one in the Tenenbaum family craves that extension of empathy more than Margot, who is always introduced by her father to polite company as his adopted child. Yet even Etheline, the more compassionate parent, betrays the same bias. She visits Margot in her bathtub sanctuary to tell her Chas is coming home. He's been very depressed. "So am I," she tells her mother, who responds in confusion: "So am I what?"

Anderson had been charmed by Gwyneth Paltrow's enigmatic turn in the 1996 adaptation[102] of Jane Austen's *Emma*. She was of established Hollywood stock, born to actor Blythe Danner and producer Bruce Paltrow. The cast had been peppered with celebrity offspring: Ben Stiller was the son of comedians Jerry Stiller and Anne Meara, while Anjelica Huston was the daughter of director John Huston and granddaughter of actor Walter Huston. All arrived to set with an apt weight of family legacy on their shoulders.

Margot (Gwyneth Paltrow), the perpetual outsider of the Tenenbaums, finds little solidarity with her mother, Etheline (Anjelica Huston).

Paltrow identified with Margot's isolation, at least in her younger years.[103] But, while she admired Anderson's work, she was unused to the stilted cadence he required of his performers. "I had a couple of moments on set where I thought, like, 'Are we making the worst movie?'" she remarked. "But luckily it turned out to be pretty good."[104]

Anderson had wanted a role for his *Rushmore* collaborator Bill Murray, and so wrote the character of Margot's current husband, Raleigh St. Clair, based on the neurologist Oliver Sacks, who he'd once read about in *The New York Times*.[105]

Ben Stiller had been one of *Bottle Rocket*'s early advocates. He'd penned a letter of admiration to Owen Wilson, before casting him in his next directorial effort, black comedy *The Cable Guy (1996)*.[106] The two had since become close friends. Anderson reckoned the actor could do something special with all of Chas's coiled-up resentment. The character isn't an outsider like Margot, but he is the unfavoured son, grief-stricken by his wife's untimely death – never prioritized, never in control, and left to endlessly practise safety drills just to feel some fragment of power.

The Tenenbaums' private miseries find an odd counterbalance in Eli Cash, who, like *Rushmore*'s Max, finds his efforts to pierce the elitist bubble to be a self-destructive pursuit ("I always wanted to be a Tenenbaum, you know?"). He's fashioned himself into an author – a "Cormac McCarthy knockoff",[107] according to the director – who writes a novel that presupposes Custer never died at the Battle of the Little Bighorn. But the Tenenbaums still look down on him. After all, they're a true *Family of Geniuses*, or so the

"I always wanted to be a Tenenbaum, you know?" Eli Cash (Owen Wilson), wandering around the life he built purely to ingratiate himself with his neighbours.

title of Etheline's book states, while Eli's critics make it a point to say that he definitively is not.

Everything about him is performative, from his cowboy wardrobe to his shirtless magazine cover, inspired by the Richard Avedon portrait series *In the American West*, which Wilson's own mother had worked on as an assistant.[108] A painting in his apartment, *Bad Route*, which features five men on dirt bikes in grimacing monster make-up, was purchased by Anderson at a New York gallery. The man behind it, Miguel Calderón, hadn't painted it himself, but had hired a nameless portrait artist to do it for him.[109]

The Tenenbaum children treat their clothes like a uniform, or like the closet of a cartoon character, willfully turning themselves into outsized parodies of arrested development. Richie has paired sports accessories with a camel suit for what appears to be the majority of his lifetime.

Anderson sent nightly emails to costume designer Karen Patch, along with the occasional sketch by his brother Eric, for roughly five months before she was even allowed to read the script. Everything was custom made, even if it bore a brand's logo, from Margot's striped Lacoste dresses, to Chas's Adidas tracksuit and Richie's FILA headband.

Each individual piece was simple, but they were paired in unusual ways that seem to speak to some internal restlessness – see how Margot wears her sports dresses with a heavy fur coat, kohl-rimmed eyes and a girlish barrette. The Tenenbaum method has since become a beloved reference point for fashion's elite, with Alessandro Michele's stint as creative director

OPPOSITE (ABOVE) Royal (Gene Hackman) with the woman he knows is too good for him, his estranged wife Etheline (Anjelica Huston). **OPPOSITE (BELOW)** Etheline is an archaeologist. So was Anderson's mother. **ABOVE** Henry Sherman (Danny Glover), whose romance with Etheline threatens to heal "two decades of betrayal, failure and disaster".

at Gucci, between 2002 and 2022, essentially turning the brand into its own Andersonian wonderland.

Etheline was a role that Anderson had explicitly written for Anjelica Huston. He'd loved her in *The Dead* and *Prizzi's Honor*, both directed by her father, and imagined she was probably the kind of woman who knew and socialized with intellectual types like the Tenenbaums.[110] She suggested they meet to have eggs Benedict, which he wasn't familiar with. "So, I introduced him formally to eggs Benedict," she said.[111] She'd liked *Bottle Rocket* very much, and quickly accepted the role.

Anderson gave her a few of Eric's drawings of Etheline in "very small suits with strange hairdos",[112] alongside photographs of the Anderson matriarch, Texas, and, eventually, a pair of her old glasses. She confronted the director and asked if she was, in fact, playing his mother. He was shocked at the suggestion.

Paltrow shared a make-up trailer with Huston, where her station was located upstairs, in an area nicknamed "the nest", to which she'd retreat at the end of each day with a cigarette and a glass of white wine.[113] Her presence was serene. On take five of the scene of Etheline bringing the young Margot her birthday cake, her hair caught fire. Huston calmly put the cake down, while Pallana swatted out the flames with a brush of his hand.[114]

For the role of Henry Sherman, who happens to share the name of Anderson's then-landlord, the director looked to Danny Glover. He knew well his performances in *To Sleep with Anger* and *Witness* (the line "I know you, asshole!" is a reference), but it was his extensive offscreen activism that

reassured Anderson that he'd bring the necessary gentility and generosity to the role.[115] Henry, in a way, exists as the promise of what could be. He makes Etheline giggle like a schoolgirl when they kiss.

Anderson had, as he did with Huston, written Royal with Gene Hackman in mind. They first met around two years before production commenced. The interaction was pleasant, but Hackman warned that he didn't like roles to be written for him, or to be presented with some stranger's idea of who he was. Anderson did it anyway. Hackman passed on the movie, twice.[116]

So, the director sent him Eric's sketch of the cast with him at the centre – which has since, regrettably, gone missing – and several dozen letters. "I was essentially stalking him," he confessed, "even though for a while I had no personal contact."

Eventually, Hackman relented. His agent was reading yet another letter over the phone when he replied, "I guess maybe I should do it." Like the rest of the cast, he'd have to be paid scale, the lowest amount an actor can legally accept, so that the production could actually afford its stars. But there was an echo of Royal Tenenbaum in his own life. One day, when Hackman was 13, his father climbed in his car, drove past his son in the street and waved, but refused to stop. He never returned.[117]

Hackman left home at the age of 16, lying about his age so he could enlist in the United States Marine Corps. He served four and a half years as a field-radio operator, before ending up at the Pasadena Playhouse College of Theatre Arts, where the students voted him, alongside his classmate Dustin Hoffman, as Least Likely to Succeed.

ABOVE Royal (Gene Hackman) and his idea of a day out with the grandkids (Jonah Meyerson and Grant Rosenmeyer): taking them to an illegal dogfighting ring. **OPPOSITE** Anderson had written Royal with Hackman in mind, though it took several dozen letters for the actor to finally accept the role.

It would take him until his late thirties to officially break into the industry, when he was Oscar-nominated for his role in *Bonnie and Clyde* (1967). He would then win twice, for *The French Connection* (1972) and *Unforgiven* (1992), in a body of work that was versatile but steadfastly honest, with roles that often commanded fear, respect or a combination of both.

It's that gravitas, slightly upturned, that Hackman brings to the part of Royal. The man thinks he's *The French Connection*'s Detective Popeye Doyle, who can barge like a steam train into people's lives, and live loud, large and selfishly.

And, yet, he can't stand to be rejected by Etheline or by his children. He's unmoored by his own vulnerabilities, by all that he realizes about his sad, broken-up family in the wake of Richie's suicide attempt. He asks Margot, attempting a truce over a butterscotch sundae, "Can't somebody be a shit their whole life and try to repair the damage?"

It wasn't an easy shoot. Hackman was a consummate professional, and he relished the technical challenges presented by Anderson's tightly controlled camera set-ups, but didn't take well to direction. On one occasion, after several takes, Anderson pointed out that he was meant to cry during a scene.[118] Hackman wanted to know where it was stated in the script. The director looked over his copy, only to discover that he'd crossed out everything bar his own dialogue. "The only valid way that I can act is from the moment, from what's happening at that particular time,"[119] the actor would explain. Anything else felt inauthentic.

Anderson admitted that, while he relished the opportunity to work with such a legendary performer, Hackman could be "very scary".[120] Stiller had attempted to break the ice by telling him how much he'd loved *The Poseidon Adventure* (1972). "It was a money job," the actor replied and walked away.[121]

On the day of Royal's scene with Etheline, in which he first announces his illness, Hackman seemed especially disgruntled. During rehearsal, Huston slapped him on the lapel of his jacket, only to aim for the face once the cameras rolled. "I saw the imprint of my hand on his cheek," she said. "And I thought he was gonna kill me."[122] It was the take used in the final movie.

Paltrow remembered the experience far more fondly. "He was kind of a bear of a guy," she said. "But I also felt something very sweet and sad in him there, and I liked him a lot. And I think he's one of the greatest actors who ever lived. You're Gene Hackman, you can be in a fucking bad mood if you want."[123] Anderson had received the worst of it. At one point, the actor allegedly called him a "cunt" and demanded he pull up his pants and act like a man.

Hackman also confessed to him, roughly two-thirds of the way into the shoot, that "I think this is gonna be it."[124] He starred in only two further films and then quit to become a novelist. His doctor had advised him that, for the sake of his own heart, he should avoid any unnecessary stress.[125]

Yet, Hackman received his best notices in years for *The Royal Tenenbaums*, alongside a Golden Globe for Best Actor in a Musical or Comedy. The otherwise critical A. O. Scott declared in *The New York Times* that he was "the only one who bursts off the page into three dimensions".[126]

The Tenenbaum household at a performance of Margot's *The Levinsons in the Trees*, which she produces after Royal finally attempts to make peace with her.

OPPOSITE (ABOVE) Wes Anderson directs his crew around the relatively compact quarters of the Tenenbaum residence.
OPPOSITE (BELOW) Paramours Margot (Gwyneth Paltrow) and Richie (Luke Wilson) share a moment together, alone, on the rooftop of their childhood home with the latter's hawk Mordecai.
ABOVE Chas (Ben Stiller), Henry Sherman (Danny Glover), Margot and Etheline (Anjelica Huston) at the dinner table.

Filming of *The Royal Tenenbaums* began in March 2001 and lasted for 60 days – a relatively short time for what was a dense, ambitious screenplay. Anderson raised his voice only once. Luke Wilson was being fitted for a suit, and, when the director would periodically turn up the level of his cuffs, the actor would surreptitiously ask the tailor to let them back down again. "He pulled me to the side and went, 'This is going to be the level of the cuffs!'" Wilson recounted. Anderson immediately regretted the outburst.

It was the first time the director had worked with a full cast of A-list stars. There was little time to rehearse, but a space in the house had been set aside as a green room, where the actors could gather and bond between scenes. Paltrow and Luke Wilson dated briefly in the months that followed.

Anderson would play the songs he intended to use on set. When *The Royal Tenenbaums* was first screened at the New York Film Festival, he warned attendees that certain copyright permissions were yet to be secured for the soundtrack.[127] Originally, the movie began with the Beatles' "Hey Jude" and ended with "I'm Looking Through You".[128]

So, Anderson asked Paltrow if she might call up Paul McCartney and secure a deal (she was close with his daughter, Stella). As it turned out, both were in East Hampton, and so she, Luke, Paul and his then-partner Heather Mills all went out to a local bowling alley.[129] McCartney loved the movie but George Harrison was on his deathbed at the time, and it became impossible to acquire the rights without his approval.[130]

Anderson reached out to Elliot Smith, whose track "Needle in the Hay" plays over Richie's suicide attempt, and tried to have him record a cover of "Hey Jude". It didn't work out. Instead, for the opening seven-minute, introductory sequence, composer Mark Mothersbaugh created an instrumental version of the song, in which each of the family members becomes associated with a different instrument. Margot, for example, is tied to the harp. It's an idea then carried on across the entire score.[131]

The Royal Tenenbaums received an early, awards-qualifying run in New York and Los Angeles on 14 December, almost three years to the day after the release of *Rushmore*. While his previous movie had attracted the right sort of attention, it was *The Royal Tenenbaums*, with its ambitious scale, cavalcade of recognizable faces, and coherence of voice, that saw Anderson fully cement the artistic reputation he'd maintain for the rest of his career.

It was here that the Anderson brand began in earnest, as critics threw around soon-to-be-clichéd terms like "absurdist",[132] "quirky", and "cockeyed genius",[133] while his detractors fretted that a world this controlled, and this precise, was doomed to turn people into perfect dolls. As Kenneth Turan in the *Los Angeles Times* wrote, "Watching *The Royal Tenenbaums* is as close as we're likely to get to being kidnapped by extraterrestrials and spirited away to their strange world."[134]

It was also the movie that earned Anderson his first Academy Award nomination, for Best Original Screenplay. *Gosford Park* was the firm favourite to win but, right before the category was announced, his co-writer Wilson was struck by a sudden, divine confidence. He leaned over to the director, who he'd told not to bother with preparing a speech, and whispered: "Get ready." Paltrow, who presented the award, opened the envelope and read the words, "*Gosford Park*". As Wilson later joked, "I went back to just saying, 'It's an honor to be nominated.'"[135]

The Royal Tenenbaums, with its ambitious scale, cavalcade of recognizable faces, and coherence of voice, saw Anderson fully cement the artistic reputation he'd maintain for the rest of his career.

OPPOSITE Wes Anderson makes himself comfortable in the trunk of a car as it's driven away by Eli Cash (Owen Wilson) and Margot (Gwyneth Paltrow).
NEXT SPREAD Margot (Gwyneth Paltrow) and Richie (Luke Wilson), whose illicit love exemplifies the tragic futility that's attached itself to the Tenenbaum name.

4 SEARCH AND DESTROY

On *The Life Aquatic with Steve Zissou*

Wes Anderson's childhood hero was the oceanographer, inventor and documentary filmmaker Jacques Cousteau.[136] He thought of him, too, as a kind of "movie star", a heroic image of the man with the camera, not unlike his early fascination with his parents' Betamax tapes of Alfred Hitchcock's work, with his name printed large and proud.

Cousteau spied for the Allies during World War II and fell in love with the open sea while in recovery from a near-fatal car accident. He designed the Aqua-Lung, the first open-circuit, self-contained underwater breathing apparatus, otherwise known as SCUBA. And he was an early convert to the environmentalist cause, spending much of his career preaching about the beauty and fragility of the ocean. "He saw it as what we'd have left when we had destroyed everything else," Anderson said.[137]

The director had been the right age to watch his documentary series, *The Undersea World of Jacques Cousteau*, when it premiered on ABC, with its English narration provided by *The Twilight Zone*'s Rod Serling. In college, he wrote a short story, not much more than a paragraph, in which he described a Cousteau-like creation, his paramour and a boat. He had no intention to elaborate on it.[138]

But his friend Owen Wilson would regularly remind him of its existence, as Cousteau quietly crept his way into Anderson's early work. In *Bottle Rocket*, a photographic portrait taken by Richard Avedon can be seen in the apartment of local crime boss Mr Henry (James Caan). In *Rushmore*, a library copy of *Diving for Sunken Treasure* by Cousteau and Philippe Diolé brings Max Fischer (Jason Schwartzman) and Rosemary Cross (Olivia Williams) together.

He told Bill Murray about the idea. At first, the character was simply called Steve Cousteau.[139] Later, he became Steve Zissou. A few other adventurers, including Norwegian ethnographer Thor Heyerdahl,[140] were used to help flesh out his edges.

A friendly orca drops in to observe an interview between Steve Zissou (Bill Murray) and journalist Jane Winslett-Richardson (Cate Blanchett).

Bill Murray and Wes Anderson take a breather between scenes on *The Life Aquatic with Steve Zissou*. Zissou is based on the oceanographer, inventor and documentary filmmaker Jacques Cousteau.

Anderson would end up making *The Life Aquatic with Steve Zissou* with Touchstone Pictures, a subsidiary of Disney, which had produced his previous two movies. Yet, shortly before release, the studio got cold feet. They feared that the homage had tiptoed into direct copyright infringement, but were equally reluctant to alert the Cousteau estate to what the director had done.[141]

Eventually, they pooled together several hundred thousand dollars, called up the Cousteaus, and told them they'd hand over the money if they promised not to sue. The family agreed, with a single caveat, that the credits should read, "With gratitude to the Cousteau Society which was not involved in the making of this film." In the director's commentary for the movie's Criterion Collection release, the word "Cousteau" is censored.[142]

Wilson had struggled to find time to work with Anderson on the script for *The Royal Tenenbaums*. He was a full-fledged celebrity now, sought out for his knavish, laid-back charm, deployed in the likes of *I Spy*, *Shanghai Knights* and *Starsky & Hutch*. For his next script, Anderson would have to turn elsewhere.

He'd recently become acquainted with Brooklyn-born filmmaker Noah Baumbach, who sent him an early draft of his movie *The Squid and the Whale* to read while Anderson was working on *The Royal Tenenbaums*.[143] The projects shared a certain amount of DNA. Both were movies inspired by the divorce of their parents, and focused on economically privileged, but emotionally stilted, families.

Anderson offered to come onboard the project as a producer, and helped finesse its screenplay. The two men discovered, in turn, that they enjoyed each

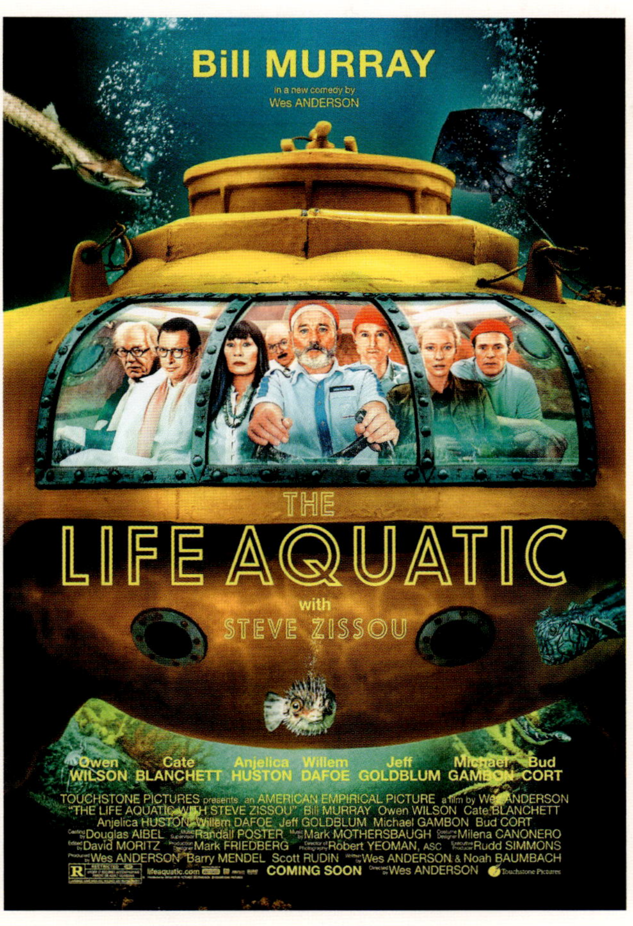

The theatrical poster for *The Life Aquatic with Steve Zissou*.

other's company, and the way their conversations seemed to flow naturally into new ideas and stories.

Anderson invited Baumbach to work with him on a script about his Cousteau-like protagonist. Baumbach had looked up to the man, too, as a child, and both would come to think of Zissou as "a kid's idea of what an adult is, or what a celebrity is".[144] This would be a film about heroes and the cheerless humanity that lies behind the facade. Both were directors on the rise, forced to reckon with the public's idea of who they were.

The pair would meet each day before lunch at Bar Pitti, an Italian trattoria in New York's Greenwich Village, and stay until after dinner. They'd talk. They'd act out scenes. Occasionally, they'd borrow a name off the menu (Zissou's private estate, Pescespada Island, is inspired by the swordfish entrée).

On the day they wrote the movie's pirate attack, they enlisted the restaurant's waiters to beef up their temporary ensemble. Anderson would note everything down in longhand, returning home each night to type up what they'd achieved. The movie, unsurprisingly, would be shot in Italy.

We meet Steve Zissou (Bill Murray) at the festival premiere of his latest documentary, about his confrontation with a mysterious creature he's termed "the jaguar shark". He watched it eat and kill his dearest friend and colleague, Esteban du Plantier (Seymour Cassel). The work is received to muted applause.

Zissou, who hasn't made a hit in nearly a decade, is rejected by his wife Eleanor (Anjelica Huston), his past lovers, his producer Oseary Drakoulias (Michael Gambon) and his financiers. He's taunted by strangers, and finds loyalty only in his crew, a miniature army of blue uniforms and red-bobbled hats. There's only one shot left to rescue his reputation. He will hunt down the jaguar shark. And he will kill it.

Murray, in the afterglow of *Rushmore* and *The Royal Tenenbaums*, was enjoying something of a career resurgence. On screen, his cynicism had turned softer and more melancholy with age, and he carried that resignation to the doors of independent cinema's hottest talents: Sofia Coppola, for *Lost in Translation* (2003), and, soon, Jim Jarmusch, for *Broken Flowers* (2005). The former had recently earned him his first Oscar nomination.

Anderson himself was in thrall to Murray's stardom. "I've never met anybody else like him," he said. "That I can absolutely certify. He really has an effect on people." He once accompanied the actor to a Sheryl Crow concert in Central Park. Afterward, as they headed to the parking garage, across Fifth Avenue, he noticed that they were being tailed by a handful of fans. By the time they reached their destination, the crowd had swelled to around forty people. Murray talked to them a little, climbed in his car, and he waved, as a king would, as they drove away.

"Working with Bill is a bit like being on a high diving board and not knowing quite how deep the water is that you're jumping into,"[145] Huston said. On the good days, she would feel spoiled by his attention and affection. Then, one day, Murray invited the entire cast to dinner but not her. She was deeply hurt. When they were reunited later on in the shoot, he asked how she'd been, and said he missed her "You're full of shit. You didn't miss me," she replied. Murray, in turn, looked confused.[146]

And so, there's certainly something of Murray in Steve Zissou, a man who draws people in and pushes them away in equal measure (Wilson once commented: "It's hard sometimes to see where Steve Zissou ends and Bill Murray begins.").[147]

Perhaps, too, there's a little of Anderson in there. Zissou is, after all, as much a filmmaker as he is an oceanographer, and his internal crisis stems ultimately from the fact he's lost control over a world as carefully curated as Anderson's, with little delineation between art and life.

Anderson, at this point, was in the honeymoon phase of his career. His last movie was an all-round hit, and had earned him his first Oscar nomination. But he had older friends and family in his life, and seemed aware of what might lie ahead of him. He and Baumbach thought, too, of Federico Fellini's *8½* and its protagonist Guido Anselmi, a celebrated director who's reached a creative impasse, and feels assailed on all sides by public expectation and private strife. "What happened to me?" Zissou wonders. "Did I lose my talent? Am I ever going to be good again?"

Zissou's movie is also called *The Life Aquatic*. It's introduced to us between parted red curtains, in the same way *Rushmore* transitions between chapters, so that we're both the audience in the movie, watching Zissou's work, and the audience outside of it, watching Anderson's.

For the documentary footage, the director used old Ektachrome stock, which, in still photography, was closely associated with the *National Geographic Magazine*. It provides a fine grain and vibrant colours. Its look then bled into the rest of Anderson's movie, with its yellow-toned, saturated glow, shot by regular cinematographer Robert Yeoman (who had also just worked on *The Squid and the Whale*).

Zissou is humiliated when reporter Jane Winslett-Richardson (Cate Blanchett), sent to write a cover profile on the man, offers up this criticism of his work: "I thought aspects of it seemed slightly fake." It's confirmation of his ultimate fear: that his work, life and personality are a ruse no one wants to buy into anymore. He's been stuck in performance mode for so long that real emotions have started to elude him. When Esteban is devoured, and Zissou resurfaces above the water, his first instinct is to ask whether the camera's still rolling.

The premiere of *The Life Aquatic* is attended by a young man named Ned Plimpton (Owen Wilson), who believes he may be Zissou's son. He introduces himself at the afterparty. Zissou invites him to join the crew of his ship, the *Belafonte*. There's potential for a relationship subplot here – Ned's great at ad-libbing, asking informative questions, which are really his attempts to bond with his maybe-father.

Zissou suggests he change his name to Kingsley Zissou, and orders him correspondence stock. He will not let him call him "Dad". "Why do you believe in this boy?" Eleanor asks. "Because he looks up to me," Zissou replies. He does not, however, mean as a father, but as a cinematic idol. A movie star.

It was important to Anderson that Wilson remained a crucial part of the movie, even if he couldn't collaborate on its script. But Ned is entirely unlike the actor's typical roles – a true innocent, a chivalric pilot for Kentucky Airlines, who's perhaps really a stand-in for every little kid who still naïvely looks up to Zissou.

It had always been Baumbach and Anderson's plan for Ned to die, after the *Belafonte*'s helicopter malfunctions and sends both him and Zissou

Jane Winslett-Richardson (Cate Blanchett) grabs a few quotes from Steve Zissou (Bill Murray) ahead of a dive.

STEVE
TEAM ZISSOU
MASTER FROGMAN

Steve Zissou (Bill Murray) shares a drink with the man who might be his son, Ned Plimpton (Owen Wilson).

plummeting into the ocean.[148] Cousteau's son and successor, Philippe, was killed in 1979, when a Cousteau Society seaplane crashed in the Tagus river near Lisbon. There were reservations. Anderson's close friend filmmaker, Peter Bogdanovich, and Baumbach's brother Nico, had both warned against the decision.

Certainly, it's an uncharacteristically brutal sequence, periodically stripped of its sound, as bloody water laps up against the camera's lens. Neither writer wanted to decide if Zissou was truly Ned's father (Eleanor, at one point, reveals that the man "shoots blanks"). His death was necessary to keep the question unanswered, so that the truth ultimately wouldn't matter. Zissou's life, at this point, has been as much illusion as it has been reality. Why change it now?

The initial tension between Ned and Zissou is spurred by the arrival of Jane, who becomes the centre of a petty romantic rivalry. She was also a Zissou fan in her youth, with her khaki uniform inspired by the English primatologist Jane Goodall.[149] She's jaded now, pregnant by her married editor, and reflects in her diary that "the Zissou of my childhood represents all the dreams I've come to regret."

When Cate Blanchett first arrived to set, Anderson kept her sequestered in her trailer. It meant that the moment she was brought out to shoot Jane's arrival on Pescespada Island – when she catches Zissou and his crew in their pyjamas, filming electric jellyfish (actually, as Jane points out, Viet-Cong man-of-wars) – it would be the first time Blanchett met her co-stars.

Eleanor Zissou (Anjelica Huston) reveals to journalist Jane Winslett-Richardson (Cate Blanchett) that "Zissou shoots blanks".

While in the middle of production on Martin Scorsese's *The Aviator*, the actor went to have a body cast fitted, which could then be used to create the appearance of a pregnancy. She fainted, which was out of character. A week later, she discovered she was pregnant. Anderson jokingly accused her of having turned into a method actor.[150] The crew put aside the prosthetic belly halfway through production as Blanchett's own stomach swelled in size.

Anjelica Huston had heard talk on the set of *The Royal Tenenbaums* that Anderson would next pursue a nautical-themed movie. She wanted in.[151] He asked Huston if she'd play Eleanor, acknowledged by her husband as "the brains behind Team Zissou". Costume designer Milena Canonero, a new addition to the Anderson ensemble, who'd worked with Stanley Kubrick on *Barry Lyndon* and *The Shining*, imagined Eleanor as a "self-made mermaid". She gave her blue hair extensions and hand-painted, pale green contacts.

Meanwhile, she outfitted the rest of Team Zissou in red caps, as worn by Cousteau's own crew, and light blue, polyester co-ords, which Anderson wanted to resemble the costumes "you'd seen on a TV show that would have aired in about 1968."

For the part of Klaus Daimler, the most steadfast of them all, Anderson had originally cast a German actor around Wilson's age, so that their characters could vie for Zissou's paternal attention.[152] He dropped out at the last minute, so Anderson decided to call Willem Dafoe, a character actor of dangerous charisma, who he'd met recently and had expressed a desire to work with him. Despite Dafoe being only five years younger than Murray, Anderson decided to keep the dynamic in place.

The director had become good friends with Bud Cort, star of *Harold and Maude*, *Brewster McCloud* and *Pollock*. So, he wrote for him the role of Bill Ubell, the bond company stooge sent to monitor the project's expenditure.[153] Cort, in preparation for the role, would rise at 4 am every day to swim. For the pirate attack scene, in which it's revealed that Bill is fluent in their spoken language, he endeavoured to master Indonesian, though Anderson stressed that only a phonetic memorization of the lines would be necessary.

At the last minute, the director found he was unable to secure the Indonesian actors needed to fill the roles, so the pirates were changed to be of Filipino origin, requiring Cort to instead speak Tagalog. He was not pleased. Still, the actor wrote five pages of his own dialogue, in which he talked about the destruction of the coral reefs. Anderson loved it, yet the producers demanded he cut out "the political stuff".

The rest of Team Zissou consists of safety expert Pelé dos Santos (Seu Jorge), camera operator Vikram Ray (Waris Ahluwalia), frogman Bobby Ogata (Niels Koizumi), physicist and composer Vladimir Wolodarsky (Noah Taylor), sound man Renzo Pietro (Pawel Wdowczak, the film's actual sound mixer) and script girl Anne-Marie Sakowitz (Robyn Cohen).

Also on board are several unpaid interns from the University of North Alaska, including Nico (Matthew Gray Gubler), named after Baumbach's brother. Gubler had met Anderson two years earlier, when he served as his unpaid intern in return for course credits at the New York University Tisch School of the Arts.

As a child, Anderson had loved to draw cutaways of houses and transportation vehicles.[154] A boat, sliced in half, was the second image to come to him after that of a Cousteau-like figure. He requested from his production designer, Mark Friedberg, two identical ships: one that was ocean-fit, and another that could be bisected for a scene in which Zissou takes the audience on a tour of the *Belafonte*, room by room, function by function.[155]

He found a pair of World War II vintage in Cape Town, South Africa.[156] They were in a pitiful state. One was stripped down into pieces and loaded on the other, which then set sail for Italy. As it passed by the Ivory Coast, its crew were arrested and held for several days.[157] Upon arrival, the bisected ship was reconstructed on Stage 5 of Rome's Cinecittà Studios, a favourite of Federico Fellini's. It stood nearly five storeys tall.[158]

At the end of the tour, the lights go down on the *Belafonte*, as if we've reached the end of a scene in a play. If Zissou's life is mere show, then it made sense to Anderson that his aquatic co-stars should hail not from reality, but from the world of movie magic. He'd already approached animator Henry Selick, who'd directed *The Nightmare Before Christmas* and *James and the Giant Peach*, about potentially working on a stop-motion adaptation of Roald Dahl's *Fantastic Mr Fox*.[159]

As a child, Anderson had loved to draw cutaways of houses and transportation vehicles. A boat, sliced in half, was the second image to come to him after that of a Cousteau-like figure.

OPPOSITE (ABOVE) Team Zissou: Vikram Ray (Waris Ahluwalia), Pelé dos Santos (Seu Jorge), Renzo Pietro (Pawel Wdowczak), Vladimir Wolodarsky (Noah Taylor), Klaus Daimler (Willem Dafoe), Ned Plimpton (Owen Wilson) and Bobby Ogata (Niels Koizumi).

OPPOSITE (BELOW) Klaus and the man he'd like to call father despite being only five years his senior, Steve Zissou (Bill Murray).

1
2
3
4
5
6
7
8
9
10
11
12
13
14
15
16
17
18
19
20
21
22
23
24
25
26
27
28
29
30
31
32
33
34
35
36
37
38
39
40
41
42
43
44
45
46
47
48
49
50
51
52
53
54
55
TEAM ZISSOU
SHOWER

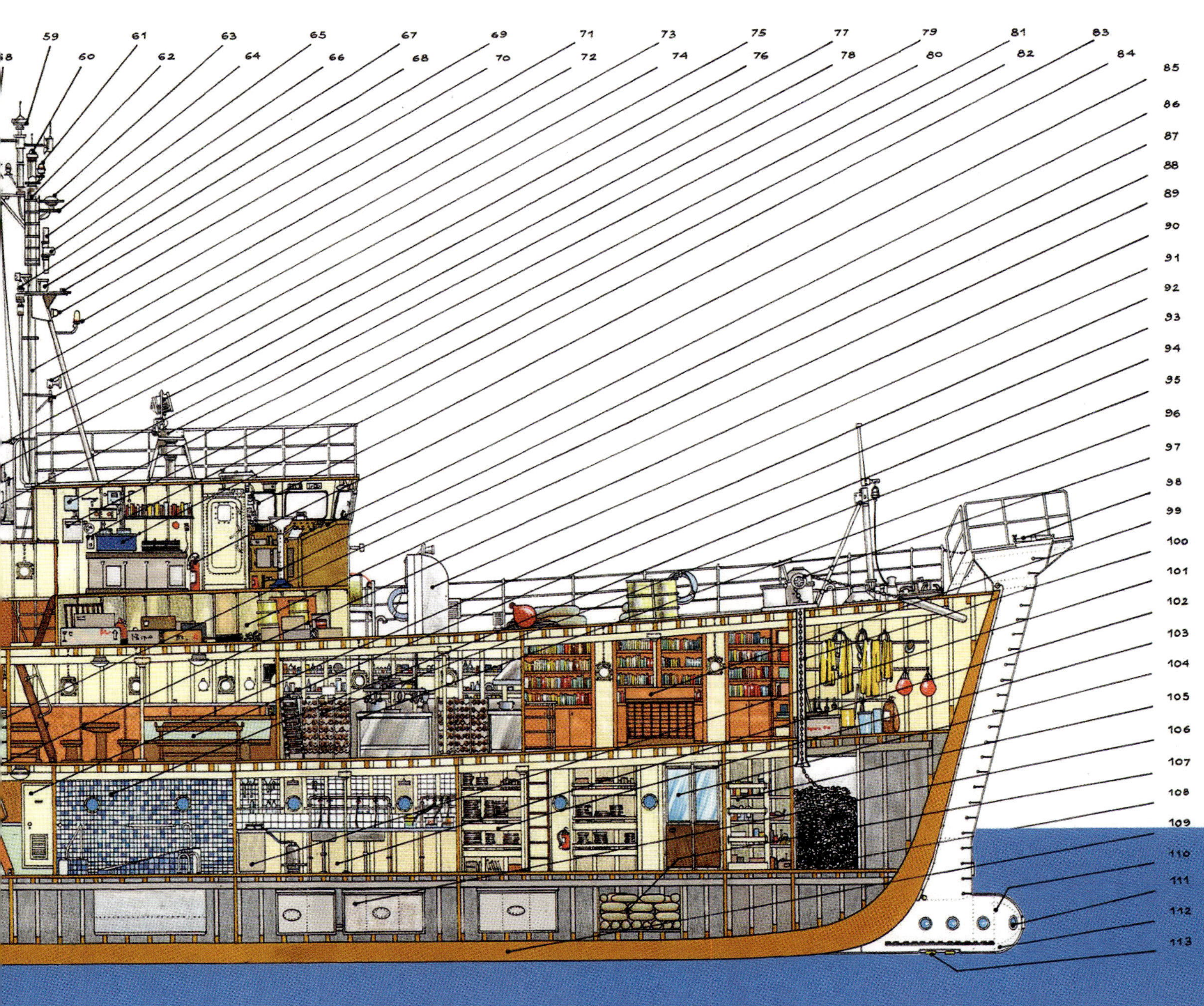

59
60
61
62
63
64
65
66
67
68
69
70
71
72
73
74
75
76
77
78
79
80
81
82
83
84
85
86
87
88
89
90
91
92
93
94
95
96
97
98
99
100
101
102
103
104
105
106
107
108
109
110
111
112
113

So, he hired Selick to create an ecosystem of imagined creatures, made with metal armatures wrapped in a lifelike and flexible silicone called Dragon Skin.[160] Anderson wanted them to be believable, even if they were implausible: a rainbow seahorse, candy-striped crabs and, of course, the eight-foot-long (2.4 metres) jaguar shark, at the time the largest stop-motion puppet ever made. One day, the legendary animator Ray Harryhausen, of *Jason and the Argonauts* (1963) and *Clash of the Titans* (1981), came to visit. He was astonished at its size.

The Life Aquatic was the first time Anderson had filmed outside America, shooting not only at Cinecittà Studios, but across the Italian coast in Naples, Ravello and on the island of Ponza. It required a few adjustments. Rome's artisans were skilled in ways he'd never seen before. But they could be stubborn, too – or, at least, rooted in their traditions. Lunch could not, under any circumstances, be delayed.[161]

It was also a place where one could easily indulge in the local culture. Not only were they surrounded by the echoes of Fellini, but Huston would spend her free time wandering into churches, in order to admire their many renditions of the Virgin Mary, a figure not entirely unlike Eleanor. Cort, meanwhile, attended the Beatification of Mother Theresa and sang for the hotel staff on a nightly basis.[162]

More pressingly, Anderson had never handled a budget remotely close to *The Life Aquatic*'s reported $50 million. He wondered, to Murray, whether it might end up looking like his own version of a Bond movie.

Misadventures occurred. While the majority of the cast were sitting in the cramped, contained set of the *Belafonte* submarine, for the scene in which Zissou finally confronts the jaguar shark, a light exploded and an instrument panel caught fire.[163] No one had agreed on a proper escape plan. Murray was chilled to the bone while the crew struggled to heat the water tanks used for underwater filming.[164] A helicopter crashed.[165] Days were wasted when boats failed to line up properly for a required shot. A gun was accidentally tossed overboard, forcing everything to come to a standstill while it was recovered by the marines.

As a result, production went 20 days over schedule, and $8 million over budget.[166] "I couldn't do the sort of controlling I like to have on this project," Anderson reflected. "I mean, just dealing with being on the water – I couldn't control things the way I usually want to, and I think some of that spills over in what you shoot."[167] Murray spent much of the press tour complaining (comically). "It wasn't like *Lawrence of Arabia* or anything," his director clarified.

The Life Aquatic earned back just over half its budget at the US box office, with a gross of $24 million,[168] and was held up as proof of indulgent tendencies by its critics. Roger Ebert branded it "terminal whimsy".[169] *Variety*'s Robert Koehler said it marked "a cul-de-sac for the gifted filmmaker",[170] while *Salon*'s Stephanie Zacharek described the filmmaker as "self-congratulatory and precociously bratty".[171]

The Life Aquatic's reputation has improved in the decades since its release, perhaps only after audiences became a little more fluent in Anderson's cinematic language. Still, the filmmaker had learned a hard lesson about his own limits. "Well, I just don't think they got it," a well-dressed admirer, played by magazine editor Isabella Blow, tells Zissou after his movie's premiere.

Yet, for a movie criticized for its emotional rigidity, the final few scenes of *The Life Aquatic* play like an open wound. Zissou comes to face-to-face

PREVIOUS SPREAD An illustration of the research vessel The Belafonte. **ABOVE** Ned Plimpton (Owen Wilson) decides to join Steve Zissou (Bill Murray).

BELOW Zissou and his team break into a remote station owned by his more successful rival, Alistair Hennessey (Jeff Goldblum).
NEXT SPREAD Hennessey and Zissou admire one of the many wonders of the ocean.

with the jaguar shark, the creature that killed his friend and (potentially) his career, and chooses to spare its life. He watches it swim by and wonders if it remembers him.

The day of the scene's shoot, Murray appeared drained. He was away from his family, trapped for weeks inside an unhappy, embittered character. He didn't speak to anyone, but sat alone and read a book.[172] Anderson started to play 'Starálfur' over the speakers to set the mood, a haunting piece by Icelandic art-rock band Sigur Rós (it features in the movie, too).

In the scene, Zissou starts to cry and every person in the submarine – who's also every person in his life – reaches out to touch him on the shoulder. "It just had a very strong feeling to it," cinematographer Robert Yeoman said. "I felt like it was a perfect culmination of all that had happened up to that point."[173] Once the scene was done, Murray seemed like a changed man, as if a weight had been lifted off his shoulders.

Zissou may say he only cares for revenge, but it's clear the jaguar shark means more to him than he could ever put in words. "I remember Scott Rudin, our producer, saying to me when I was writing it, 'What is the metaphor with the shark?'" Anderson remarked. "I said, 'I don't know but I like that we're thinking of it as a metaphor. Let's just let it be a metaphor.'"[174] There's certainly some sense of resolution there. Zissou, faced with his critics and his obstacles, is allowed to find peace. Anderson soon would, too.

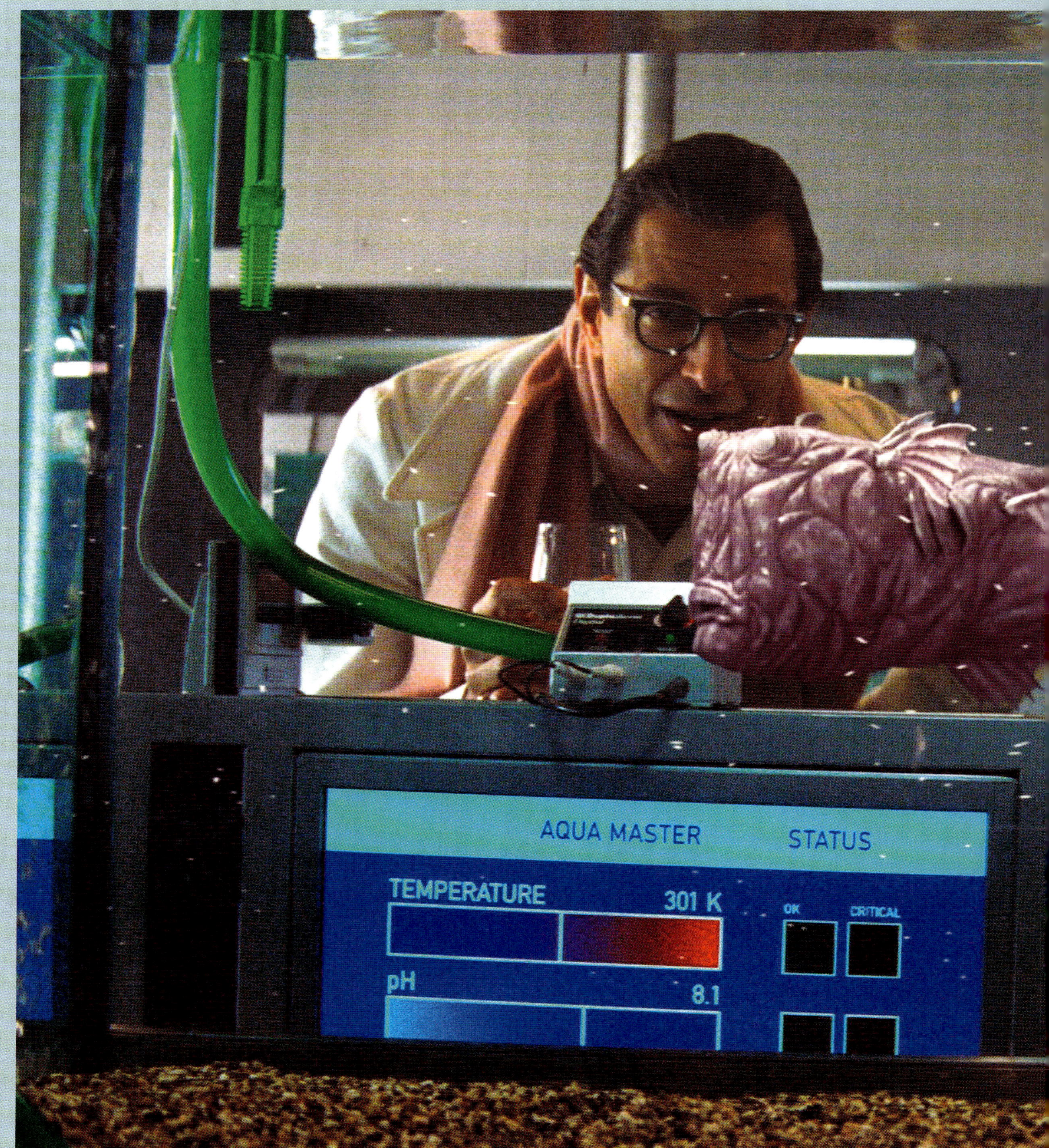
AQUA MASTER
STATUS
TEMPERATURE
301 K
OK
CRITICAL
pH
8.1

5 ABHIJAN

On *The Darjeeling Limited*

In 2005, Jason Schwartzman and Wes Anderson both found themselves in Paris. The actor had arrived in the city to shoot Sofia Coppola's *Marie Antoinette*, in which he played the guileless young king Louis XVI. The director was at the tail end of *The Life Aquatic*'s publicity tour. Schwartzman suggested he stay a few extra nights at his apartment so he could sightsee.[175] Anderson was there for three months.[176]

"We were like a married couple," Schwartzman said. Each night, after the actor had arrived home from work, they'd venture out into the streets to walk the dog and talk about their lives. Stories, inevitably, turned into ideas. Anderson filled his notebook with them. After about three weeks, he suggested they bring Schwartzman's cousin Roman Coppola "in on this". Schwartzman had no idea what "this" was. Walking the dog? "This movie we're writing," Anderson replied, matter-of-factly.[177]

As it turns out, the director had stumbled on his next project. He, Schwartzman and Coppola would write a movie about a trio of brothers traversing India by train. "It will be the most personal thing we could possibly make – let's try to make it even too personal," he explained.[178]

The Life Aquatic had swelled into something beyond his grasp. Its relative failure, then, had made him yearn for the intimate and the low budget, a real adventure free from the usual encampment of crew members and makeup trailers. "I felt like I was getting some things off my chest, I guess," he'd confess.

Anderson's oldest friend Sanjay, who he'd met when he was eight years old, hailed from the southern Indian city of Chennai, named Madras at the time.[179] He'd tell Anderson stories about his birth country, about the places, people and traditions that existed far beyond the limits of the young Texan boy's world.

The Whitman brothers – Jack (Jason Schwartzman), Francis (Owen Wilson) and Peter (Adrien Brody) – set forth. *The Darjeeling Limited* encapsulates Anderson yearning for freedom after the big-budget pressures of *The Life Aquatic with Steve Zissou.*

Later, Anderson discovered the work of Satyajit Ray, one of the great masters of cinema, whose overwhelming authorial control over his own work (he wrote, cast, scored and edited his movies, even designing his own credit titles and publicity materials) no doubt had an influence on Anderson's hermetic approach to his cinema.

Ray was born in Kolkata, West Bengal. Alongside a small circle of fellow intellectuals, he founded the Calcutta Film Society in 1947, which would eventually lead him to French director Jean Renoir, who came to India to shoot *The River* (1951), in which the Ganges becomes the ever-flowing, symbolic backdrop to a young woman's awakening passions. Ray helped him find his locations, and the two discussed his long-simmering desire to adapt the classic novel *Pather Panchali*. Renoir was encouraging.

The film he'd make, released in 1955, depicted rural Bengali life with truthful, startling beauty. It's one of the most astounding declarations of artistic intent ever made, the beginning of a career ruled over by empathy, by the desire to root out small details and uncover hidden struggles, in a way that would actively help shape post-partition Bengali culture.

When Ray died in 1992, the city of Kolkata came to a standstill. Anderson is hardly the only great American director enthralled by and indebted to his work – he's been cited by Martin Scorsese, Francis Ford Coppola, John Huston, George Lucas, and Quentin Tarantino, among many others.

Years later, Scorsese invited Anderson to see a new restoration of *The River*.[180] He had a hunch that it was something the director should see. On his way out of the screening room and into the street, Anderson made a resolution. Somehow, some way, he was going to shoot a movie in India. It took all those daily constitutionals in Paris for the story to fall into place.

Ray's music would become an integral part of *The Darjeeling Limited* – not only what he composed for his own work, but for several Merchant Ivory movies, including *Shakespeare Wallah* (1965). Anderson played it everywhere: while writing, while on set, while location scouting, or merely while travelling with Schwartzman and Coppola.

"It was really not just the soundtrack to the movie," Anderson said. "For us, it was a soundtrack for the making of the movie."[181] He sent his music supervisor, Randall Poster, to Kolkata, and to the Satyajit Ray Film Society, who made their entire archive available to him.[182] Several pieces, including from *Charulata* (1964) and *Teen Kanya* (1961), appear in the final movie.

Coppola started out working visual effects and second unit direction on his father Francis Ford's 1992 horror, *Bram Stoker's Dracula*, before making his own feature debut, *CQ* (2001). He'd phoned up Anderson during the shooting of *The Life Aquatic* to see if he needed any help. He did, desperately, but had no idea what to ask for. Coppola turned up in Italy anyway, at 5am, and within hours was directing second unit footage of a ship being towed.

Conveniently, he was also in Paris to direct second unit on his sister Sofia's movie. And so, Anderson, Schwartzman and Coppola would rendezvous in cafés and restaurants, late at night, or in the apartment, where Coppola would sit on the floor, Schwartzman would sit on the sofa, and Anderson would pace the room.[183] When they finally parted ways, they would instead stage daily four-hour conference calls.

They aimed, through their work, to reach a state Coppola would describe as being "in the forest" – to feel as if they were headed somewhere they'd been before without a map, guided only by the faintest memory and the

ABOVE Francis (Owen Wilson), Peter (Adrien Brody) and Jack Whitman (Jason Schwartzman) are confronted by The Chief Steward (Waris Ahluwalia). **LEFT** The theatrical poster for *The Darjeeling Limited*.

odd, recognizable feature. "It's a sensation of rediscovering something that already existed," Coppola explained. "We were just finding it again."

Anderson knew how his movie would begin: with an American businessman missing his train, a part that would allow Bill Murray to have a small cameo. He worried the actor would say no – it's a long way to travel for a few minutes of screen time – and so he promised him the businessman was less of a character, more of a symbol. "Oh, I can do a symbol," the actor replied.[184] Of what, is entirely the viewer's choice, though it's worth noting that the father of the three brothers died a year earlier.

The director was certain, too, of how he wanted things to end, with the siblings finding their vanished mother, Patricia (played by Anderson's go-to, Angelica Huston), living in a convent in the Himalayas.[185] He would mail the actor a figurine of a nun in the mail – two, in fact, after he'd forgotten that he'd sent her the first. It was his way to let her know that he'd come up with a new role for her.[186] She, of course, eagerly accepted. Briefly, when she was six, she had toyed with the idea of becoming a nun.[187]

Soon, the brothers acquired names: Francis, Jack and Peter Whitman. Each was a concoction of experiences belonging to the writers, their friends and various acquaintances. Yet, in the process of working and acting out scenes, a new approach coalesced: Anderson would always play Francis, while Schwartzman would play Jack, and Coppola would play Peter.[188]

The Whitmans, when we first meet them, have become strangers to each other, hollowed out in the pursuit of vain, empty distractions. An invitation from Francis brings them to India, and to their cabin on The Darjeeling Limited. He turns up with a face swaddled in bandages, the result of a motorcycle accident that we later learn was a deliberate suicide attempt.

"A: I want us to become brothers again like we used to be, and for us to find ourselves and bond with each other," he informs Jack and Peter. "B: I want us to make this trip a spiritual journey where each of us seek the unknown and we learn about it. C: I want us to be completely open and say yes to everything, even if it's shocking and painful." They should expect a daily schedule, printed out, laminated, and slipped under their door by Francis's assistant Brendan (Wally Wolodarsky).

Quickly, they retire to their individual corners to smoke cigarettes, swallow pills and down bottles of cough syrup, raising their heads up from these activities only to argue or trade secrets with one brother that must be kept from the other. While their bodies may traverse sacred places, through temples and shrines, their minds are back home in New York. They bicker over material possessions: an expensive belt, a stolen shoe or their dead father's sunglasses.

Schwartzman, naturally, would end up in the role of Jack, while Owen Wilson would play Francis. His bruised and battered look, created with the help of makeup artist Frances Hannon, was inspired partially by a man Anderson had once seen in St Peter's Basilica in Rome.[189] He came, it appeared, directly from the hospital, his eyes framed by tears, as he prayed and lit a candle. The director couldn't help but imagine what near-death experience had brought him to this place.

Anderson had been a fan of Adrien Brody since his breakout role in Steven Soderbergh's Depression-era drama, *King of the Hill*.[190] The part was explicitly written for him, one of a string of high-profile roles he took after winning the Academy Award for *The Pianist* (2002).

Anderson had written a short about a man and a woman,[191] old lovers who partake in a barbed, but sincere reunion in a Parisian hotel room. "If we fuck, I'm going to feel like shit tomorrow," she laments. She does so anyway. Schwartzman would play the man, marking the first time he'd work with the director since *Rushmore* (a small role in *The Royal Tenenbaums* was cut, with the character's name, Mordecai, given to a falcon instead). Natalie Portman would play the woman. Yet, as the script for *The Darjeeling Limited* progressed, it became clear that the man and Jack were the same person.

Anderson, at this point, had been spending more and more time in Paris, and was determined to make something in the city. He loaned out equipment from Panavision, and called in as many favours as he could. Portman flew over during a break from filming Miloš Forman's *Goya's Ghosts* in Spain. The director picked Hotel Raphael as his location – he'd stayed in a yellow room there once, and it seemed to him to be a readymade set. He worked quickly, with a small crew, and shot the movie in two and a half days.

Hotel Chevalier is, in practical terms, a prologue. It's also a motivating piece of backstory for Jack, who spends much of *The Darjeeling Limited* pitiably checking the answering machine of Portman's character, Rhett. When that fails to produce any resolution, he attempts to reignite his desires with the train's stewardess, Rita (Amara Karan). She has her own story, one of restlessness, and a fitful affair with the Chief Steward (Waris Ahluwalia).

Jack, for her, is a brief sexual interlude. He doesn't get it, lingering outside her cabin door hoping for a kiss good night and playing her the same song he seduced Rhett with, Peter Sarstedt's "Where Do You Go to My Lovely?". Karan, London-born to Sri Lankan parents, and an Oxford graduate, quit a promising role at an investment bank in order to pursue acting. She had to enlist her friends to teach her how to smoke.

Hotel Chevalier also forms the short story that Jack, a writer by trade, presents to his brothers at the end of *The Darjeeling Limited*. He claims all his characters are fictional when they are, quite nakedly, not. Perhaps it's a bit of an in-joke for Anderson.

Anderson, eventually, suggested they finally see India for themselves. In March 2006, the director packed his monogrammed luggage and joined Schwartzman, Coppola, his friend Waris Ahluwalia (who was born in Amritsar, Punjab) and producer Alice Bamford.[192] They stayed for five weeks. The printer they brought on the train with them blew up when Anderson plugged it into the wrong outlet. "How could I know that?" he insisted. "I don't understand electricity like that."

The writers adopted Francis's motto – "say 'yes' to everything" – and became indistinguishable from the characters they'd created. "We became like brothers ourselves,"[193] Anderson noted. They might head to a temple, scripts in hand, and act out a scene, often in places they'd later shoot in, or jump in a rickshaw and drive aimlessly through the streets.[194] If they met new people, they'd usually convince those people to be in their movie.

Anderson eventually suggested they finally see India for themselves. The director packed his monogrammed luggage and stayed for five weeks.

OPPOSITE (ABOVE) Jack (Jason Schwartzman) pursues a frustrated romance with the train's stewardess, Rita (Amara Karan).
OPPOSITE (BELOW) The Whitman matriarch, Patricia (Angelica Huston), is eventually found living in a convent in the Himalayas.

A crouched Wes Anderson offers a little guidance to Owen Wilson, Adrien Brody and Jason Schwartzman as they prepare for a scene in the train's dining car.

One day, they were brought to a village in the Rajasthan desert, where the elders invited them to participate in a traditional welcome ritual. Seated together on the floor of a hut, they watched as one of the elders steeped opium in a small leather pitcher, as one might a bag of tea, and poured it into his hand. They were encouraged to take one sip or three from his cupped palm. All decided on three.

"It felt like half a Xanax," Anderson recalled. "But when we stood up and started to go out of there, we all shared this feeling, like, 'This is a great village.'"[195] It ended up as a major location, where the Whitmans attend the funeral of a young boy, with many of the people they met that day cast as actors.

For the role of the grieving father, Anderson sought out Irrfan Khan, a legend in Indian cinema who'd pointedly branched out into the British and American industries with roles in Asif Kapadia's *The Warrior* and Ang Lee's *Life of Pi*. The local cast would flock to him. He wasn't familiar with Anderson's work, but, after his first day on set, he watched *The Royal Tenenbaums* and returned an admirer. He shared his thoughts with the director. Suddenly, Anderson didn't feel like such a novice directing one of the all-time greats.

Another key influence on *The Darjeeling Limited* was John Cassavetes's *Husbands*, in which three men in crisis jet off to England in an (ultimately unsuccessful) attempt to purge their anxieties. It's a desperate, egocentric exercise that shares much of its DNA with the Whitmans's excursion to India. Francis believes he can trim a little spiritual enlightenment off the country's decorative edges, without investment into any god, community or

ABOVE The Whitmans – Jack (Jason Schwartzman), Francis (Owen Wilson) and Peter (Adrien Brody) – rush to make a second train, The Bengal Lancer, at the very end of their journey.
NEXT SPREAD The Whitmans haul across a field their monogrammed luggage, designed by Marc Jacobs.

faith. He brings with him some half-remembered feather ceremony, inspired by the Havasupai tribe of the Grand Canyon.

Francis is a tourist, cheerily ignorant of the inauthenticity of the tourist mindset, or what a fool he sounds like after he and his brothers are kicked off the train for their boisterousness and for the release of a poisonous snake. "We were just trying to experience something," he implores.

The Darjeeling Limited warns against casual Orientalism, and the exoticizing of India by white Westerners with heads full of saffron-dipped dreams. In a piece for the *Los Angeles Times*, published on its release, writer Swati Pandey pointed out that Anderson's trademark fixation on trinkets avoided the usual "cheap shots" by creating an "equality of gaze" that is "at once Orientalist and self-fetishizing" – equally bewitched by the cut of the Whitmans' suits as it is by sounds and colours of the marketplace.[196]

But it's a movie that also reveals the limits of Anderson's perspective, guilty as it is of the same impulses it seeks to critique. The American tourists can only be shaken out of their narcissism by a confrontation with true faith, after Peter fails to save the life of a boy whose boat tips over into the river. Here, India – and, more pointedly, the death and suffering of Indian people – is reduced to a vehicle for the amelioration of white protagonists on the behalf of a white director.

As Pandey continued, it "relies too heavily on setting-as-story, of lands that magically make epiphanies deeper and love affairs more meaningful." Anderson himself admitted that, at the end of it all, he and his co-writers were still "tourists there; that's all we can ever be there." He was moved by what he found to be

J.L.W.
3

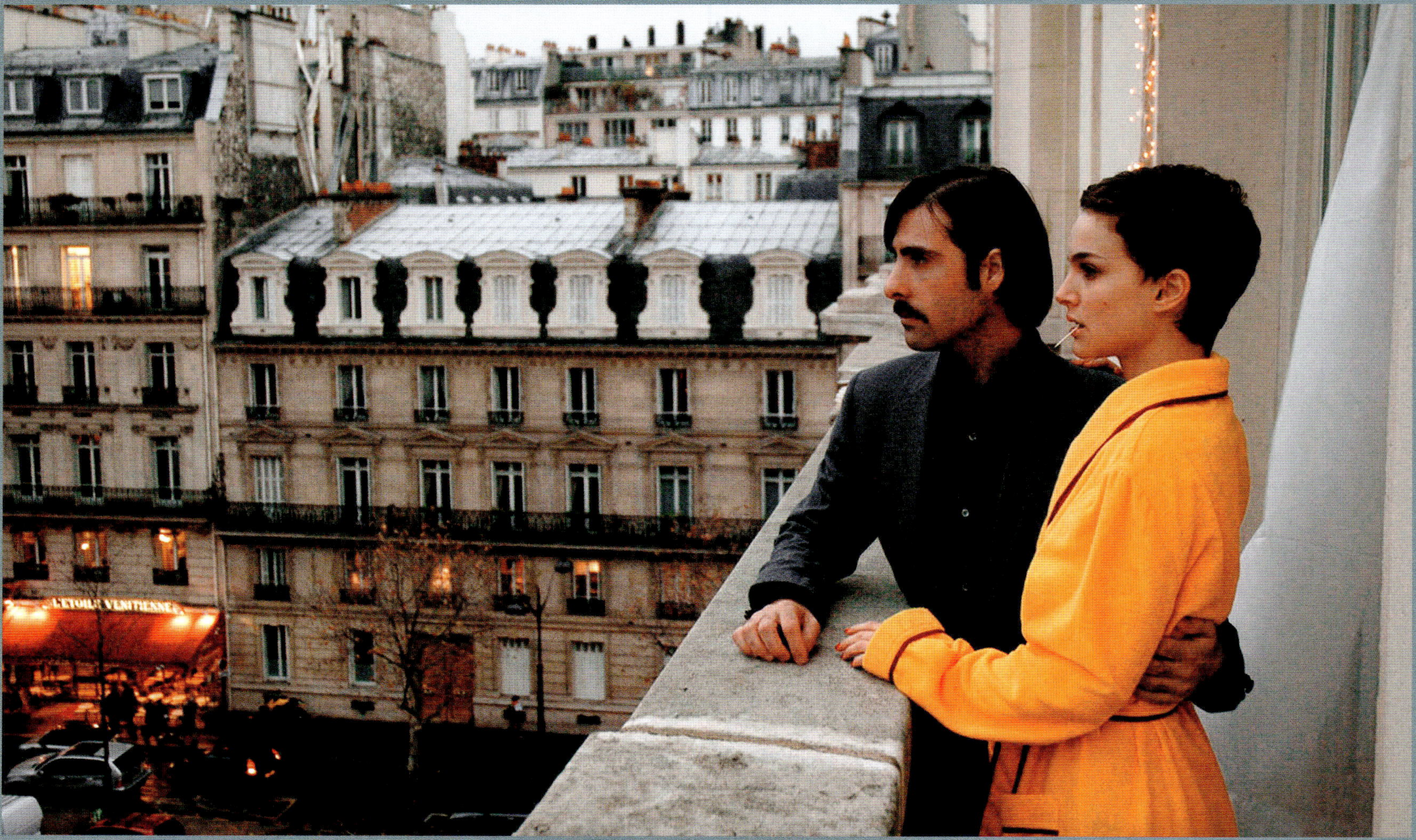

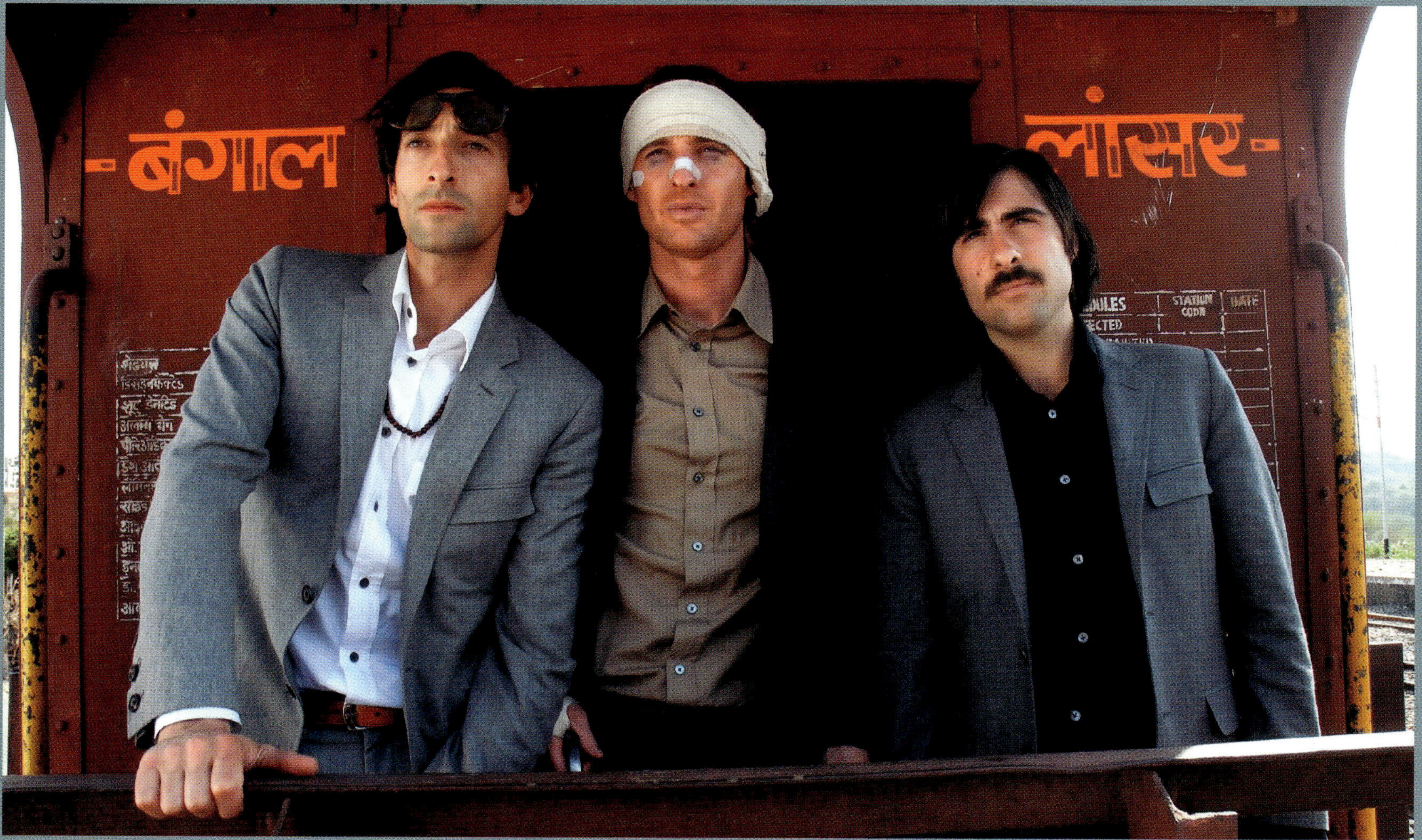

-बंगाल
लांसर-
STATION CODE
DATE

OPPOSITE (ABOVE) Jack (Jason Schwartzman) and Rhett (Natalie Portman) look out at Paris from the balcony of their room at the Hotel Chevalier.
OPPOSITE (BELOW) Peter (Adrien Brody), Francis (Owen Wilson) and Jack Whitman look out at their discarded luggage from the rear of The Bengal Lancer.
ABOVE The Chief Steward (Waris Ahluwalia) of The Darjeeling Limited.

a country that possessed such a breadth and abundance of religion. "Then you get sensitive and wonder if that sounds kind of naive," he continued. "I just hate to sound self-protective and defensive; I'd rather just express our real feelings about it."

Certainly, India or, at least, the dramatic shift in surroundings, had helped fuel Anderson's new desire for creative spontaneity. On a budget of $16 million,[197] less than half of *The Life Aquatic*'s, the director tailored his set to be as adaptive and intimate as possible. Suits were prewired with microphones. Actors did their own makeup. There were no trailers to retreat to.[198] "Wes was kind of like the fourth brother," Brody reflected. "We're all so similar in intangible ways – it's almost a little weird."[199]

Filming largely took place in the north-western desert region of Rajasthan. Anderson and his crew worked quickly, often venturing out into the city streets without a lighting set-up, allowing real people, busy with their own lives, to enter the frame. He took the same attitude while collaborating with local craftsmen, having committed himself to embracing the unexpected.

If a house, without prompt, was painted blue and pink, and covered with flowers, so that it no longer matched the others, then it would remain that way.[200] It was Anderson's way of learning about the country and, hopefully, to make his movie more honest. As producer Lydia Dean Pilcher observed, "I think India kind of co-directed the movie with Wes, and I think he liked that."[201]

The director had become friends with Marc Jacobs, then the creative director of French fashion house Louis Vuitton, after being introduced by one of his muses, Sofia Coppola. Anderson hired him to create the bespoke

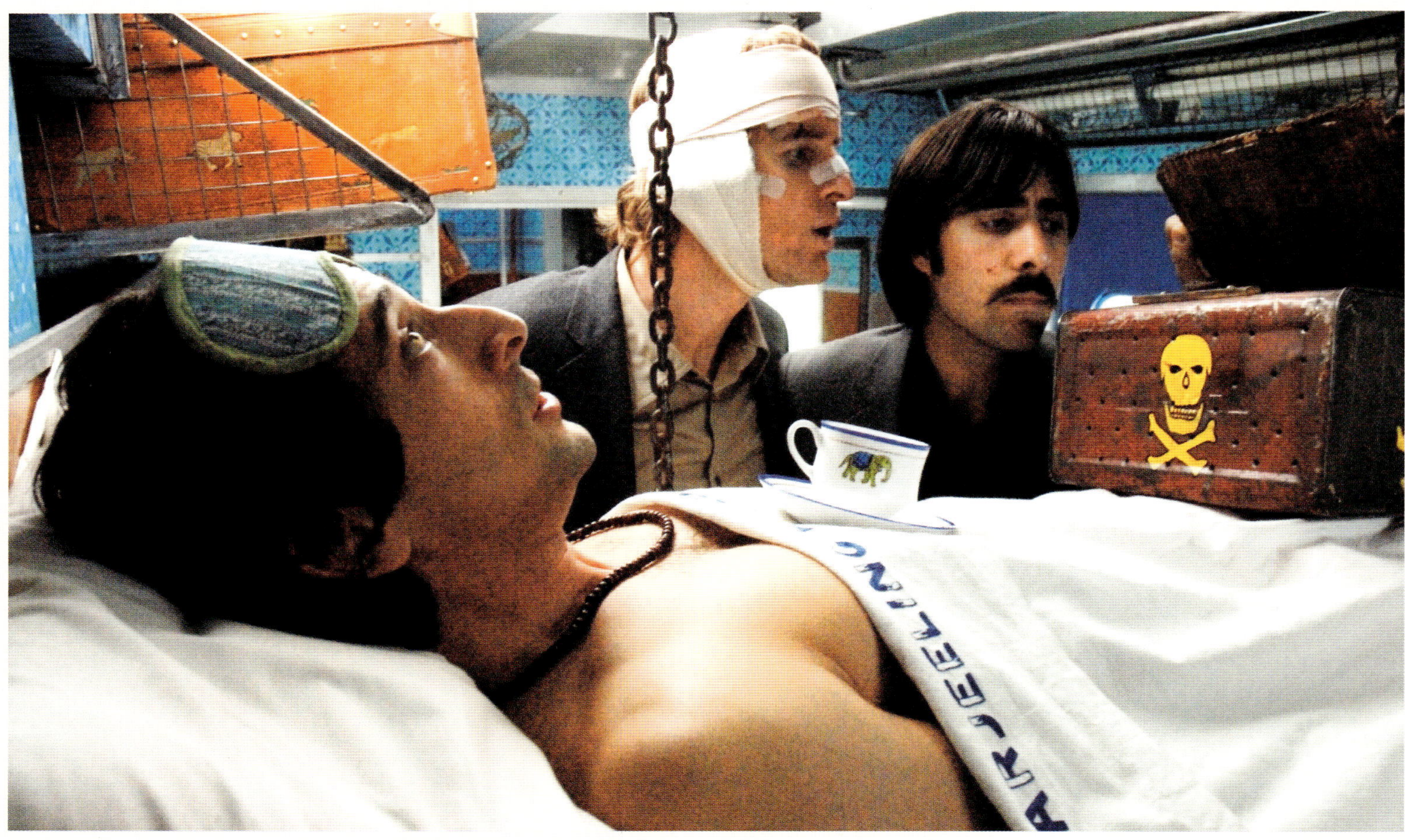

Peter (Adrien Brody) lies as still as a corpse while revealing to Francis (Owen Wilson) and Jack (Jason Schwartzman) that his poisonous snake has escaped its box.

luggage collection the Whitmans inherit from their father, its pattern of safari animals passant and palm trees designed by the director's brother Eric.[202]

Anderson himself, however, specified the colour of the lining and the accessories within, including one appendage intended to house a tennis racquet.[203] At the end of the shoot, the pieces were sold off to buy ambulances that could serve the local Rajasthan villages.[204]

Jacobs would also provide the men's suits, subdued but luxurious in their neutral palette, while Milena Canonero returned to design the other costumes. Jack is barefoot in the movie purely because he's barefoot, walking across plush carpet, in the *Hotel Chevalier* short.

It was perfect for Jack, Anderson thought, since he was exactly the sort of man who'd unnecessarily create discomfort for himself – for the experience, the story, or, perhaps, some vague notion of rerooting himself back into the earth. Schwartzman stopped wearing shoes around seven weeks before filming began, so that they'd harden and become callous.

For Patricia's convent, Anderson and his production designer, Mark Friedberg, took inspiration from Michael Powell and Emeric Pressburger's *Black Narcissus*, in which a sexual fever spreads among nuns high up in the Himalayas.[205] They used a house in Udaipur, the former residence of George Everest, the nineteenth-century Surveyor General of India whose name was borrowed for the mountains' highest peak.[206]

Anderson knew that his movie needed a real, moving train. He could not be talked out of the idea, no matter how impractical it seemed, so he requested from India's North Western Railway the use of a broad-gauge train

Wes Anderson watches the monitor while his regular cinematographer, Robert Yeoman, stands ready behind the camera. Working with a budget of $16 million, the director tailored his set to be as adaptive and intimate as possible.

with ten coaches which could be stripped down and renovated for three months.[207] It was acquired, but only after a substantial amount of bureaucracy.

Friedberg, alongside art director Adam Stockhausen and graphic artist Mark Pollard, used a blend of Rajasthan-style patterns and colours, combined with an Art Deco flair that evoked the 20th Century Limited, a New York passenger express that was advertised as "the most famous train in the world". On its exterior, local painters added hundreds of hand-drawn elephants, similarly to how truck drivers might decorate their vehicles.[208]

Certain modifications were required, of course. Duplicate sets were built on opposite sides of the train, so a scene could be shot both in the morning and in the afternoon. Sliding walls, and a dolly track attached to the corridor's ceiling, allowed the camera to move seamlessly within spaces. In one scene, an argument between the brothers, Schwartzman had to be physically guided by the key grip, Sanjay Sami, who oversaw the camera equipment. "They would just grab me by the back of the coat and yank me," the actor said.[209]

The train ran on the railway network, fitting within existing schedules and departing each morning from a station in Jodphur. It therefore demanded stringent professionalism from its cast and crew – if you were late to set, the set would no longer be there.[210]

If the train was forced to stop unexpectedly, for example due to animals wandering onto the track, a piece of lumber would be used to rock the carriages to simulate motion, or a section would be unhooked and loaded onto a truck, which headed out into the desert. "The idea was

that, no matter what the logistics," Pilcher said. "We would never stop shooting, ever."[211]

Anderson and his co-writers had struggled to pin down the film's emotional climax. The Whitmans have finally confronted their mother, but she feels no penitence for having abandoned her children in their hour of need. She won't fall to her knees and beg their forgiveness. They'll have to work out their own resolution. But how? Coppola, suddenly, remembered an old acting exercise, in which participants would work through a scene's beats using only their eyes.[212]

This is how Patricia achieves peace with her sons, and how her sons achieve peace with each other. "Maybe we can express ourselves more fully if we do it without words," she suggests. The camera spins around their circle of faces, before drifting down the length of a train carriage, each cabin occupied by a past memory: Rita, Rhett, the businessman who never caught his train, the man-eating tiger said to stalk the convent grounds.

The shot was achieved in a single take. A car was gutted and filled with a feline puppet manufactured by Jim Henson, along with a fake forest, Natalie Portman and Bill Murray, the two actors having flown over specifically for the scene.[213]

Everything the Whitmans need to heal is already stored in their own hearts. Running late again to catch another train, the brothers shed their luggage, a vision Anderson has warned against reducing to pat metaphor. What they leave behind is what belongs to their father, the ghost of his legacy – "I think they take the emotional baggage with them," the director added. As Francis tells Peter and Jack, after he unravels his bandages and looks at his still-scabbed face in the mirror, "I guess I've still got some more healing to do."

Released by Fox Searchlight, with the hope it would drum up a little awards interest, *The Darjeeling Limited* opened to middling reviews and only $12 million at the domestic box office,[214] the lowest return on an Anderson movie since *Bottle Rocket*. Yet, Anderson's bid to let loose (in a way only Anderson can) had a revelatory effect on some of his most stubborn critics.

The Guardian's Philip French, who confessed he'd "never taken to the cultivated eccentricity and arbitrary conduct" of the director's characters, found himself "oddly moved".[215] *Salon*'s Stephanie Zacharek, meanwhile, wrote that it was "the first of Anderson's movies that has elicited even the mildest scrap of affection from me: I feel warmly toward it, although I reserve the right to remain wary of its aging-hipster gimcrackery."[216]

An even greater reward was found closer to home. Schwartzman showed the movie to his younger brother, Robert. He seemed reluctant to share his reaction at first. He wanted to sleep on it. He phoned Jason the next day, his voice suddenly agitated. He was scared by the prospect that they, like the Whitmans, might one day drift apart. Maybe they should take a trip.

"It wasn't India," Schwartzman said. "It was someplace forty-five minutes away or something. But he was like, 'We should go away for the weekend, and spend the night and just get to know each other and talk and find out where we are all in our lives, because we can't let this happen to us.'"[217]

ABOVE Rita (Amara Karan) leans out of the train's window to enjoy a cigarette.
OPPOSITE (ABOVE) Bill Murray in the role of a symbol, the businessman who misses his train.
OPPOSITE (BELOW) Peter (Adrien Brody), Jack (Jason Schwartzman) and Francis Whitman (Owen Wilson) examine their laminated itineraries.
NEXT SPREAD Jack, Peter and Francis visit a temple in search of enlightenment.

6 VULPES VULPES

On *Fantastic Mr. Fox*

At the turn of the millennium, Roald Dahl's widow, Felicity, received a phone call from Los Angeles. Someone had inquired after the rights to her late husband's novel *Fantastic Mr Fox*, a short but sprightly tale about a wily canid who outsmarts the local farmers in order to steal food for his family. "Do you think we can really make a film of that?" Dahl wondered.[218] Her agent cautioned her against meeting the young filmmaker quite yet. His work, it's said, was an acquired taste. It may not be to her liking. Let him send her his movies first, so she could see for herself.

And so, Wes Anderson's *Bottle Rocket* and *Rushmore* turned up on Dahl's doorstep. She watched both. "Blimey, here's somebody with a bit of talent," she thought to herself, now that she'd been inducted into the director's wistful imagination.

She agreed to meet Anderson in New York, where he was about to shoot *The Royal Tenenbaums*, arriving uptown for lunch at a "very small, but very smart" restaurant the director had picked.[219] And there he was, dressed a little like Mr Fox himself, modest but gentlemanly. "Goodness, what are we doing here?" she asked. "The cheese soufflé is fantastic," he replied. By the end of the meal, she was certain Anderson would do right by her husband's work.

Anderson's mother had purchased a copy of *Fantastic Mr Fox* at a Texan book fair, when the director was roughly seven years old.[220] He wrote his name on a sticker, placed it on the book's title page and brought it with him wherever he went, well into adulthood.[221] Dahl's fastidious prose, whimsical but keen to the uglier, darker impulses of human nature, appealed greatly to the boy.

For years, the director had wanted to make a stop-motion animated movie. It's a difficult, laborious medium. Each frame is a single photograph,

Mr Fox (George Clooney) leads the local critters underground to safety and security. Writers Wes Anderson and Noah Baumbach were immediately drawn to the image of the character as an irresistibly charismatic Cary Grant type.

populated by puppets that are moved in the smallest increments to simulate life.

"You're a bit aware of the illusion," Anderson has said. "Which is a very effective illusion, but you're a bit aware of how the illusion is being created."[222] The same could be said of when he draws back the red theatrical curtains in *Rushmore*, or bifurcates a ship in *The Life Aquatic*. We're reminded that this is all created by the caring, impassioned hand of an artist. It seemed as if stop-motion might be the perfect medium to tell the story of *Fantastic Mr Fox*.

Anderson asked Dahl if he might visit her at her home, Gipsy House, in Great Missenden, England, where Roald had written the novel, among other classics *Charlie and the Chocolate Factory*, *Matilda* and *The Witches*.[223] It was autumn when the director arrived, and he began to dream of a muddy palette, with pink and orange skies streaked like a painting by Mark Rothko, and grass made of yellow terrycloth. There are no blues and no greens in his movie.

Dahl gave Anderson a pair of rubber boots, and one of her husband's old fishing hats, and took him out to see a large beech tree.[224] He recognized it immediately from the illustrations Donald Chaffin had created for the book's first edition – this was Mr Fox's home. A year later, the tree keeled over, and was quickly overtaken by brambles.[225]

It was autumn when the director arrived, and he began to dream of a muddy palette, with pink and orange skies streaked like a painting by Mark Rothko.

She brought him, too, to Roald's writing hut, filled with knick-knacks that seemed to tell his life's story. Here was the surgical valve he invented, which was used to save his son's life when he contracted hydrocephalus, and there was a ten-pound (4.5 kilograms) ball of aluminum foil made of discarded Cadbury's chocolate wrappers. She left him to examine the author's own archive, filled with early drafts and illustrated notebooks.

Anderson ventured a new proposition: if Dahl would allow it, he'd love to stay at Gipsy House with his *Life Aquatic* co-writer, Noah Baumbach, while they worked to adapt *Fantastic Mr Fox*. She not only agreed, but set aside an office space for them with a desk, printer and dedicated phone line.[226] And so they worked steadily away, inspired by the same things that once moved her late husband.

Fantastic Mr Fox, as a book, was too short for a feature film. Anderson and Baumbach would need to expand its horizons. The writers added a before and an after, and sprinkled in neuroticism and a few marital troubles. Mr Fox's thievery became the life's passion he and Mrs Fox left behind in order to raise their son, Ash (in the novel, there are four fox children, though none have names or individual identities).

Now, Mr Fox is a newspaperman, yet 12 years at the job have left him feeling insignificant. "Does anybody actually read my column?" he cries. Frustrated, he rustles up a team for "one last job" – a strike on three farms owned by Walt Boggis, Nate Bunce and Frank Bean. A miniature system of bureaucracy was put in place, too, with a badger attorney and a weasel estate agent.

OPPOSITE (ABOVE) Mr Fox (George Clooney) and Mrs Fox (Meryl Streep), the latter working on one of her landscapes.

OPPOSITE (BELOW) The new, dream abode of the Fox family, a move that brings with it disastrous consequences.

Dahl was their guide, their lighthouse. Always, they tried to imagine what he might have written. And the more time they spent in Great Missenden, the more their movie become about the author himself. Dahl had written memoirs for his young audience, which gave them an unusual familiarity with the wizard behind the curtain of their favourite stories.

Mr Bean, his wife and their home were modelled to slightly resemble Roald, Felicity and Gipsy House. A flint mine near the village became a hiding place for the foxes, and one of its pubs, the Nag's Head, found itself in the movie's town square.

Mr Fox's study looks strikingly similar to Roald's writing hut, with its green upholstered armchair and felted writing board. Anderson sent a researcher to photograph every piece of furniture and every memento at Gipsy House in order to recreate them in miniature.[227] When Felicity Dahl, whose first name was given to Mrs Fox, first went to visit the movie's sets, she burst into tears.[228]

Anderson and Baumbach were aware that they were Americans, with a certain dry, American sensibility. So, while Mr Fox has several of Dahl's own documented traits[229] – a cavalier impulse for showmanship, matched with a hint of emotional immaturity – they decided that he and the other creatures should be voiced by American actors, while the humans would remain British.

Unusually for Anderson, he hadn't written these parts with anyone in mind, though he and Baumbach were drawn immediately to the image of Mr Fox as the irresistibly charismatic Cary Grant.[230] Due to practical limitations (the actor had been dead since the '80s), they were led to the next best thing, George Clooney.

"You want him to be the hero when he's at his worst," Anderson said of the actor. "And he's often at his worst in *Mr Fox*."[231] Cate Blanchett was, at first, considered for the role of Mrs Fox, but her newly founded theatre company kept her home in Australia.[232] Anderson instead reached out to the indomitable Meryl Streep, whose image of motherhood comes with its own, fierce sense of independence.

A new addition to Dahl's story was the rivalry between Ash, small in stature and large in resentment, and his visiting cousin Kristofferson, named after the country singer and actor Kris Kristofferson.[233] The latter is a natural sportsman, and is humbly self-assured in ways that attract the attention of Ash's crush, Agnes (Anderson's partner, Juman Malouf, a Lebanese artist and designer who he'd met in 2009).

Anderson had initially been inspired by an old after-school special he'd seen on television as a child. But, when he cast his younger brother, Eric, as Kristofferson, Eric suggested the relationship might actually be based on Anderson and their older brother, Mel Jr. – a taller, less troubled, better behaved physician who had excelled in school and could play piano by ear when he was five years old. "I didn't feel competitive," Anderson confessed. "I felt inferior. Simply inferior."[234]

Owen Wilson voices Coach Skip, an albino river otter who oversees the school's games of whack-bat, whose incomprehensible rules reflect Anderson's own confessed inability to grasp how cricket operates. Bill Murray voices Mr Fox's attorney, Mr Badger.

At first, the actor decided the character should have a Wisconsin accent, being that the creature is the mascot of the University of Wisconsin.

Wes Anderson and Felicity Dahl arrive together at the world premiere of *Fantastic Mr. Fox*, held in London.

Cousins Kristofferson (Eric Anderson) and Ash (Jason Schwartzman) finally put their differences aside and work as one.

He drove around for days listening to local public radio stations. When he demonstrated the voice for Anderson, the director rebutted that Mr Badger was more of a Savile Row type. The accent, reluctantly, was dropped.[235]

Adrien Brody voices a mouse. Michael Gambon was originally cast as Rat, before Anderson realized he'd be better suited as the farmer Frank Bean, with Willem Dafoe taking his place.[236] Wally Wolodarsky plays Kylie, a loyal opossum sidekick to Mr Fox, whose eyes swirl in hypnotic spirals whenever he's overstimulated.

Voices in an animated movie are typically recorded in a sound studio. But Anderson wanted his actors to work as a collective, within real environments, in the way Aardman Animations took to the streets to interview real people, then matched claymation zoo animals to their voices for their *Creature Comforts* short and series.[237]

In the fall of 2007, he invited several of his actors, including Clooney, Murray, Schwartzman and his brother Eric, alongside a sound man, to a Connecticut farm he'd found through friends of both Eric and Clooney. They recorded scenes in fields, in forests, and near ponds, or in the attic, basement or barn of the farmhouse. The natural soundscape seeped into the movie.

The cast, scripts in hand, could work through around 30 pages a day.[238] They climbed, dug, growled and snarfed down French toast and biscuits.[239] "It was kind of like being at summer camp," Anderson observed.[240] This was the undomestication of pampered Hollywood folk – thematically fitting for a movie about the free, feral creature that lives inside of each of us.

For Mr Fox to put aside his thievery, or the feeling of his teeth latched onto a chicken's neck, is to deny his true nature. The corduroy suit and desk job can only conceal so much. When the farmers drive him, his family and his neighbours into the local sewers, he rallies them with a speech in which he rechristens them with their Latin, scientific classifications. It feels older, more primordial. He's not Mr Fox, he's Vulpes Vulpes.

The film ends with Mr Fox, having successfully liberated Kristofferson from Mr Bean's clutches, motoring his way home. He spies a wolf in the distance, far away on a mountain crag. Mr Fox has always attested to having a phobia of wolves. Yet, we know the truth – really, it's a fear of his untapped desires. Mr Fox and the wolf salute each other with a raised fist.

When Anderson was set to record the scene, he realized it might be good to have someone stand in as the wolf, even if they didn't have any lines. "I can be the wolf," Murray suddenly volunteered, his hands buried in his pockets.[241]

He took off, becoming a tiny speck on the horizon. And he played the part beautifully. "It almost felt like maybe he had practiced it," Anderson said. "It seemed like a fully conceived wolf performance."[242] He took out his camera phone and recorded it, so that animators could then use the footage as a reference, making the most of Murray's perfect nonchalance.

Anderson also supplied his own homemade videos of him acting out brief gestures or demonstrating how certain characters should move. Animatics, essentially a moving storyboard set to the audio track, were then created. Christian De Vita, lead storyboard artist, recalled how Anderson would send him stamp-sized drawings on sticky notes, hotel notepads and restaurant napkins.

It was the antithesis to the spontaneous methodology he'd applied to *The Darjeeling Limited*, and Anderson found such pleasure in the process that animatics would become a much larger element of his filmmaking, even when working in live action. While there's a stillness to the director's work that contravenes the traditional rules of animation, in which movement is necessary for the illusion of life, the animatics allowed him to map out exactly how his signature shots would work in this new medium: the deep focus, long takes and tight close-ups.

He wanted, too, for his characters to reflect stop-motion's storied history: the Rankin/Bass holiday specials (most famously, 1964's *Rudolph the Red-Nosed Reindeer*) that formed part of many an American childhood; the work of Willis H. O'Brien, who created the original, 1933 King Kong puppet; and of his protégé Ray Harryhausen, famous for the battling skeletons of *Jason and the Argonauts* (1963) and the snake-haired Medusa of *Clash of the Titans* (1981).[243] Anderson thought his foxes should have actual fur, and be made in a variety of sizes, as they were for Ladislas Starevich's whimsical medieval fable, *Le Roman de Renard (1937)*.

Animators, typically, take great pains to avoid what they term the "boiling" effect, an unintended visual ripple caused by the slight movement of fabric or hair in between shots. Anderson, however, asked that they embrace such imperfections, to the degree that they'd occasionally blow gently on the puppets' heads.[244] Water was made out of Saran Wrap,[245] smoke out of cotton balls,[246] and fire out of carved soap – all, typically, used as temporary placeholders, here made an integral part of the movie's visual language.

ABOVE Meryl Streep and Wes Anderson pose with a trio of vulpine puppets: Ash, Mrs Fox and Mr Fox.
OPPOSITE (ABOVE) The opossum Kylie (Wally Wolodarsky), whose eyes swirl in hypnotic spirals whenever he's overstimulated.
OPPOSITE (BELOW) Rat (Willem Dafoe), the wily security guard of farmer Frank Bean.

CIDER
CUVÉE 2006

Belgian illustrator Félicie Haymoz led the character design, creating around 15 sketches for each of the 40 characters.[247] Some were easier to nail down than others. When it came to Petey, the human troubadour voiced by Pulp frontman and Anderson's friend, Jarvis Cocker, the glasses never seemed to come out right. Photographs were taken of every near-sighted and far-sighted employee at the studio, from which the director could make his final selection.

Haymoz's drawings were then used as a reference by the puppet makers Mackinnon & Saunders, who used steel ball-and-socket armatures – skeletons with almost as many joints as the human body – wrapped in foam latex or silicone. The main puppets were around 12 inches (30.5 centimetres) tall. Their heads were covered in small joints and paddles, which would allow the lip to curl or the eyebrow to rise.

Five different scales were created, the largest a pair of human-sized fox hands (for a close-up shot) and the smallest the "mini-micros" as big as a human thumbnail,[248] with a single wire running through them. At that size, especially, the puppets were known to frequently break. Seventy had to be made for the whack-bat scene alone.[249] Producer Allison Abbate would compare the animation process to "painting the Sistine Chapel on the head of a pin".[250]

The animal fur was partially artificial, plucked off toys, and partially real, sheared from goats. Hair for the human characters, meanwhile, was harvested from the scalps of studio employees. Anderson, according to Ian MacKinnon, stated that he wanted Mr Fox to wear a yellow corduroy suit, "the sort of suit you'd see on any man walking down the street in Paris. And we were in Manchester, thinking, 'Well, we don't see many men walking down the street in suits like that!'"[251] Thankfully, the director provided his own fabric, sent directly from his personal tailor (he then ordered himself a matching suit).[252]

For Rat, a beatnik who moves with balletic, *West Side Story* flair, a red-and-white striped sweater was knitted by hand using tiny, whittled needles, with an embroidered badge reading "Bean Security" in 1.5 mm tall letters.[253] It took six weeks to make.

Anderson treated his miniaturized world seriously. He'd photograph buildings, or the odd architectural detail, and send them to production designer Nelson Lowry to recreate.[254] While looking over the supermarket set, Anderson pointed out a mistake to producer Jeremy Dawson. "Stores don't put bread in the refrigerator," he said. Dawson joked, "Here they do," only for the director to respond, "I'm saying a serious thing. Maybe we shouldn't have bread in the refrigerator."[255]

Originally, Anderson had wanted to entrust the project to *James and the Giant Peach*'s Henry Selick, who, as a result of their early conversations, had created *The Life Aquatic*'s stop-motion marine life. Suddenly, Selick's own *Coraline*, based on a Neil Gaiman novella, was green-lit and the two parted ways.[256] *Fantastic Mr. Fox* would be made for significantly less, on a budget of roughly $40 million,[257] with Mark Gustafson in the role of animation director.

Wes Anderson corrals his pint-sized, inanimate cast of characters. The puppet heads were covered in small joints and paddles, which allowed animators to control individual expressions.

The main puppets were around 12 inches tall. Five different scales were created, the largest a pair of human-sized fox hands and the smallest the "mini-micros" as big as a human thumbnail.

It was shot at a former distillery in East London, named 3 Mills Studios, where, on the first day of shooting on 6 June 2008, a 2,200-pound (1 metric ton) German warhead from World War II was found and detonated.[258] The sound of the explosion was used in the movie, for when the farmers blow the Fox residence sky high.

The UK had, in the past few decades, become a hub for stop-motion animation, thanks in part to the rise of Wallace & Gromit creators Aardman Animations. When Murray came to visit the set, he observed: "There was more talent in one factory than I've ever been closeted with. I've never been with so many talented people in one place."[259]

Once the puppets and sets had been built, Anderson assumed he'd reached the end of his contribution. He'd facilitate his vision, hand it off to the animators, and, in return, receive a completed movie.[260] Instead, he found himself at his desk in Montparnasse, Paris, where he now lived part-time, scrutinizing individual frames. Animators worked towards a target of ten seconds of film a week,[261] across roughly 30 stages at once, shooting a total of 621,450 frames.[262]

A new system named FishCat, after its creators Rupert Fishwick and Matthew Kitcat, allowed animators to hit a "Live to Wes" button on their computers in order to send him a real-time stream of their work. Owen Wilson went to visit Anderson in Paris, but found that he rarely left his apartment. "It seemed like his work was never over," he said. "Because he could control the whole universe of the movie."[263]

It wasn't unusual for a stop-motion director to be largely absent from set. The same had been true of Tim Burton, when he made *Corpse Bride* (2005). But Anderson's confessed naïveté about the medium, and the way he guided animators away from the smooth and fluid towards the distinctly handmade, was a source both of inspiration and frustration.

"He's pushed it further than I would have been comfortable pushing it," Gustafson confessed. "He definitely doesn't have some of the reservations that I have from working with this stuff for years. But that's good. I came here to be challenged. And he's certainly challenged me."[264]

The animators, when interviewed, tended to agree: it wasn't an easy shoot, but the result was worth it. "When I saw the film, it all comes together," Peter Saunders, of Mackinnon & Saunders, said. "[Anderson] was right and I was wrong."[265] However, in an article in the *Los Angeles Times*, one of the first to be published about the movie, cinematographer Tristan Oliver accused the director of being "a little sociopathic", adding: "contact with people disturbs him. This way, he can spend an entire day locked inside an empty room with a computer. He's a bit like the Wizard of Oz. Behind the curtain."[266]

"There were issues on both sides," he later clarified.[267] Anderson agreed. "It took us a long time … to get into sync," he said. "It's not crazy for him to be upset, since you're in the middle of the stress of production and the crew is dealing with a director who won't take no for an answer."[268]

OPPOSITE (ABOVE) Bill Murray takes a nap mere inches away from a burning inferno.
OPPOSITE (BELOW) Wes Anderson inspects one of the puppets for Mr Fox, created by the Greater Manchester-based studio Mackinnon & Saunders.

Mr Fox (George Clooney) shares one of his visions. Our hero must learn that there's a greater satisfaction to be found in providing not just for oneself, but for the wider community.

Even if Oliver's "sociopathic" comment was unwarranted, the conflict had a funny way of pointing out that Anderson may have more in common with his protagonist than he imagines. Both he and Mr Fox are leaders and visionaries. And both have had to find the balance between an individual's drive and their fealty to their community. Certainly, the latter leans more towards egotism. In *Fantastic Mr Fox*'s first scene, Mr Fox asks his wife if she'd like to take the shortcut or the scenic route, then the hole under the horse fence or the bridle path, only to override her twice.

Here, Mr Fox's fixations link back to very Andersonian ideas of class and status. Life in a fox den makes him "feel poor" (despite Mrs Fox's reminders that even if they're poor, they're happy), so he moves his family into a house under a tree, and then plans several elaborate heists to pay for it.

One chopped-off tail, and the deliberate flooding of their home later, Mr Fox finds himself in the sewers with all his neighbours, their material possessions flushed away. All they have is each other now, and our hero learns the pleasures of stealing not just for his own benefit, but for his community. "We'll eat tonight and we'll eat together," he declares in the movie's final scene.

It's a simple way to enhance the fable at the centre of Dahl's story, which Anderson and his music supervisor Randall Poster then garnished with music from old children's shows and movies, like Disney's *The Ballad of Davy Crockett* series and the animated *Robin Hood*. For the score, he reached out to Alexandre Desplat, composer of one of Anderson's favourite soundtracks, for Jonathan Glazer's *Birth*.[269]

Farmers Walter Boggis (Robin Hurlstone), Frank Bean (Michael Gambon) and Nathan Bunce (Hugo Guinness) enact their vengeance.

It only took Desplat about a week to compose the movie's score. He and Anderson had developed an instant connection. "He's very mischievous," Desplat explained. "And that's something that when you start working with Wes that you have to understand and capture first."[270] Recording took place at London's Abbey Road, famous for its association with the Beatles, and a choir of children were invited to sing a ditty set to a few of the book's opening lines: "Boggis and Bunce and Bean. One fat, one short, one lean." To ease their nerves, the director brought in several character puppets.

Anderson and Baumbach, while writing the script, had come across the original manuscript for *Fantastic Mr Fox*, which featured a different finale.[271] Here, the foxes dig a hole up into the supermarket, where they find an inexhaustible feast. Dahl's publisher had suggested he change it to provide his audience with a better moral – instead of stealing from the innocent, the foxes should target the storehouses of the farmers who tried to kill them.

But Anderson was drawn to the supermarket scene, and its vision of liminal suburbia, with its aisles that seem to stretch on into eternity. Poster had once played Anderson the Bobby Fuller Four's "Let Her Dance", from the mid-1960s, and they'd agreed they should find a place for it in one of their movies. Here it was, as the wild creatures dance for joy.[272]

A pair of early test screenings went well, though the studio requested that Anderson make some basic changes: get rid of the cigarettes and any trace of blood. He did not comply. Still, 20th Century Fox hoped for a

major hit, an easy sell of a kid's movie with friendly, talking animals. Some of the trailers didn't even bother to feature Anderson or Dahl's names.

"With *Fantastic Mr Fox*, I thought that I was taking less of a risk than I ever had," the director said. "I thought, 'I'm going to do an animated Roald Dahl story. Hey, this will guarantee me an audience,' which, then, in the course of making the movie, I think I managed to prevent that from happening."[273] It earned $21 million at the US box office, more than *The Darjeeling Limited* but less than *The Life Aquatic*.[274]

At least the reviews were positive. Even his more sceptical critics seemed, for the most part, charmed, though many of them dusted off the very same quip about his style – as *Reverse Shot*'s Jeff Reichert wrote, "there are few American filmmakers currently working who are more fastidious about composition than Wes Anderson, and in a sense he has been making animated films all along."[275]

Anderson and his collaborators were pressed on two particular subjects: would children like the movie? And would Dahl have approved? Felicity provided an answer to both. "I think Roald would have loved it," she said. "I can hear him quietly laughing as we watched it."[276] Furthermore, she'd screened it twice for the family, and when her 13-year-old grandson was asked whether his peers would enjoy it, he replied: "Well, they'll be pretty boring if they don't."

More tellingly, critic A. O. Scott, writing for *The New York Times*, seemed to finally pinpoint the growing mystique that now circulated Anderson. "Not everyone will like *Fantastic Mr Fox*," he noted. "And if everyone did, it would not be nearly as interesting as it is. There are some children – some people – who will embrace it with a special, strange intensity, as if it had been made for them alone."[277]

There are some children – some people – who will embrace it with a special, strange intensity, as if it had been made for them alone.

OPPOSITE (ABOVE) Mrs Fox (Meryl Streep) and the rest of the mammalian community at work preparing a feast.
OPPOSITE (BELOW) The feast in question, with a toast from Mr Fox (George Clooney).
NEXT SPREAD Mr Fox (George Clooney) in the office of his attorney, Mr Badger (Bill Murray).

7
LE TEMPS DE L'AMOUR

On *Moonrise Kingdom*

Wes Anderson remembers the girl from fifth grade. It's Valentine's Day, and the classroom walls are covered with small, white lunch bags adorned with students' names, makeshift mailboxes for children to deposit their cards and gifts. The girl's bag looks as if it's fit to burst. There's a golden necklace in there – not from Anderson, of course. He said and did nothing.[278]

But he dreamed about her all the same, and that memory, decades later, would be transformed into a story and then into a movie, *Moonrise Kingdom*. It was what he would come to call "the autobiography of something that didn't happen", about what he might have done if he'd acted on those transformative pangs of first love, that felt to him as if he'd been dropped to the bottom of the sea.[279]

Set in 1965, it follows a pair of 12-year-olds, Khaki Scout Sam Shakusky (Jared Gilman) and Suzy Bishop (Kara Hayward), who run away into the wilds of a fictional New England isle, New Penzance. They evade all adult authority: Suzy's parents, a frosty couple of lawyers (Frances McDormand and Bill Murray); Sam's leader, Scout Master Ward (Edward Norton); and the local policeman, Captain Sharp (Bruce Willis). It ends with a dedication to Anderson's partner, Juman Malouf.

Anderson was inspired to create New Penzance after spending time on Naushon Island, near Cape Cod, with his friend Wally Wolodarsky, who'd appeared in many of his movies.[280] It's only accessible by boat, and has no paved roads, cars or stores.[281] It's as if it were pickled in time. The setting of 1965 came without much thought,[282] yet New Penzance is a convenient stand-in for an America on the brink of a cultural awakening. Sam and Suzy's rebellion is but a taste of what would come, as college students rose up against the Vietnam War and *Easy Rider* (1969) spat in the face of conformity.

Cousin Ben (Jason Schwartzman) leads the fugitive couple, Sam Shakusky (Jared Gilman) and Suzy Bishop (Kara Hayward). The yellow suitcase contains Suzy's most precious belongings, her books.

Moonrise Kingdom would be a movie that understood the child's world, and would see from their perspective. Anderson thought of *Small Change* (1976), by the French director François Truffaut, which pushed adults to the periphery and brought its camera down to the eye level of its juvenile protagonists.[283]

For research, he watched Ken Loach's historical drama *Black Jack*, from 1979, which he'd stumbled across in a video store in London and dealt with eighteenth-century children's preoccupations with death and insanity. Waris Hussein's *Melody* (1971) also proved relevant, with its own intentionally myopic story of two children who declare their love, to the befuddlement of their parents.

When Sam runs away, he brings with him scout gear, his BB gun, bed rolls, cooking supplies and a tent. Anderson had briefly joined the scouts, drawn by the allure of its rules and uniforms, but found that he wasn't much of a camper.[284] He'd joined Troop 55, and so named the group in *Moonrise Kingdom* after his thwarted ambitions. When Suzy runs away, she brings her kitten (kept by Hayward after the movie was shot, and named Gino),[285] a portable record player, binoculars and a suitcase.

It's filled with fantasy books, with titles like *The Girl From Jupiter* and *The Francine Odysseys*, inspired by Susan Cooper's young adult novels, which

ABOVE The theatrical poster for *Moonrise Kingdom*.
OPPOSITE Suzy Bishop (Kara Hayward) and Sam Shakusky (Jared Gilman) prove their love to one of very few adult allies, Cousin Ben (Jason Schwartzman).

Moonrise Kingdom **would be a movie that understood the child's world and would see from their perspective.**

were rooted in Arthurian legends and English folklore. When Anderson read her books, as a child, he wanted to believe in magic powers so profoundly that he became convinced that scientists would simply one day confirm it all to be true.[286] Such a delusion isn't so far removed from the headiness of young love, he observed.

And so, in a way, he began to think of *Moonrise Kingdom* as one of the books inside Suzy's suitcase – not magic in a literal sense, but filled with the enchantment of a child's innocence. The story had been on Anderson's mind since before he'd begun work on *The Darjeeling Limited*.[287] He spent roughly a year trying to write a script, but could only manage around 14 pages,[288] having hit a wall right at the point Sam and Suzy meet in a field.[289] They're about to run away. He couldn't figure out what happened next.

He turned to his friend and frequent collaborator Roman Coppola, who read his pages and then peppered him with questions: "Who is this kid? What do his parents think when he runs off like this?" "Well, Sam is an orphan," Anderson replied.[290] A flashback was added and, suddenly, the rest of the movie fell neatly into place.

The two worked together a little more formally, as Anderson bounced ideas off Coppola, and Coppola offered up a few of his own childhood memories. In fourth grade, a girl had passed him a note that said, "I think you're cute. Call me."

He did, but had nothing to say. All hopes of romance were quashed. Still, he dreamed of running away with her.[291] His mother, documentarian Eleanor Coppola, would use a bullhorn in the house to summon her children.[292] It was the inspiration for Suzy's mother doing the same. After a month, the script was complete.

It was clear no audience would buy into Sam and Suzy's love without the right actors at the helm. But Anderson knew from *Rushmore*, when Jason Schwartzman turned out to be nothing like the Max Fischer in his head, not to set any kind of expectations. Instead, nearly a year before cameras rolled, casting director Douglas Aibel was sent out to scour the American school system for the perfect unknowns.[293]

Anderson watched thousands of children reading over the same set of lines. He'd started to hate what he'd written. Then, suddenly, there was Kara Hayward, and she spoke as if she were the one making these words up on the spot. Jared Gilman landed the role mainly because of his post-audition interview. His hair was long and he wore bug-eyed glasses secured to his head with a strap, like the basketball player Kareem Abdul-Jabbar.[294] Something about his look, voice and mannerisms amused the director.

It was the first movie for both of them. For the month before filming started, Anderson had Hayward and Gilman travel every Monday to Rhode Island, where the movie was shot, to rehearse.[295] He'd give them tasks, too – not only to get them into character, but to familiarize these middle-schoolers with the concept of having a job.[296]

Hayward was given books to read, and she learned how to apply Suzy's signature blue eyeshadow so she could do her own hair and make-up. Anderson wanted her look to be what a 12-year-old could plausibly achieve.[297]

Gilman pursued canoeing and was taught how to cook on a campfire. They wrote letters to each other as Suzy and Sam, to simulate the correspondence they share in the movie. At first, they communicated over email, before Anderson realized it'd be better if they mailed them in the traditional way.[298] Hayward was a professional and never sulked.[299] Gilman knew a lot about movies, and asked questions about how it all worked. Between scenes, they mostly did homework.[300]

Anderson was highly aware of the delicate nature of his story, and that he was asking these young actors to play out a romance. Midway through production, during the scene in which Sam and Suzy are married by another Scout elder, Ben (Jason Schwartzman), the director took Hayward and Gilman aside and suggested they hug to break the ice. The dance scene on the beach, where they first kiss, was the very last thing the two of them shot.

A miniature troupe of child actors was collected around them. Jake Ryan plays Suzy's younger brother, Lionel – Anderson discovered the boy was a natural comic, and he went on to cast him in a Sony commercial he directed, in which Ryan improvises a short story about robots.

Anderson says he relates somewhat to Suzy. She carries with her a pamphlet, stolen from her parents and titled "How to Cope with the Very Troubled Child". The director once found one on the refrigerator in his father's house.

Despite having two brothers, he knew that he was the "Very Troubled Child" in question.[301] It's an anecdote the director shared early on in the press tour for *Moonrise Kingdom* and seemed to instantly regret. He lamented: "I just don't want to have told something too personal."

It's a confession about a confession that anyone in New Penzance might themselves share. The people here cling to their secrets. Suzy's mother and Captain Sharp are having an affair. Sam hasn't told anyone at camp that he's an orphan. His and Suzy's plans for escape are made in private, their destination the little-known 3.25 tidal inlet, renamed by them as Moonrise Kingdom and wiped off the map by the storm that descends in the movie's climax. Suzy's books are all stolen from the library. "I think I just took them to have a secret to keep," she says.

None of the adults know what to do with these strange, sad kids. Sam's foster parents, when informed of his disappearance, tell Captain Sharp that they simply "can't invite him back at this time", because "he's emotionally disturbed." Suzy's in the materially privileged position, with her home and two parents, but there's something indescribably unsettled about her psyche.

She has fits of rage, in which she throws a brick through the kitchen window or picks a fight at school. "Poor Suzy. Why is everything so hard for you?" her mother wonders. Perhaps that's why she believes orphans like Sam, or the characters in her books, have lives that are "more special". Their sorrow has a source. "I love you, but you don't know what you're talking about," Sam responds.

In *Moonrise Kingdom*'s opening scene, when the camera travels through the doll's-house-like Bishop home, its family members remain isolated in their chambers, in their own worlds. When characters talk over the phone,

A quartet of fretful adults: Mr Bishop (Bill Murray), Mrs Bishop (Frances McDormand), Scout Master Ward (Edward Norton), and Captain Sharp (Bruce Willis).

SCOUT MASTER
K.S.N.A.
LEADERSHIP

the director shoots them in split screen and then lets the camera linger a little after the receiver is put down, to see them in private meditation.

Suzy's binoculars try to pierce through the veil. It's how she first discovers her mother and Captain Sharp's affair, and how she first sees Sam when they meet in the field. "I pretend it's my magical power," she explains. But loneliness is loneliness; the only difference for children is that the wounds are fresh and the love is brighter.

That lack of delineation between the adult and child worlds found its way into the movie's musical landscape. Suzy, with her teal-shaded eyelids and pink minidress, models herself after the French chanteuse Françoise Hardy, and carries around her record *The "Yeh-Yeh" Girl From Paris!*. At the beach, she plays Sam "Le temps de l'amour".

Integral to the movie, too, is the work of Benjamin Britten, who'd always been interested in extending the adult world of classical music to children. When he was ten, Anderson appeared alongside his older brother in a production of Britten's *Noye's Fludde*, created to be performed in a community hall or church, with a chorus of nonprofessionals and children.[302] He and his best friend Sanjay were a pair of otters.[303] Replicas of their costumes are worn by Sam and Suzy during the movie's climax, with the lovers having first met during a performance of the opera.

One of Anderson's earliest ideas for *Moonrise Kingdom* became its opening scene: siblings trapped inside during a rainstorm, listening to Britten's *The Young Person's Guide to the Orchestra*, which breaks down Henry Purcell's "Rondeau" from the *Abdelazer* suite to demonstrate the individual contributions of the orchestra's instruments.[304]

The version used is Leonard Bernstein's arrangement – another composer with a keen interest in sharing his work with the younger generations. Alexandre Desplat provided the rest of the score, with its own broken-down, narrated version of the theme played over the credits.

While the adults are all confounded by Sam and Suzy's love, some are more sympathetic than others. Captain Sharp, a "sad, dumb cop" in Suzy's eyes, eventually steps up to the plate and adopts Sam, so that we can be reassured the young lovers won't be separated anytime soon.

Anderson, this time, hadn't written any of these characters with a particular actor in mind.[305] He did think of James Stewart, that Old Hollywood star who radiated both decency and humility, and wanted someone audiences would immediately recognize as a figure of authority.

Naturally, that path led him to Bruce Willis, who'd emerged from early television fame, thanks to the romantically charged detective series *Moonlighting*, to become one of America's greatest action heroes – *Die Hard* (1988) was followed by *The Last Boy Scout* (1991) and *Armageddon* (1998).

"You can tell when somebody's a cop," Anderson said. "There is something that's often projected from an actual policeman, and Bruce Willis has this cop authority, where even if he's playing something away from what he normally plays, you would never question whether Bruce Willis is the police."[306]

OPPOSITE (ABOVE) Mr Bishop (Bill Murray), Suzy's father, relaxes in the family home.
OPPOSITE (BELOW) Social Services (Tilda Swinton), whose fire-red hair and midnight-blue cloak recalls the the Technicolor fantasies of Powell and Pressburger.

Anderson, this time, hadn't written any of these characters with a particular actor in mind.

Scout Master Ward (Edward Norton) observes the construction of a rickety, too-tall treehouse. Norton had served as a Cub Scout, receiving an honourable mention for a balsa wood sailboat he'd painted to look like an orca.

Bill Murray, who was cast as Suzy's father, seemed fond of Willis. Both wore their fame lightly. "He's rolled as a movie star for a long time, so it's a little different for him coming into Wes Anderson's world, where no one gets movie-star treatment," he said. "But Bruce absolutely delivered. He was really game. It was like, Let's play."[307] He claimed the actor delivered "one of the biggest laughs of any movie I've ever been in", when he's left dangling from the church tower after a lightning strike, limp like a puppet but with Sam and Suzy holding on for dear life.[308]

Anderson thought of Edward Norton for the role of Scout Master Ward, since he'd always believed his face could have been painted by Norman Rockwell, the great documenter of America's cultural history.[309] Norton famously played troubled young men – in his 1996 debut, *Primal Fear*, as a rehabilitated neo-Nazi in *American History X* (1998), or in *Fight Club* (1999).

But Anderson saw what the actor considered to be "the inner Scout Master Ward in me":[310] he'd developed superior survival skills as a pilot and white-water raftsman.[311] He was a Cub Scout, too, and had received an honourable mention for a balsa wood sailboat he'd painted to look like an orca. Norton experienced what he would describe as "freedom in bondage" under Anderson's meticulous vision.[312] Sometimes, he'd simply ask the director to deliver a line and then copy its intonation.[313]

Frances McDormand was cast as Suzy's mother, and Murray described the scenes he shared with her as "like dancing at night after a few glasses of champagne". Tilda Swinton plays the ominous figure referred to only

Suzy Bishop (Kara Hayward) sees the truth of the world through her trusty binoculars. It's how she first discovers her mother (Frances McDormand) and Captain Sharp's (Bruce Willis) affair.

as Social Services, with luminous pale skin, fire-red hair, and a midnight-blue cloak, as if she's just walked out of one of Powell and Pressburger's Technicolor dreams. When Anderson reached out to her, she wrote back promptly: "When do I need to be there? Tell me the dates. Yes. I'm happy to read the script, too."[314]

Anderson had always wanted to work with Harvey Keitel, one of Martin Scorsese's tough guy muses. He convinced him to play on that image for the role of Commander Pierce, a semi-legendary figure in the troop. The actor had been in the marines, and before that, the scouts.[315]

Bob Balaban took on the role of narrator, both a prophetic figure who warns of the storm that will strike the island in three days' time, and an active contributor to the narrative, who informs the characters that his knowledge of cartography has clued him into where the runaways are heading.

The use of animatics on *Fantastic Mr. Fox* had opened Anderson up to a whole new level of precision and control. He used them here instead of basic storyboards, for the first time in live action, in order to plan out longer or more complex sequences.[316] He even travelled to the locations to pre-shoot and pre-edit certain scenes without his actors.[317]

"We were the most prepared on a day-to-day basis that I've ever been," he said. This led partially to the decision to build more sets than he'd done before, including that of the Bishop family home, inside a disused Linens 'n Things store.[318] The rooms were laid out horizontally, so the camera could pass through them on a dolly track (essentially a cart pushed along rails).[319]

When *Moonrise Kingdom* opened in the United States, it broke records for a film of its size and earned $45 million.

Production designer Adam Stockhausen combined details from various houses they'd visited while location scouting: the Bishop playroom is a recreation of one in a house on Cumberland Island, off the coast of Georgia; household items were loaned from the single home that sits on Comfort Island, up near the border with Canada; and the shingled walls were inspired by Rhode Island's Ten Chimneys, once home to the famous Broadway actors Lynn Fontanne and Alfred Lunt.[320]

"I also had the idea that maybe the house could have the atmosphere of a rickety old place in some book where the kids go up into the attic and reach through a broken board and find a fragment of a forgotten map and set off on an adventure," Anderson said. The house's exterior is the Conanicut Island Lighthouse, off the coast of Rhode Island, and the church is Newport's Trinity Church, which locals claim George Washington once attended.

Anderson went to visit the rector in her office there, and spotted a needlepoint of the church fixed to the wall behind her desk. He decided to use it, and to have needlepoints created of the other main locations, only to discover the woman who'd originally crafted it was now aged 96. They were made in the Philippines instead.[321] A treehouse sitting precariously at the top of the slimmest and tallest of trunks was created in half-scale. Two trees were stacked, one on top of the other, to get the necessary height.

An old house was acquired for Anderson to lodge in with his editor, Andrew Weisblum, and director of photography, Robert Yeoman. All the actors were to stay at a hotel, but when Norton found out about the arrangement, he asked if they had a spare guest room. He stayed there for the duration of the shoot. Murray then moved in. So did Schwartzman. They had their own cook. It was a happy little arrangement.[322] Actors did their own hair and make-up, and would take vans out to set already in costume.[323]

Norton compared the experience to being part of a repertory theatre, like Orson Welles's famous Mercury Theatre players. "There's a romance to that when you're an actor," he said. "I used to dream a lot about how fun it would be to be in a troupe like that."[324]

They worked quickly, with a small crew – Anderson switched from his usual anamorphic 35 mm film and shot, instead, on super 16 mm film on smaller, more mobile cameras.[325] Some would have to be held in one hand, with the operator looking down through the lens at the top of the camera, meaning the movie could actually be shot at a child's eye level, like Truffaut's *Small Change*.

All this guerrilla fashioning suited Anderson's slashed budget. *Fantastic Mr. Fox* had not fared well at the box office, so *Moonrise Kingdom* had to be made for significantly less, around $16 million.[326] Thankfully, the rewards were far sweeter: it was selected to open the 2012 Cannes Film Festival, the first time Anderson's work had been shown at the year's most prestigious cinematic showcase, and it received some of the most enthusiastic reviews yet.

OPPOSITE (ABOVE) Suzy's parents (Bill Murray and Frances McDormand).
OPPOSITE (BELOW) Our runaway heroes, Suzy Bishop (Kara Hayward) and Sam Shakusky (Jared Gilman).

Some critics certainly wheeled out the familiar, derogatory terms – "obsessive",[327] "twee", inaccessible" – but even the harshest among them could no longer deny that there really was something special about this guy. Maybe his fans weren't such oddballs, after all. As MUBI *Notebook*'s Ignatiy Vishnevetsky admitted: "Anderson, it seems, has finally and thoroughly gone up his own ass – and yet the film happens to be one of his best and most inviting works."[328]

The critical turnaround led *The New Yorker*'s Richard Brody to pen a rebuttal to the narrative that the director had changed his stripes. "*Moonrise Kingdom* is not a drastic departure from Anderson's first six features but rather an intensification of their characteristics, or even just their more explicit revelation," he wrote. "To love *Moonrise Kingdom* at the expense of *The Darjeeling Limited* or *The Life Aquatic with Steve Zissou* is to love it lightly."[329] Audiences pretended that Anderson had attuned himself to them, when it was very much the other way round.

When *Moonrise Kingdom* opened in the United States, it broke records for a film of its size, and earned $45 million – double what Anderson's supposed sure-fire hit *Fantastic Mr. Fox* had made.[330] But a young Gilman didn't really register its success until Halloween rolled around and, suddenly, neighbourhoods were filled with Sams and Suzys.

"It became a minor cliché," he joked. "But ultimately, it's because it was a movie that, for lots of people, was instrumental in one way or another. It's something I can look back on and say, 'Yeah, that was an instrumental movie for me, too.'"[331]

OPPOSITE Captain Sharp (Bruce Willis) on patrol.

PLYMOUTH
NEW PENZANCE ISLAND
362 164
POLICE

ZZ
ZZ
ZZ
ZZ
ZZ
ZZ
GRAND BUDAPES
MENDL'S

8 UNGEDULD DES HERZENS

On *The Grand Budapest Hotel*

Wes Anderson had never heard of Stefan Zweig[332] until he stumbled across a copy of the Austrian writer's 1939 novel, *Beware of Pity*, in a Parisian bookshop.[333] In it, a young lieutenant keeps his engagement to a paraplegic baroness a secret for fear of public humiliation. It leads to her suicide. He read the first page. "Okay, this is a new favorite writer of mine," he thought to himself, and bought it immediately.[334]

Zweig, who was born into a wealthy Viennese Jewish family in 1881, was once one of Europe's most celebrated authors. He'd been part of Vienna's thriving cultural and intellectual scene, where the city's packed coffee houses would sing with philosophical chatter, with the sharing of ideas and the cross-pollination of disciplines. Zweig knew the psychoanalyst Sigmund Freud, the novelist James Joyce, the sculptor Auguste Rodin, the composer Richard Strauss, the poet Rainer Maria Rilke and the physicist Albert Einstein.

He was a devoted collector of items associated with European accomplishments, such as Ludwig van Beethoven's desk. But he was forced to watch it all – his magnificent, enlightened Europe – slip into the hands of hatred, authoritarianism and decay. The Nazis burned his world to the ground.

His memoir of that time, *The World of Yesterday*, published in 1942, tells the story of unendurable loss. The continent marched into World War I with a head full of blind patriotic optimism and misplaced glory, only for it to sicken into the brutality of Hitler's regime. Zweig had begun to write *The World of Yesterday* in 1934, when he fled his home in Salzburg – first to London, later to Brazil.

The day after he sent it to his publisher, 22 February 1942, he and his second wife, Lotte Altmann, took a fatal dose of barbiturates. They were found in bed, still holding hands. Now artefacts of an old, lost world, his books drifted into obscurity.

The Grand Budapest Hotel falls under the control of the fascist Zig-Zags, whose insignia evokes that of the Schutzstaffel, the Nazi paramilitary organisation otherwise known as the SS.

Anderson, at this point, spent most of his time in Europe, either in Paris or at his partner Juman Malouf's home in Kent, England.[335] He was surrounded by the ghost of Zweig's dreams. "This is such familiar historical territory," the director confessed. "The reason I want to engage with it is because this series of events in Europe are somehow still right in the middle of our lives. And anyway, it's – the impact is we just feel it in kind of a daily way somehow."[336]

At first, he considered a direct adaptation of *Beware of Pity*. But he'd been drawn in, too, by *The Post Office Girl*,[337] published posthumously in 1982, in which a naïf is invited to stay at a grand Swiss hotel, at the pleasure of a wealthy aunt. She dresses the part. She imitates aristocratic airs. Yet, the illusion can only be maintained for so long. Her humble origins are uncovered, and she's sent home in disgrace.

An idea began to form: not to adapt Zweig, but to capture some of his essence, as Anderson had done with Satyajit Ray in *The Darjeeling Limited* or J. D. Salinger in *The Royal Tenenbaums*. A hotel would be one part of his movie.

Another would draw on Zweig's most trusted framework, in which a narrator meets someone who, in turn, tells him the novel's story.[338] Anderson's tales already came in visible packaging, presented behind drawn-back stage curtains or inside the pages of an opened book. *The Grand Budapest Hotel*, his tribute to Zweig, merely adds a few new layers.

It opens in the present day, as a young woman approaches a bust of the "Author", based on a similar monument to Zweig in Paris, in the Jardin du Luxembourg,[339] and pulls out a copy of his book, indeed titled *The Grand Budapest Hotel*. Anderson cuts to the "Author" (Tom Wilkinson), in 1985, as he paraphrases Zweig's words: "People think the writer's imagination is always at work, that he's constantly inventing an endless supply of incidents and episodes; that he simply dreams up his stories out of thin air. In point of fact, the opposite is true. Once the public knows you're a writer, they bring the characters and events to you."

He then introduces us to the next time period: 1965, in which he, as a young man (Jude Law), comes upon the Grand Budapest Hotel while in recovery for "a form of neurasthenia common among the intelligentsia of that time". It's been remodelled in a functional if drab, Soviet palette of orange, green and brown. The "Author" alludes to faded glory and eventual demolition. For now, the building seems to exist in a state of pre-death, haunted by solitary travellers in secluded corners.

Yet, it's here that the "Author" finds its owner, Zero Moustafa (F. Murray Abraham), whose embattled dignity becomes an immediate object of fascination. What tethers him to this place? Zero tells his story as the film, once more, retreats inside itself in order to seek out the old man's youth. He was a lobby boy (Tony Revolori), then, back when the Grand Budapest Hotel was at its height and ruled over by the most refined of concierges, M. Gustave (Ralph Fiennes).

The "Author", certainly, is meant to represent Zweig. But so is M. Gustave, as he watches his cultivated life be dismantled, piece by piece, by

Anderson, at this point, spent most of his time in Europe, either in Paris or at his partner Juman Malouf's home in Kent, England.

OPPOSITE (ABOVE) M. Gustave (Ralph Fiennes) with his preferred company, old and rich blondes.
OPPOSITE (BELOW) The "Author" (Jude Law) as a young man, enjoying the hotel's thermal baths.

Madame D. (Tilda Swinton) clings tightly to her lover, M. Gustave (Ralph Fiennes), as they're accompanied in the elevator by lobby boy Zero (Tony Revolori).

the advance of fascism. He doesn't live in a real Central Europe, but in the Andersonian one, in the fictional town of Lutz, in the fictional country of Zubrowka.

The encroaching conflict combines elements of both World War I and World War II, with the Nazis represented by the Zig-Zags, whose insignia seems to evoke that of the SS, the paramilitary Schutzstaffel. All actors speak in their own accents, whether American, English or Irish.

The Grand Budapest Hotel exists, partially, in the continent of the cinematic imagination, as conjured by European directors who'd settled to work in Hollywood during the '30s. The Englishman Edmund Goulding made *Grand Hotel* (1932), which observes a series of dramas ignited between guests at a lofty Berlin establishment.[340]

Anderson's film is at its heart, a caper in which Gustave and his newly minted protégé, Zero, discover that one of the former's many elderly paramours (he makes his business pleasure, and vice versa), the Dowager Countess Céline Villeneuve Desgoffe-und-Taxis (Tilda Swinton), has died. And Madame D., as she's known, has bequeathed a priceless work of art, Van Hoyt's *Boy with Apple*, to him. Her terrible son, Dmitri (Adrien Brody), is furious. He wants to get his hands on it, by any means necessary.

There's murder by poison here, followed by decapitation and severed fingers. "The dark cloud over civilization at that time is being expressed by people getting dismembered and brutalized," Anderson reflected. "I've certainly never been inclined to have people get chopped up in movies before, and I feel like that's because that's what this world was coming to."[341]

Wes Anderson counsels his actors Tony Revolori and Ralph Fiennes on the most convincing way to drive a tiny, pink pastry delivery truck.

Anderson first sought out his Zubrowka online, in the archives of the US Library of Congress's Photochrom Collection.[342] It contains thousands of ink-based photolithographs, in rich colours, from the 1890s to the 1910s, of landscapes across Europe, the Middle East and North America. One particularly struck him, a view of the Hotel Pupp in Karlovy Vary (then Carlsbad).[343] In the nineteenth century, it was a popular spa resort for the European aristocracy. Yet, its luxuries were brought to an abrupt end by the outbreak of World War I.

Once the script was completed, Anderson sought out the places he'd seen in these photolithographs. He was accompanied by his producer, Jeremy Dawson, and others, as they travelled around visiting hotels in Germany, Austria, Hungary, Poland and the Czech Republic.[344] Some places appeared much the same, while others had changed dramatically, often under the influence (and concrete) of Soviet-era practicality.[345] Those sites would come to shape the Grand Budapest Hotel of the '60s.

He'd had his hopes set, ultimately, on the Hotel Pupp as a primary location. Yet, while the building itself remained untouched, the surrounding area proved simply unworkable. There were too many car parks and blocked views.[346]

So, the Grand Budapest Hotel became a figment of pure imagination. Anderson picked out specific elements from his travels – Karlovy Vary's The Hotel Bristol Palace, high up on a hill, or Switzerland's Glessbach and its funicular – and blended them into a model built 14 feet (4.26 metres) wide and 7 feet (2.13 metres) deep.

It was housed in Germany's famous Babelsburg Studios (where Fritz Lang's *Metropolis* and Josef von Sternberg's *The Blue Angel* were shot),[347] and was set against a mural painted to invoke the weathered, Gothic romance of Caspar David Friedrich's landscapes.[348] The movie would be shot in Germany, too, for both practical and financial reasons.[349] Yet, Anderson was set against using Babelsburg for anything other than his model work. He needed a real location, where his fantasy could take root.

He and his team found Görlitz early on in their search.[350] A town on the German-Polish border, largely untouched by World War II, it had become a popular filming location. Quentin Tarantino's *Inglorious Basterds*, *The Reader* (which won Kate Winslet an Oscar) and George Clooney's *The Monuments Men* had all been shot there. Production on *The Grand Budapest Hotel* would be forced out a day early when *The Book Thief* rolled into town.[351]

In Görlitz, Anderson found the perfect space for his hotel: the Görlitzer Warenhaus, a Jugendstil department store, built in 1913, up for lease and with five floors nestled around a large atrium and skylight.[352] It became the production's base camp, with offices, the wardrobe department and the camera room all stationed on the top two floors,[353] and the rest transformed into The Grand Budapest, with false walls to create rows of hotel rooms.[354]

It was made to look "a bit like a cake", in Anderson's words, in confectionary shades of pink, purple, and royal red. Then, built on top of the main set, was the sixties version of the hotel, with its dreary decorative scheme.

"Not necessarily the most cheerful colours," Anderson said, "but colours I feel might have been chosen because they're easy to clean. The difference between the dirty version of this orange and the clean isn't so extreme." The sixties scenes were shot first, after which the layer was peeled away to reveal the more glorious thirties set beneath.

Anderson, by now, was a more efficient filmmaker than ever before. His use of animatics in order to pre-visualize nearly 90 per cent of the movie made it clear which shots he needed,[355] and which sets had to be built – and "the set might end right where the camera ends," noted Dawson.[356] It's what allowed the film to appear so intricate, on a relatively limited $31 million.[357]

Other locations seemed to almost magically fall into place. Görlitz's civic centre became the hotel's cavernous dining room.[358] An abandoned building on the town square housed the bakery, both Gustave and Zero's rooms and even Madame D.'s coffin.[359] A series of tall, brick smokestacks alerted Anderson to the presence of hidden, disused thermal baths, used for the scene in which the elder Zero and the "Author" first meet.[360]

Anderson commissioned *Boy with Apple*, the centre of his story's drama, from an English painter named Michael Taylor.[361] The director supplied him with reference pictures of sixteenth-century mannerist portraits by Bronzino, Holbein and Cranach, wanting the boy to hold the apple with a prideful, exaggerated flourish. As he instructed, the painting should be "not very funny, just a bit funny".[362] A young dancer named Ed Munro sat for the portrait. It took about four months to complete. Anderson kept it afterwards, and hung it in his office.

Wes Anderson with Jude Law, in the role of the "Author", sat together in the Grand Budapest Hotel lobby. It's unclear whether their matching suits are an intentional choice.

DINING ROOM
ELEVATOR
CONCIERGE
THERMAL BATHS

An Egon Schiele-inspired work, an erotic piece of two nude women with jagged, slightly skeletal bodies, is haphazardly hung up to replace *Boy with Apple* when Gustave decides to simply take his rightful inheritance before Dmitri notices. It was commissioned from Rich Pellegrino, an artist discovered at the San Francisco-based Spoke Art Gallery's *Bad Dads* exhibition, a yearly show of work directly inspired by Anderson's movies.[363]

Irish graphic designer Annie Atkins created all of Zubrowka's many letters and signs, using vintage typewriters, screen printers and calligraphy.[364] Editions of the *Trans-Alpine Yodel* newspaper feature accurate weather forecasts and articles written in full by the director.

For years, Anderson had wanted to make a movie in the Academy Ratio, the square-like format of 1.37:1, the standard from 1932 to 1952, after which the threat of television pushed Hollywood to expand into widescreen.[365] But multiplex movie theatres weren't equipped to project the Academy Ratio until the early 2010s, when most had converted to digital video projection.

And so, Anderson took advantage of the technology to create a movie in which each time period is presented in a different aspect ratio: the standard 1.85:1 for the present day, widescreen 2.40:1 for the '60s, and 1.37:1 for the '30s.

Alexandre Desplat's Mitteleuropa-inspired score, meanwhile, was filled with stringed zithers, cimbaloms and balalaikas, alongside alphorns and a monk-like chorus of men's voices. "It had to have a bit of mud under the shoes," Desplat said.[366]

Before Anderson discovered Zweig, he'd been working on a story with British artist and writer Hugo Guinness. A friend since 1998,[367] Guinness had created artwork for the Tenenbaum household and voiced Farmer Bunce in *Fantastic Mr. Fox*, but had never written with the director before. Anderson believed him to be "very knowledgeable about art, and he had some particular turns of phrase that were not in my lexicon".[368] Guinness, humbly, stressed that his contribution to the script "wasn't much more than to make Wes laugh".[369]

Their idea was based on a mutual friend of theirs, an art dealer by trade.[370] He liked to make friends with people much older than him, and tended to adopt their somewhat antiquated mannerisms.[371] He also, like Gustave, wore around six squirts of cologne each day.[372] They wrote several scenes involving this character, though the story wasn't set in the past, and he wasn't a hotel concierge.[373] They made little progress and eventually set the project aside.

When *The Grand Budapest Hotel* was born, the character slotted neatly into place. They wrote Gustave with only one actor in mind: Ralph Fiennes, a man of the stage gifted with measured intensity, famous for his roles as villains in *Schindler's List* (1993) and the Harry Potter series. Gustave, however, could bring out what Anderson considered to be the "very gentle side of his personality . . . I don't want to say courtly, but his manner is that he is extremely polite."[374]

For years, Anderson had wanted to make a movie in the Academy Ratio, the square-like format of 1.37:1.

OPPOSITE (ABOVE) M. Gustave (Ralph Fiennes) and his incarcerated allies make their escape.
OPPOSITE (BELOW) An older Zero (F. Murray Abraham) in a moment peace in the lobby of the Grand Budapest Hotel.

VISITORS
ARE REQUESTED
TO REFRAIN
FROM CIGAR SMOKING
IN THE LOBBY

M. Gustave (Ralph Fiennes), ready for service. Fiennes had once worked as a house porter at London's Brown's Hotel, before a brief promotion to hall porter.

The director sent Fiennes an email, informing him that he had a script he'd like him to read, if he could let him know which part he liked most. "That was a psychological game," Anderson joked. "I've always had this thought that the best way to get an actor to not want to be in your film is to offer them a part. The number of times I've had someone say, 'Well, I like everybody else's parts – I'm not so sure about my guy.'"[375]

Thankfully, Fiennes was drawn to Gustave. In his younger years, he'd worked as a house porter at London's Brown's Hotel, before a brief promotion to hall porter, which required a uniform. He quit to attend drama school.

Fiennes decided that Gustave, too, started out as a porter, at the bottom of the hospitality ladder – the impoverished son of a shoemaker, who carefully adjusted his personality so that he could nestle his way into the lives of his wealthy clientele.[376] Anderson would always encourage Fiennes to speak faster, so much so that the actor feared it would turn into "gibberish". It never did. He had excellent diction.[377]

For the role of Zero, Anderson was once more set on finding a young unknown. Before even the script was completed, casting director Douglas Aibel was dispatched on a worldwide search. They found him, eventually, in Anaheim, California.[378] Tony Revolori had landed his first role in an ad for baby food, at the age of two. Since then, he'd regularly attended auditions with his older brother Mario.[379]

Both were brought in for a callback for Zero. Four days later, Tony was contacted by his agent: Anderson wanted to meet him in Paris. He

Zero (Tony Revolori) with Agatha (Saoirse Ronan), the Mendl's baker he falls in love with and whose pastries prove crucial to Gustave's liberation from imprisonment.

flew there for a total of 17 hours. But the meeting went well, and he was offered the role.[380] Anderson had liked his owl-eyed, attentive look, a useful trait for a lobby boy always expected to anticipate demand. "He's somebody who could be in a Buster Keaton film," the director remarked.[381]

He ensured Revolori had around four months to prepare, in which he acted out scenes at home with Mario (who'd forgiven him for beating him to the part), and received notes from the director in return.[382] He also worked in a hotel for a week, resetting rooms and cleaning out the pool. He was nervous about meeting Fiennes. But, on their first day, the actor turned to Revolori in a half-finished costume covered in pins and ushered him in for a hug. His fears dissipated instantly.

The rest of the cast was populated with Anderson collaborators old and new. F. Murray Abraham, famous for his role as Salieri, Mozart's embittered rival, in *Amadeus* (1984), provides the older Zero with a rich, mellifluous bass. He was only needed for a week. "I cried when I had to leave the set," he said. "I really did. I loved everybody."[383] Two notable French actors, Léa Seydoux, as the maid Clotilde, and Mathieu Amalric, as the butler Serge X, also appear. Almaric had been the French voice of Mr Fox.

Saoirse Ronan, known then for her roles in *Atonement*, *The Lovely Bones* and *Hanna*, plays Agatha, who works in the local bakery, Mendl's, and falls in love with Zero. She's crucial to the plan to spring Gustave out of his unlawful imprisonment, having been accused of Madame D.'s murder, and recover *Boy with Apple* from its hiding place in the Grand Budapest. She has a birthmark in the shape of Mexico on her right temple.

OPPOSITE (ABOVE) Ludwig (Harvey Keitel), a tattooed convict and an unexpected ally.
OPPOSITE (BELOW) The Grand Budapest Hotel's lawyer, Deputy Vilmos Kovacs (Jeff Goldblum).
ABOVE Agatha (Saoirse Ronan) creating confectionery magic in Mendl's bakery.

A local pastry chef devised Mendl's signature creation, the courtesan au chocolat, in collaboration with prop master Robin Miller.[384] It's a delicate, pastel tower made of filled choux puffs dipped in icing, smuggled into Gustave's prison cell as a necessary luxury. It arrives in a box that opens with the single flourish of an untied bow, achieved on set by the pull of a fishing line.[385] Gustave slices it into quarters for his cellmates to share. It's Anderson's hand in the shot since, according to Jeremy Dawson, no one else possessed "the scalpel-like precision" needed.[386]

Returning members included Harvey Keitel, as the convict Ludwig. Never one to short-change a character, the actor invited his fellow inmates to stay and bond for 48 hours in the prison used as a location.[387]

Adrien Brody was cast as Dmitri, while Jeff Goldblum was asked to be the Grand Budapest's lawyer, Deputy Vilmos Kovacs, as, according to Anderson, "there aren't so many people who you can hand pages and pages and pages of legal text and say, 'Entertain us with this.'"[388]

Anderson had now comfortably been established as a true actor's director. He could call anyone, and they'd say yes without hesitation – that is, outside of Angela Lansbury,[389] who had to turn down the role of Madame D. An aged-up Swinton happily took her place, swathed in velvet hand-painted with Gustav Klimt-inspired designs and trimmed with black diamond mink by costume designer Milena Canonero.[390]

Willem Dafoe plays Dmitri's right-hand man Jopling. Anderson wanted him to have sharp, canine teeth, but Dafoe suggested instead that he fasten them to his bottom jaw, letting them poke out like a bulldog.[391]

Once Gustave escapes from prison, he's aided by the Society of Crossed Keys, a secret guild inspired by the not-so-secret Les Clefs d'Or association for hotel concierges. It's crammed with Anderson favourites: Fisher Stevens (an old friend, in his first appearance in the director's films), Wally Wolodarsky, Waris Ahluwalia, Bob Balaban and Bill Murray.

When Revolori first met Murray, the actor threatened to toss his father into the hotel's swimming pool, as he'd reportedly done to a showbiz parent on the set of *Moonrise Kingdom*. Thankfully, Mr Revolori passed the test and remained dry.[392]

The entire cast and crew were lodged in Görlitz's Hotel Börse. Its owner was given a role as the Grand Budapest's receptionist, yet would somehow magically return behind the front desk of his own establishment before its residents returned from set at the end of each day.[393] Malouf painted portraits of the actors in costume to hang around the place.[394] Actors put on costumes in their rooms, and had their hair and make-up done in the lobby.[395] One room became a DVD library of Anderson's influences.[396] Goldblum would play jazz piano in the evenings.

At its premiere at the 2014 Berlin Film Festival, it was declared an immediate triumph. *The New Yorker*'s Richard Brody described Anderson as "a liberated filmmaker",[397] while *Sight & Sound* magazine wrote, "*The Grand Budapest Hotel* is his most complete fabrication yet, a fanatically and fantastically detailed, sugar-iced, calorie-stuffed, gleefully overripe Sachertorte of a film."[398] *Rolling Stone*'s Peter Travers even warned audiences they might want to "lick the screen".[399]

ABOVE The villainous Dmitri (Adrien Brody) and his right-hand man Jopling (Willem Dafoe).
OPPOSITE The Grand Budapest Hotel at its most glorious, here a model built 14 feet (4.26 metres) wide and 7 feet (2.13 metres) deep.

1876
GRAND BUDAPEST

It became Anderson's best performing movie, with a global box office of $163 million,[400] though the director's pastiche of Europe was surprisingly most popular with the Europeans. An unusual 62 per cent of its gross came from outside the US.[401]

It was also the first of Anderson's creations to win an Academy Award – four, in fact, for Best Costume Design, Best Makeup and Hairstyling, Best Original Score, and Best Production Design. He lost Best Picture and Best Director to Alejandro González Iñárritu's *Birdman*, though they were tied in nominations.

The Grand Budapest Hotel is the most accessible of Anderson's films, not because he's tempered his voice (quite the opposite, in fact), but because it argues so clearly for the moral worth of his creations. Zero, it's revealed, is an orphaned refugee in search of a home and a purpose. He finds it in Gustave, and in The Grand Budapest, because beauty in Anderson's world isn't merely an aesthetic, but a way to live. Beauty is kindness. Beauty is basic decency.

When Gustave and Zero first fall foul of the authorities, as Zubrowka lies on the knife edge of fascism, they're saved by an officer (Ed Norton) who remembers how generously Gustave treated him when he was a boy and his parents would frequent the hotel. He earns the loyalty of his cellmates because he never belittles them, telling Ludwig that his map of their escape route "shows great artistic promise". And when apologizing to Zero for an unkind word, he not only speaks for himself, but declares, "this is beneath the standards of The Grand Budapest Hotel. I apologize on behalf of the hotel."

Gustave sees goodness both in people and in places. Anderson does, too. Zero and Agatha's relationship becomes the whispered soul of his movie – a warm, precious love which allows cinematographer Robert Yeoman to melt the director's dioramas into soft focus and a kaleidoscope of carnival lights.

The older Zero lets us know, abruptly, that Agatha and their son died from fever. That is why he returns to the Grand Budapest, not out of some faint loyalty to Gustave, but to what Gustave taught him about the world. "The hotel I keep for Agatha," he tells the "Author". "We were happy here."

OPPOSITE Zero (Tony Revolori) and M. Gustave (Ralph Fiennes) gaze out of their train window at Zubrowka, a country free-falling into darkness.
NEXT SPREAD Zero (Tony Revolori) and Agatha (Saoirse Ronan), after a safe landing into a pile of Mendl's pastry boxes.

Heizung

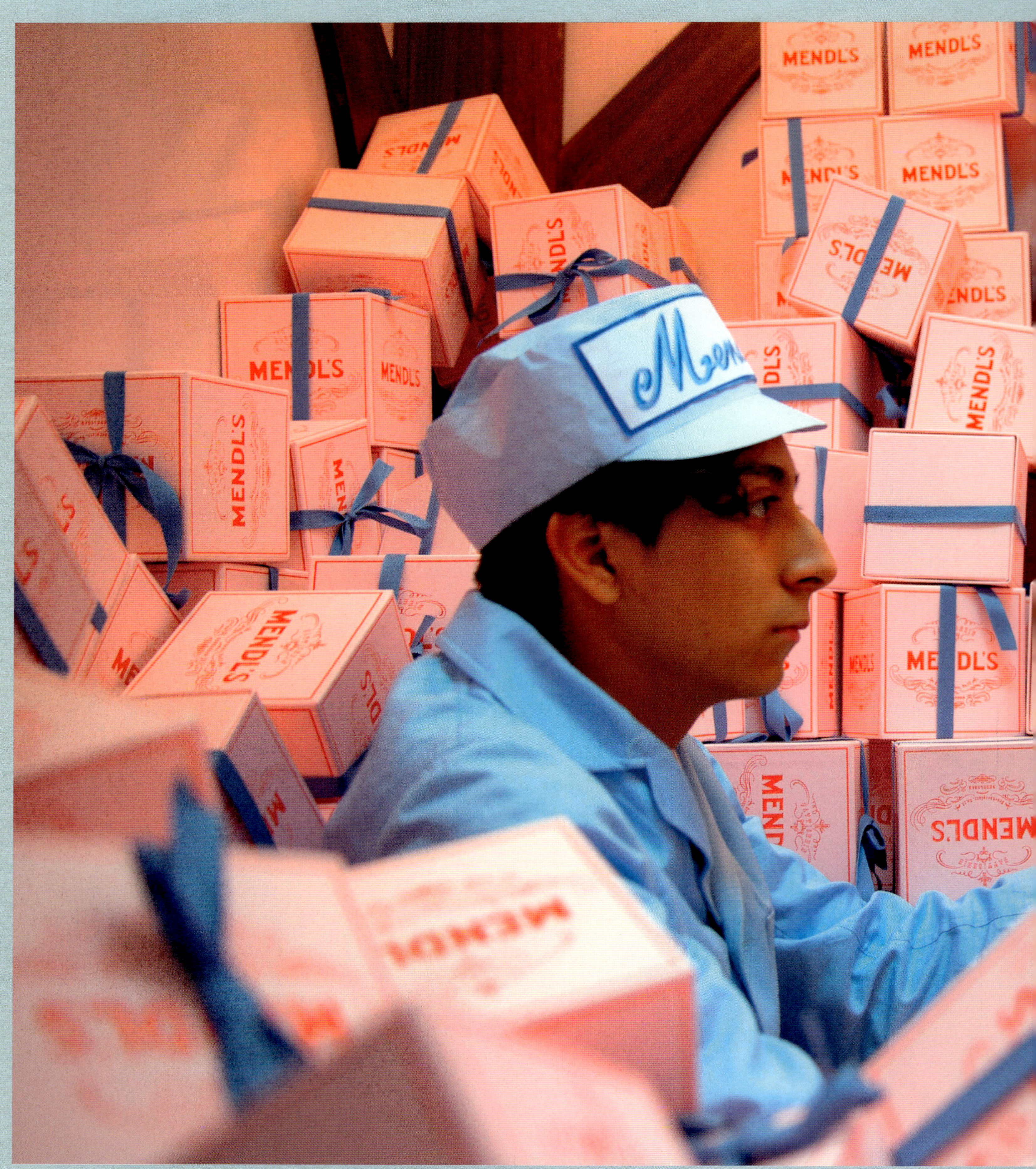
Mendl's
MENDL'S
MENDL'S
MENDL'S
MENDL'S
MENDL'S
MENDL'S
MENDL'S
MENDL'S

MENDL'S
MENDL'S
MENDL'S
MENDL'S
MENDL'S
MENDL'S
MENDL'S

ドギー
ショップ
クリニック

9
NORA INU

On *Isle of Dogs*

London's Isle of Dogs, a thumb-like protrusion into the River Thames, is not, regrettably, a canine paradise. For most of its history, it's functioned as a shipping dock, driving historians into conflict over the origins of its name. Some say it's where the greyhounds of King Edward III once resided. Others, that it derives from an insult dreamed up by Elizabethan satirists Ben Jonson and Thomas Nashe.

Yet, when Wes Anderson spotted road signs referring to the place, while in production on *Fantastic Mr. Fox*, he preferred to think on the fantasy.[402] A true Isle of Dogs. The director is not a dog person, per se, though his family owned a black Labrador named Chief when he was a child.[403] But he had the idea for a story about strays living on a garbage dump.[404] He'd also been ruminating on his longtime fascination with Japanese cinema, sparked at university and compounded by a visit to the country over a decade later.[405]

"It really changes you, and I like the idea of being changed in that way," Anderson said. "You sort of pick the thing that you want to learn about, and making a movie is a great way to have that chance." So, the strays would live on a garbage dump somewhere in Japan. He reached out to his friends and collaborators Jason Schwartzman and Roman Coppola, and work on a script began.[406]

Isle of Dogs is set 20 years in the future, in the fictional city of Megasaki. In its prologue, a Newfoundland dog named Jupiter (F. Murray Abraham) narrates the legend of The Boy Samurai and the Headless Ancestor. "Before the age of obedience, free dogs roamed at liberty, marking their territory," he tells us.

Yet, the cat-allied Kobayashi dynasty declares war on hound-kind, who are saved only by the boy warrior's defection from his own species. He decapitates the Kobayashi leader. Dogs, defeated, are domesticated. They

A glimpse of what life in the city of Megasaki can be when man and canine live in harmony, the nefarious plans of the cat-loving Kobayashi dynasty having been defeated.

Mayor Kenji Kobayashi (Kunichi Nomura) declares that all canines are to be sent to Trash Island. He claims it will protect the citizens of Megasaki from a flu outbreak.

live under humanity's thumb until Mayor Kenji Kobayashi (Kunichi Nomura) banishes them to Trash Island under the pretence of a canine flu outbreak.

The animation process on *Fantastic Mr. Fox* had been far from smooth, but Anderson remained undeterred. He now returned to London's 3 Mills Studios, and to many of *Fantastic Mr. Fox*'s animators and artists, confident now that he knew how better to work with them. His direction, once more, was provided from his home in Paris, using the same system of email communication.[407]

And, just as he'd vowed, he brought back cinematographer Tristan Oliver, having already hired him for *The Grand Budapest Hotel*'s stop-motion sequence, despite their minor public fracas – a sign that it was much more of a concern to the press than it was to them. "He's a really, really nice guy," Oliver said. "So, I like him. Being frustrated by somebody doesn't mean that you don't like them."[408]

Fantastic Mr. Fox's introduction of animatics into the process had offered Anderson a new confidence, which, in turn, pushed him to enlarge his scope and push his ambitions. It took two years, 240 sets on 44 stages, and 130,000 stills to make *Isle of Dogs*.[409] "It's a bigger movie," Anderson said. "But it was much more efficiently done."

Kunichi Nomura, a Japanese writer-director-DJ-designer, had helped Sofia Coppola secure numerous Tokyo locations for *Lost in Translation* (2003).[410] He had a cameo role in its karaoke scene, partying alongside Bill Murray. In the following years, she'd occasionally email Nomura to ask him to look after visiting friends.

Spots (Liev Schreiber) and the rest of the Trash Island canines, aided by the boy Atari Kobayashi (Koyu Rankin), make a final stand against their own extermination.

One turned up and introduced himself as Wes. They had some drinks. The next day, Wes emailed: "Oh, I had fun. Can we meet again?" He agreed. Days later, Nomura's new acquaintance asked if he liked movies, and if, perhaps, he'd like to see his new one. "Oh, that's … are you Wes Anderson?" Nomura replied.

He was. The director invited him to make a cameo appearance in *The Grand Budapest Hotel*, as one of the Soviet-era guests. Nomura had to source his own costume. Some time later, Anderson sent another email, which this time read: "I'm thinking of making this stop-motion film set in Japan. Would you help?" According to Nomura, "A short e-mail from Wes is a bad sign. Because he's going to start a whole thing." He was right.

Nomura would translate large portions of its script, advise on the movie's cultural authenticity, cast its Japanese voice actors, direct their performances and initially record all the Japanese dialogue.[411] Apparently, Anderson thought Nomura's voice sounded "very evil mayor", so he kept the role as Kobayashi.[412]

"Kun had absolutely no reluctance about saying, 'That's not good. That's wrong, that's not Japanese,'" Anderson said. "We wanted it to be authentic, and he would explain things to us, like the way you might explain cricket to someone, or how you wear clothes this way and not that way."[413]

Adam Stockhausen served as production designer for six months, beginning in April 2015, before handing the reins over to Paul Harrod so he could work on Steven Spielberg's *Ready Player One*.[414] Anderson wanted a different look to *Fantastic Mr. Fox*, with less of that Rankin/Bass charm,[415] and more of the flat-lit, boldly coloured, graphic look of ukiyo-e, or Japanese woodblock prints.[416] Coppola had gifted Anderson his first one. He'd since amassed quite the collection.[417]

Stockhausen and Harrod settled on a retrofuturistic Japan, 1963's vision of the future,[418] where mid-century and traditional design co-habit the Megasaki skyline, with influences from the biologically inspired, post-war Metabolism architectural movement.[419] Brick Mansion, Kobayashi's home, is based on Tokyo's Imperial Hotel, designed by Frank Lloyd Wright, while the Municipal Dome, where he conducts his speeches, is inspired by a kabuki theatre in Kyoto.[420]

"The movie is a fantasy," Anderson clarified. "And I would never suggest that this is an accurate depiction of any particular Japan. This is definitely a reimagining of Japan through my experience of Japanese cinema."[421]

Yet, details still mattered, and the movie features a dazzlingly complex sequence in which a sushi chef prepares a bento, or boxed meal, garnished with poisoned wasabi. It's the crucial ingredient in a bid to assassinate Kobayashi's political rival, Professor Watanabe (Akira Ito), head of the Science Party, who has discovered the cure for the canine flu.

Anderson was inspired by one of his favourite sushi chefs, based in Paris. His hands were photographed, and then replicated in clay form. "Wes wanted it to be recognizable for sushi chefs to look at it and understand how it was made," said animation director Mark Waring. "The way you hold the knife, the way you cut, the techniques – all of that had to be factored in."[422] Internal magnets were used so that the silicone fish puppet could be pre-cut, its insides already painted to look like flesh, and then sealed back together so it could be "sliced" on camera. It took six months to shoot.[423]

Anderson's movie pays tribute to the entire breadth of Japanese cinema, from the domestic dramas of Yasujirō Ozu, to Studio Ghibli's Hayao Miyazaki, to the kaijū, or monster, genre begun by *Godzilla* (1964). Yet it is, by far, the most indebted to Akira Kurosawa, the Japanese master who scaled human emotions like mountains, who absorbed Western influences and reshaped them by his own hands, who adapted Shakespeare, Tolstoy and Dostoevsky and, in turn, inspired so much of the Western canon.

Ingmar Bergman, Federico Fellini, Andrei Tarkovsky, Stanley Kubrick and Robert Altman have all cited his work. Coppola met him as a child (recalling him to be "a very tall, a very elegant guy"),[424] when his father, Francis Ford, worked with him on a commercial for Suntory whisky, the same brand promoted by Murray's character in *Lost in Translation*.

When Kurosawa suffered professional disaster after his high-profile departure from the 1970 war film *Tora! Tora! Tora!*, Francis Ford and a post-*Star Wars* George Lucas used their clout to secure financing for his 1980 epic, *Kagemusha*.

"Akira Kurosawa is one of those international superstar directors and such a striking person," said Anderson. "For a young director, that's one of the people you look to and say, 'That's what I aspire to be.'"[425] For *Isle of Dogs*, he imagined how Kurosawa might try to tell this story in live action.

When the alphas square off against a rival pack over the contents of a trash bag, Anderson cuts between close-ups and wide shots in order to mimic *Seven Samurai* (1954), famously adapted by John Sturges into a Western for *The Magnificent Seven* (1960).

Anderson's movie pays tribute to the entire breadth of Japanese cinema, from the domestic dramas of Yasujirō Ozu, to Studio Ghibli's Hayao Miyazaki.

Atari Kobayashi (Koyu Rankin) leads his crew in search of Spots (Liev Schreiber), his best friend and guard dog.

OPPOSITE (ABOVE) Rex (Edward Norton) tells Duke (Jeff Goldblum), Boss (Bill Murray) and King (Bob Balaban) that he can no longer bear the taste of garbage.
OPPOSITE (BELOW) Mayor Kobayashi (Kunichi Nomura) takes a soak. The character was inspired by actor Toshirô Mifune.
ABOVE Chief (Bryan Cranston) confronts Rex.

He replicates Kurosawa's startling use of stillness, too, as trash rolls by, caught up in a gust that bristles canine fur. Mayor Kobayashi is modelled on one of Kurosawa's closest collaborators, actor Toshirô Mifune, specifically as he appeared in the 1963 police procedural *High and Low*.[426]

Anderson's stories of families, both inherited and found, had always butted up against ideas of class, privilege and community, but *The Grand Budapest Hotel*'s direct entanglement with the themes of fascism and immigration had taken the director to a darker and more explicitly political realm of the human spirit.

Here, the residents of Trash Island are in dire straits – diseased, starved and hopeless. The alpha pack, Rex (Edward Norton), King (Bob Balaban), Duke (Jeff Goldblum) and Boss (Bill Murray), all mourn their former domesticity, as dog food commercial stars and baseball mascots. Only their leader, Chief (Bryan Cranston), came to the place as a stray. Duke talks of a dog that committed suicide, hanged by his own leash.

There's no future to be found in the ruins, and though Chief may pine over Nutmeg (Scarlett Johansson), the silky haired show dog, she shoots him down: "I wouldn't bring puppies into this world." This, arguably, is Anderson at his bleakest. At one point, an early scene saw humans test their poison on a chihuahua. The director showed it to Hackley, the seven-year-old son of his friend (and frequent star) Wally Wolodarsky. "He was not comfortable with it," Anderson said. The moment was excised.[427]

The movie needed dogs with matted fur and hungry eyes. Andy Gent, the head of the puppets department, and his team of more than 70 artists,[428] sculpted initial designs in a jack-o-matic style, in which clay is swiftly applied to a wire armature.[429] Anderson provided feedback. More clay dogs were sculpted.

It was important that the audience recognized them as canines, but not necessarily that they looked and moved exactly like them. Instead, they all have four stick limbs, rather than proper hind legs,[430] and fur cut largely from the same alpaca and merino wool used to make teddy bears.

The artists' dogs often wandered around the workshop, as a source of moral support and inspiration – Gent's own chocolate Labrador Charlie made for a fine muse.[431] But ideas came from all places. Jupiter's dignified jowls were based on British star of stage and screen Charles Laughton.[432] Nutmeg's colours were inspired by a Gucci store. Very few of the dogs are made to look like specific breeds. Instead, their appearance is based on the idea of their personalities.[433] One thousand puppets were eventually created, five hundred human and five hundred canine, in a variety of scales.

The canine puppets were built, like the foxes before, with articulated facial armatures, so that animators could individually adjust their brows and mouths.[434] The human puppets, however, made use of replacement faces, one for every mouth position needed to create the illusion of speech, and for all manners of expression. Normally, an animation studio would 3D print these. Anderson insisted they were all hand-sculpted.

Human skin was made out of slightly translucent resin,[435] based on sketched designs by illustrator Félicie Haymoz. Angela Kiely painted every freckle on the face of Tracy (Greta Gerwig), the rebellious American exchange student who rallies against Kobayashi. Anderson would always demand, "more freckles". In the end, there were 321 of them, in shades of orange and brown, painstakingly replicated across her replacement faces.[436]

Anderson also called on Maggie Haden, a puppet builder and costume designer who'd already worked on *Fantastic Mr. Fox*, to create a miniature wardrobe for the characters.[437] Kobayashi's jacket alone took three months. At one point, Haden had selected an extremely fine cotton for the mayor's shirt, only to see it projected onscreen and realize, in horror, that it looked entirely different scaled up on a puppet's body. "I sort of screamed," she said. "It looked like he was wearing a sack – a shirt made of a sack – and it just looked terrible." Silk was used from that point forward.

As a gesture of fortitude, Kobayashi ensures that the very first dog banished to Trash Island is Spots (Liev Schreiber), the best friend and guard dog of his orphaned ward, Atari (Koyu Rankin). The boy steals an aeroplane and crash-lands on the island, where he meets Chief and his companions, and enlists them in his search.

There was a "slight miscommunication" between Haden and Anderson. "I thought Wes wanted him in a silver spacesuit. I think he meant 'silver white'," she said. "Wes really liked it. He thought it looked slightly absurd – and he really liked that – and it looked a little bit Ziggy Stardust, which I really liked."

As with *Fantastic Mr. Fox*, Anderson was reluctant to use anything built by a computer. Yet, VFX remained an essential part of the process, necessary to

ABOVE Atari Kobayashi (Koyu Rankin) guides Rex (Edward Norton) across Trash Island's many, distinct districts.
RIGHT A character poster for Spots (Liev Schreiber).

combine separately shot elements to create a cohesive, but richly detailed, whole. An in-house team, led by Senior Visual Effects Supervisor Tim Ledbury, touched every single frame in the movie.[438] Their work, too, involved removing rigs used to hold up puppets, ensuring the replacement faces never jarred with each other, preventing Tracy's freckles from slipping around her face, and filling out the odd crowd.

Gathering a cast together was far less of a challenge. "One thing about an animated movie is that you can't really say, 'I'm not available.'" Anderson joked. "We can do it any time. We can do it at your house. There is no excuse."[439] Many were old familiars: Bill Murray, Edward Norton, Bob Balaban, Jeff Goldblum, F. Murray Abraham, Harvey Keitel, Kara Hayward, Jake Ryan, Frances McDormand (as an interpreter) and Tilda Swinton (as a prophetic pug, The Oracle).

Angelica Huston had wanted to be a dog, but the director couldn't find a role for her, so she was instead credited as "[Mute] Poodle".[440] Others, including Greta Gerwig, Liev Schreiber, Scarlett Johansson, Koyu Rankin, Ken Watanabe, Yoko Ono and Bryan Cranston, were new inductees into the Anderson clan.

The director spent two days recording with Cranston, Norton, Murray and Balaban in a studio in New York that resembled a log cabin. "We spent hours talking and barking and becoming more dog-like in the process," said Murray. "We had to unpack what we felt about dogs. It was a really unusual experience."[441] Cranston brought his own background to the role. As a child, his family had been evicted from their home, and he had to sleep for a while on his grandparents' couch, suddenly made to feel like a stray pup.[442]

Others recorded in one-on-one sessions, all over the world. Rankin was eight at the time, not twelve like his character, which Anderson joked was "like casting a twenty year old to play a sixty year old, almost. The years make such a difference at that age. But he just has a great voice, and the puppet we ended up designing is inspired by his performance."[443]

The artists' dogs often wandered around the workshop as a source of moral support and inspiration.

Alexandre Desplat once more provided the score. At the heart of it are Japanese taiko drums, in all sizes, quiet and loud, soft and harsh. "I think that when you go out of the film, you still have these drums resonating in your chest, because it's so obsessive and relentless, and it creates a lot of angst," he said.[444]

Karol Watanabe served as a taiko composer and advisor. When Anderson arrived at his studio to help compose a few riffs, he took to the instrument surprisingly quickly.[445] Desplat then added more Western elements, to evoke the idea of a mid-century political thriller, or the sharp quality of a dog's bark, using saxophones, recorders, French horns and a chorus of men repeating the words "Yoko, Ono".

It's a deliberate cultural clash. As the opening titles inform us, "All barks have been rendered into English." Japanese characters speak in Japanese, unsubtitled but sometimes translated by machine, onscreen text or human character. Anderson had always preferred to watch movies undubbed, in their original language.[446] He and his co-writers initially started with a narrator, before realizing that in-movie interpreters would be necessary, which eventually led to the creation of Tracy.[447]

"Translation became part of our subject matter, I think," said Anderson.[448] While there was a narrative need to use certain tricks, so that an English-speaking audience could keep up with the plot, what's most important are the places where translation doesn't occur, such as the scenes shared between

Atari, Chief and his crew. The language barrier becomes dangerous when it's used to construct otherness, and when it's coupled with an unwillingness to understand another's perspective.

Chief wasn't always a stray. He belonged to a family once, but bit a kid, not on purpose. "I guess he scared me," he confesses. "I bite." A dog doesn't understand how it's viewed by its owners. It has no way to communicate how it feels. It can't tell them it means no harm. When Spots is first presented to Atari, still in his hospital bed, recovering from the bullet train accident that killed his parents, he's fitted with a translation device. Tears start to run. "I can hear you," he says.

And, yet, like *The Darjeeling Limited* before it, it seemed as if Anderson was a little guilty of the same othering his movie rails against. The release of *Isle of Dogs* ignited a major conversation about the contemporary state of cultural appropriation, with the primary accusation being that, by not using subtitles for the Japanese dialogue, Anderson was in fact marginalizing his Japanese characters within their own movie.

Opinions on the matter were mixed, shared between both Japanese and Japanese-American viewers, whose differences in experience are unavoidably shaped by their direct or indirect exposure to exoticization and racism. "It's hard to call it offensive, exactly, and yet, it's not devoid of a kind of opportunism," wrote Vulture's Emily Yoshida. "It's not a crime, but it's certainly something to unpack."[449]

While there had been cultural consultancy at all levels of production, from Nomura's contributions to the script, to the work of graphic designers

Atari searches high and low for Spots. The movie used 240 sets on 44 stages, and 130,000 stills.

ABOVE Atari Kobayashi (Koyu Rankin) appeals to the Trash Island dogs for help, showing them a photograph of his beloved pet, Spots (Liev Schreiber).
NEXT SPREAD The Megasaki skyline. At its centre is the Municipal Dome, where Mayor Kobayashi (Kunichi Nomura) conducts his speeches. It's inspired by a kabuki theatre in Kyoto.

Erica Dorn and Chinami Narikawa,[450] Yoshida's piece points out that certain choices betrayed conscious or unconscious inauthenticity. The name "Megasaki City" means nothing in Japanese, and makes use of a nonsense kanji character.

Others, like *The New Yorker*'s Moeko Fujii, pointed to carefully embedded jokes created purely for Japanese viewers, like the way a particular scientist may speak in the flat, clipped tone of a character on Japanese daytime television.[451]

Most troubling was the inclusion of Tracy, whose speaking voice, at times, literally overrides Atari's. "All these coy linguistic layers amount to their own form of marginalization," wrote the *Los Angeles Times*'s Justin Chang. "Effectively reducing the hapless, unsuspecting people of Megasaki to foreigners in their own city."[452]

Reviews otherwise were largely positive, with critics picking up on Anderson's new unruly streak, splattered across that Kurosawa palette and in the viciousness of its violence. "It is by turns savage and soulful, mangy and refined, possessed of an unmistakable pedigree and yet boldly resistant to categorization," Chang wrote elsewhere in his review.

Anderson's daughter, Freya, was born in 2016, not long after production had started. "She's seen me sitting at my computer for sixteen hours a day and knows this movie better than everybody," the director joked.[453] In fact, she'd grown so accustomed to watching dailies that the pair developed a shorthand. When Freya demanded to see the "doggies", it meant it was time to let her into her father's world.[454]

ホクサイビール
シネマ
ドギー
チヨップ。
日本一の美しさ

パチンコ

NOUS NE SOMMES! PAS "SLEEPY!"
NOUS NE SOMMES! PAS "SLEEPY!"
NOUS NE SOMMES! PAS "SLEEPY!"
CHAMBRES
DE
JEUNES
FILLES

10
NOUS NE SOMMES! PAS SLEEPY!

On *The French Dispatch*

At the age of 12, Wes Anderson sat his parents down and gave them a set of handouts. They detailed what he believed to be the most persuasive reasons why they should let him go to school in Paris. Each of them was a lie. Really, he knew nothing of the country, beyond what an old classmate who'd moved there had told him. His parents, shockingly, declined the request.[456] Yet, the director's Francophilia could not be so easily quashed. He learned first of the place through the movies, and the work of Jean-Luc Godard, François Truffaut, Jean Renoir and Jacques Tati.

In 2005 he acquired an apartment in Paris and began to reside there part-time. "Walking down a street I've never been down before is like going to a movie or something," he confessed. "Just wandering the city is entertainment."[457] Anderson had become an American transplant in Europe, what his friend and collaborator Hugo Guinness liked to call "reverse emigration".[458] There was an idea for a movie in there somewhere.

At the age of 16, Anderson was sitting in his school library, facing a wooden rack of periodicals. One in particular, with a striking illustrated cover, caught his eye and he began to read the first story he found inside – "Letter from New Delhi", a regular column by Ved Mehta on Indian social and political affairs. "I thought, I have no idea what this is, but I'm interested," he recalled.[459]

It was *The New Yorker*, a magazine founded in 1925 by Harold Ross and his wife Jane Grant, an oasis for sharp-witted satire, elegant reportage and fiery literary imagination. Its historic contributor list is a real who's who – Truman Capote, Toni Morrison, F. Scott Fitzgerald, Margaret Atwood, among countless others.

When Anderson saw a commercial for subscriptions on television, he begged his parents to sign him up.[460] On this, they acquiesced. Later, when

The student revolutionaries in "Revisions to a Manifesto" demand that the boys be allowed in the girls' dormitories. The detail is borrowed direct from the real history of the May '68 protests.

he discovered that the University of California in Berkeley was discarding a set of 40 years of bound copies, he bought them for six hundred dollars.[461]

An idea had started to form in his head: an omnibus movie, set in France, that would pay tribute to his most beloved publication. At first, it had no framing structure, but would simply be a set of stories like one might find in a magazine, with at least one presented as a work of pure fiction. This, he decided, would be a short story written by a Japanese author. Except, the idea grew and grew, until its burst out of its confines and became its own beast, 2018's *Isle of Dogs*.

The first story of *The French Dispatch* had existed in some form, on paper, for over a decade. It's about a painter, imprisoned, and his muse, the guard.[462] Anderson then gathered his regular collaborators – Guinness, then Roman Coppola and Jason Schwartzman – to corral a full feature. One section would deal with rebellious students, another with a chef.

One short piece at the front would establish the movie's location, the fictional Ennui-sur-Blasé, while a prologue and epilogue would introduce the publication at its heart, the fictional *The French Dispatch*, published by the American-bound *Liberty, Kansas Evening Sun*. It would be dedicated to the writers of *The New Yorker*, with a short list of figures who either served as inspirations, or were otherwise foundational voices at the magazine, listed at the very start of its credits.

The French Dispatch starts with death. The magazine's founder and editor, Arthur Howitzer Jr. (Bill Murray), has suffered a fatal heart attack. In his will, it's stated that the publication must cease printing. This will be its final issue. Howitzer is king and father to his writers. As Angelica Huston's cool-toned narrator informs us, "These were his people." His various assistants and errand boys were not. He fires one on the spot for interrupting him during a meeting. When the young man's eyes start to water, he points up to the sign above his door: "NO CRYING".

There's a little of Ross here, and a little of his successor, William Shawn. Murray's trademark misanthropy nods to the former, his careworn sentimentality to the latter. "Ross had a great feeling for writers," Anderson said. "It isn't exactly respect. He values them, but he also thinks they're lunatic children who have to be sort of manipulated or coddled, whereas Shawn seems to have been the most gentle, respectful, encouraging master you could ever wish to have."[463]

The best of Howitzer's "lunatic children" have been gathered for the final issue. We begin with Herbsaint Sazerac (Owen Wilson), the cycling reporter, who measures the pace of life in Ennui-sur-Blasé. Through him, Anderson demonstrates all that he's learned about the French character, as Ennui awakens: old men light their pipes, housewives beat the dust off their carpets, and canines scamper about the place.

Sazerac is invested in all that is mundane and profane: corpses pulled from the river, hives of rats in the metro, the elderly abandoned by their dreams, the sex workers, the building site awaiting a shopping centre, the choir boys on a criminal rampage.

Sazerac is based on Joseph Mitchell,[464] whose *New Yorker* essays were born mainly from curious observation, as he turned down the streets the literary elite tended to ignore, and talked to the kind of people they tended to forget. In "Thirty-Two Rats from Casablanca", he lavished attention on New York's rodent population.

ABOVE *The French Dispatch*'s founder and editor, Arthur Howitzer Jr. (Bill Murray). The character is based partially on the founder of The *New Yorker*, Harold Ross, and on his successor, William Shawn.
OPPOSITE The theatrical poster for *The French Dispatch*.

The character's favoured mode of transport, however, is a characteristic borrowed from his actor. "Owen is always on a bike in real life," Anderson said. "It wouldn't be unheard of, if you were in Berlin or Tokyo or someplace, to see Owen Wilson riding up on a bicycle."[465]

The first story proper, "The Concrete Masterpiece", is delivered via lecture by J.K.L. Berensen (Tilda Swinton), a former employee of the Kansas art mogul Upshur "Maw" Clampette (Lois Smith).

Berensen resembles Rosamond Bernier,[466] once the Paris Editor of *Vogue*, who was a familiar to many of the great geniuses, including Frida Kahlo and Diego Rivera, Henri Matisse, Pablo Picasso and Joan Miró. She not only documented their work and their lives, but breathed their air. Berensen, with her red candy floss hair, and matching kaftan, is much the same.

"The Concrete Masterpiece", in part, deals with delusion. The subject of Berensen's lecture, and the object of her intense fascination, is Moses Rosenthaler (Benicio del Toro), a literal tortured artist. He's in prison for murder, is deeply disturbed, and paints to keep his hands busy because "otherwise I think it's going to be a suicide."

Anderson explicitly wrote the part for del Toro,[467] knowing that he has a way to present such extremity of character and emotion as simple matter of fact. Rosenthaler paints in pigeon blood, shackle grease and flames. At first, the actor wanted his character to breathe fire. A specialist arrived on set, ready to train him, and commenced his demonstration. His beard ignited almost immediately. "Okay, well – that's it for that," del Toro said in response. In the finished movie, Rosenthaler simply daubs the canvas with a torch.

The larger point here is that the artist is a dangerous man, and entirely upfront about it. Berensen, in her lecture, seems to stumble off script for a moment, as she recalls the time he made an aggressive sexual advance on her in his basement studio.

It's a rare moment of disarray and hesitation within Anderson's highly organized universe. The spotlight on her switches off and silence hangs in the air, just for a beat, before she returns to the podium, her hostess grin restored, and continues her speech.

Julien Cadazio (Adrien Brody), an art dealer briefly incarcerated for fraud, stumbles across Rosenthaler's paintings. He makes a conceited assumption that the work, between these two men, carries the same worth – pure capital. "All artists sell their work, it's what makes them an artist," he insists. His stubbornness on the matter drives him to madness and violence.

Art, to Rosenthaler, is an expression of private feeling. In this case, it's a dedication to his prison guard, Simone (Léa Seydoux), who subverts the typical power dynamic of the genius-muse relationship. She snaps at him and swats at him, and gives him a brief taste of the electric chair to rouse his spirits.

Rosenthaler's masterpiece, commissioned by Cadazio, is painted on the hobby-room walls, an impractical and deeply uncommercial choice of canvas. Cadazio, infuriated, starts a brawl. Yet money still prevails, when Clampette has the entire room airlifted overseas to her own gallery back home, which comes with its own gift shop. Anderson presents this without direct commentary. But there's a touch of sadness to how desolate the place seems, empty of visitors, stranded out in the middle of a cornfield.

Lucinda Krementz (Frances McDormand) introduces the next piece, "Revisions to a Manifesto". Anderson had once heard McDormand rebuke a haughty French waiter with the words, "Kindly leave me my dignity."[468] So, he wrote the role with that spirit in mind, as well as that of journalist Mavis Gallant, who'd observed the student demonstrations in Paris, in May 1968.

They'd risen up, at first, in protest against their materialist and imperialist society. It spread then to the workers, and the union of these two groups brought France's economy (and nearly its government) to its knees. On all fronts, they were met with brutal suppression by the authorities.

Of Gallant's work, Anderson noted, "it's a foreigner's perspective, but she's very clear-sighted about all of it. Clarity and empathy. She went out every day, alone, in the middle of the chaos."[469] Certain lines of dialogue were transposed directly from her writings on May '68, including her observation that the students were graced by "the touching narcissism of the young".

Gallant was far more sympathetic to the cause than many of her peers. But, she noted, too, when their idealism inched towards absurdity. In "Revisions to a Manifesto", the revolution starts with the demand that the boys be allowed in the girls' dormitories, a detail borrowed direct from history.

What Krementz documents is a clash, that's really a romance, between two students, Zeffirelli (Timothée Chalamet) and Juliette (Lyna Khoudri). Both are inflamed by the certainty their world is sick, and in need of change, though their youth means they're still in the process of turning that extremity of feeling into something concrete. It's not really about the girls' dormitories. But no one's quite sure yet what it is about. Zeffirelli struggles to write his manifesto. Krementz helps – she's done this before. He's drawn to her. They have sex.

McDormand strongly disagreed with the idea her character and Zeffirelli had any intimate relations. Anderson told her not to share her reservations with Chalamet. "However, I did," said the actor. "Timothée's reaction was basically, 'Huh.'"[470] The director was diplomatic, but firm in his decision, communicated through the sounds of creaking bedsprings heard outside Krementz's bedroom door. "I think it works," McDormand relented.

Ultimately, Krementz is there less to shape the protestors' ideas but, with her wisdom, remind these young people that they are far more aligned than they think. Juliette is the idealist, the purer radical. Anderson told Khoudri to watch Jacques Rivette's *Le Pont du Nord*, since its protagonist, played by Pascale Ogier, wears the same leather jacket and motorcycle helmet, and conducts herself with the same ferocity.[471] Conflict, for these young people, is also flirtation.

When one of Zeffirelli's pack, Mitch-Mitch (Mohamed Belhadjine), is conscripted, Juliette chastises him for facilitating imperialist aggression. Zeffirelli, meanwhile, tends towards forgiveness. That's his friend. He had no choice. And it's easy for Juliette to talk, from the privileged confines of their regular meeting spot, the café Le Sans Blague.

He still wants to worship Tip-Top (Jarvis Cocker), his favourite pop artist, while she rebukes him as "a commodity represented by a record company

Gallant was far more sympathetic to the cause than many of her peers. But, she noted, too, when their idealism inched towards absurdity.

OPPOSITE (ABOVE) Reporter Herbsaint Sazerac (Owen Wilson) tinkers with his trusty bicycle.
OPPOSITE (BELOW) One of the student revolutionaries, Zeffirelli (Timothée Chalamet).

owned by a conglomerate controlled by a bank subsidized by a bureaucracy sustaining the puppet leadership of a satellite stooge government".

These differences matter, and they don't. Even if the lovers eventually ride off into the night, Zeffirelli, we're told, was later electrocuted atop the pirate radio tower and drowned in the river, his ideas discarded in favour of a widely reproduced photograph, now fodder for posters and T-shirts. It is, like "The Concrete Masterpiece", another emotionally ambivalent conclusion.

"I am convinced they are better than we were," Krementz reflects. Chalamet, a French-American star and favourite of directors Greta Gerwig and Luca Guadagnino, had family members who took part in the May '68 protests. He found it a striking coincidence.[472] The actor delivered lines in both French and English on set, though only the latter were used in the final edit.

Anderson's final story, "The Private Dining Room of the Police Commissioner", is a piece recalled on the spot by Roebuck Wright (Jeffrey Wright), while appearing as a guest on a TV chat show (hosted by Liev Schreiber's unnamed character). It was the last element of the movie to be written. It's also the most direct in communicating the central idea behind *The French Dispatch*, of the sacred loneliness of the foreigner – a cut above the tourist, always observant, yet not quite one with their new home.

Anderson was familiar with James Baldwin's work, particularly his 1956 novel, *Giovanni's Room*, about a young, gay American living in Paris, deeply alienated by his sexuality.[473] Howitzer first meets Roebuck in the Ennui-sur-Blasé jail, because, as the writer warns, "love the wrong way and you will find yourself in great jeopardy." The editor offers him freedom not only in the literal sense, by paying his bail, but through the gift of work, of a space to express his isolation.

The part was written for Jeffrey Wright, who happened to be on his way to Paris when the director called him. They had lunch at Le Select, in Montparnasse, which Baldwin frequented. The author had settled in the city in the hope he could create distance between himself and the claustrophobic cruelty of American racism.[474]

Anderson and Wright talked. When the director sent him the script, it was one of the most dazzling pieces of writing that had ever landed on the actor's lap.[475] He signed on immediately, and joined what he'd describe as "a highly palatable asylum".

Roebuck's soul is, at least partially, Baldwin's, but his work is a tribute to A. J. Liebling, gourmand and author of *Between Meals: An Appetite for Paris* (1959). "The Private Dining Room of the Police Commissioner" begins when Roebuck attends a private dinner held by the Commissaire de la Vilatte (Mathieu Amalric), and prepared by Nescaffier (Stephen Park), legendary in his ability to deliver fine dining in practical forms, suited to working officers.

The dinner, however, is interrupted by the kidnapping of the Commissaire's son Gigi (Winsen Ait Hellal) by a gang (two are played by Edward Norton and Saoirse Ronan). They, in return, demand the release of seemingly the Ennui underworld's sole accountant, the Abacus (Willem Dafoe).

Cycling reporter Herbsaint Sazerac (Owen Wilson) recounts how an old market has been demolished in favour of a multi-level shopping center and parking structure.

NOUS NE SOMMES! PAS SLEEPY!

A gang member (Saoirse Ronan) and her kidnapped target, the Commissaire's son Gigi (Winsen Ait Hellal).

A shoot-out occurs, followed by a vehicular chase, facilitated only by Nescaffier's heroic sacrifice. He cooks a meal with poisoned radishes, sampling them to throw the criminals off the scent. His iron chef's stomach saves him from certain death.

Here is where Roebuck's article ends. Yet, Howitzer insists on the reinstatement of a deleted passage, in which Roebuck and Nescaffier share a moment alone, to talk of life in a foreign land, "seeking something missing, missing something left behind". Journalists, at least in Anderson's world, are solitary creatures, and their curiosity about other people is driven by a sense of dissatisfaction.

It's their source of hope: that if they can observe, they can learn and, if they learn, they can find something to live for. "I have spent a lot of time in America and watched American films," Seydoux reflected. "So I know what it's like to feel as if a culture other than yours is a part of you. I feel like Wes wanted to make a movie about that phenomenon – that feeling that you can hold a culture within yourself even though you weren't originally born into it."[476]

That spirit lives within Ennui-sur-Blasé, a city that's precisely French, yet built brick-by-brick by a traveller's wonderment. Production designer Adam Stockhausen and his team first started on Google Maps, wandering France through a virtual lens.

They created a list of locations, sent out scouts to snap pictures, visited a few themselves, before settling on the ideal spot: Angoulême, a city in the southwest, spread across a plateau overlooking the river Charente, a

ABOVE Imprisoned artist Moses Rosenthaler (Benicio del Toro) and his two guards (Léa Seydoux and Denis Menochet).
NEXT SPREAD Arthur Howitzer Jr. (Bill Murray) and a waiter (Pablo Pauly) look over plans for the final issue of The French Dispatch.

beautiful scribble of meandering streets, stairways and arches, in all shades of medieval and neoclassical architecture. In its prime, it was the paper-making capital of Europe, and now hosts an annual comic book festival.

Although there were over 125 sets created for the movie, Stockhausen and his team, as before, built only what was needed for the shot. Anderson's animatics remained their North Star. What couldn't be built on location was created inside a factory that formerly manufactured felt-tip pens, in what became a small hub of workshops, production offices and storage space.[477]

Another factory, used in the production of equipment for the French navy, was transformed into the prison of "The Concrete Masterpiece". Since the movie isn't tied to any year, or any decade particularly, Stockhausen could draw from a wide range of influences, while the pieces set decorator Rena DeAngelo sourced from flea markets and estate sales dated from the '20s right up to the '70s.[478]

Cast and crew stayed at the Hotel Saint Gelais, whose proprietor Yannick Lamuraille joked that, "from the moment that the production began, we stopped being a hotel and restaurant and simply became Wes's house."[479]

Extras were drawn from the local populace, both human and feline. Anderson insisted that the cats wrangled for a shot of Ennui's rooftops were all untrained, domestic pets. "Even though we never had more than forty cats on set at once, that's still an enormous amount of cats," said second unit director Martin Scali. "It took weeks to figure out and three or four days of shooting for this three-and-a-half-second shot."[480]

THE
FRENCH
DISPATCH
ROEBUCK WRIGHT
1
2-3
4-5
24-25
26-27
34-35
FILLES
GARÇONS

OGRESS
N.12
OF
ETION
10-11
12-13
14-15
16-17
18-19
20-21
8-9
BERENSEN
CADAZIO
ROSENTHALER
38-39
40-41
42-43
44-45
46-47
RAC
62-63
64-65
66-67
68-69
72

FRANCE
COMMISSARIAT
ENNUI
ACCÈS LIBRE 
POUR TOUS LES
GARÇONS
BOYS
ALLOWED
BOYS
ALLOWED

OPPOSITE (ABOVE) Nescaffier (Stephen Park), a chef famous for his ability to deliver fine dining to working officers.
OPPOSITE (BELOW) Zeffirelli (Timothée Chalamet) and a member of the university administration (Sharif Andoura) negotiate through a game of chess.
ABOVE Roebuck Wright (Jeffrey Wright) at dinner with the Commissaire (Mathieu Amalric), the Commissaire's oldest friend (Hippolyte Girardot) and the Commissaire's mother (Mauricette Coudivat).

Javi Aznarez, an illustrator published in *The New Yorker* and *The Washington Post*, came to doodle across the set walls, and create a set of fictional covers, proudly displayed over the movie's credits.[481] There are some morbid pieces – an artist on a river bank, painting a drowning man, and a pianist slumped over his piano, a bullet hole in the window glass – but the humour is dry, and so very cosmopolitan.

"The cover of the dead pianist is a fantasy from my childhood," Aznarez said. "At my parents' house we had a neighbor who gave piano lessons. At first, it may seem very bucolic to hear a piano in the background, but when it plays every day you feel like murdering the neighbor."

Rosenthaler's body of work, a creation of somewhat naïve genius, posed a greater challenge. His abstract portraits of Simone were inspired by Willem de Kooning, Jackson Pollock, Frank Auerbach and Anselm Keifer, but were never intended to directly evoke their style.[482]

Instead, they had to feel like a revelation that could believably trigger riots wherever they were displayed. Sandro Kopp, Swinton's partner and a longtime friend of Anderson's, was hired, and he brought with him two aides: Edith Baudraud and Sian Smith, the latter first introduced to him when she worked as an assistant for her aunt, Lynne Ramsay, on her 2010 film *We Need to Talk About Kevin*, which co-starred Swinton.[483]

Kopp was given two and a half months to create ten paintings that, in the movie, take Rosenthaler three years to complete.[484] There was also the matter of the artist's earlier, figurative creations. Anderson wanted these painted from life, which meant Smith had to spend a day wandering

Angoulême in search of cherries, for a picture of a fruit bowl. They were out of season. Red currants, eventually, had to be brought in as a substitute.[485]

Miniatures were used to add detail to the city, such as the sign atop *The French Dispatch* offices or the aeroplane Clampette uses to fly from Kansas to France. Tristan Oliver oversaw a four-week shoot, spread across Berlin's Studio Babelsberg and London's Arch Film Studio, where puppet maker Andy Gent had a space.[486]

"The Private Dining Room of the Police Commissioner" features a three-minute, animated police-car chase, written into the original screenplay, and similar in look to Hergé's comic series, *The Adventures of Tintin*. It was produced in Angoulême itself, and took a team of around fifteen people roughly seven months to complete. Anderson would check in on a daily basis.[487]

Alexandre Desplat's score is centred on the piano, as played by Jean-Yves Thibaudet, also heard on the soundtracks for *Atonement*, *Pride & Prejudice* and Jane Campion's *The Portrait of a Lady*. But Desplat saw, in Anderson's script, an element of the Dadaist – surreal, provocative and playful – and so mixed in unexpected instruments, in unusual combinations.[488] The tuba, banjo, bassoon and harpsichord all have a part to play.

It's not stereotypically French but, as the composer admitted, "it's charged with my own melancholy and my own French soul." "Revisions to a Manifesto", meanwhile, makes use of the pop songs Zeffirelli might listen to, including Cocker-as-Tip-Top's cover of the '60s hit "Aline".

Anderson and cinematographer Robert Yeoman had originally only planned to shoot "The Concrete Masterpiece" in black and white, the rest in colour. But something clicked. Here, they had an opportunity to use colour sparingly as a way to exemplify the art and beauty that these journalists prize: the unveiling of a painting, the presentation of a meal, or the brilliant blue of Saoirse Ronan's eyes. This was combined with a shift in aspect ratios, from 1.37:1, associated with the French New Wave, to the wider 2.39:1, as well as an unusual placement of subtitles on the screen, in order to imitate the look and layout of a magazine.

The French Dispatch was proof that Anderson, now, had no more hesitations when it came to artifice. "At a certain point, I just decided I'm going to do whatever I wanted," he said.[489] He could trust that raw emotion would break through any layer, however tweaked and perfected. When the debut of *Simone, Naked, Cell Block J. Hobby Room* descends into a brawl, a freeze-frame tableau is created by simply having the actors stand in place, with objects dangled from the ceilings.

A flashback to a younger Rosenthaler (Tony Revolori) ends when the older one walks into frame and swaps places with him. The walls of Le Sans Blague open up like a set on a theatre stage. It took 45 takes, according to Chalamet, to nail the scene in which Zeffirelli pins a poster of Tip-Top to the wall. "If generality is the enemy of art," the actor said,[490] "then Wes deserves a statue."

The movie's most ambitious shot tracks Roebuck through the Ennui police station, through walls, horizontally and backwards. Usually, this kind

Arthur Howitzer Jr. (Bill Murray) offers advice to Roebuck Wright (Jeffrey Wright). A journalist who has never completed a single article (Wally Wolodarsky) hovers in the background.

NOUS NE SOMMES! PAS SLEEPY!

WES ANDERSON

of trick would be achieved using a Steadicam, a motion-stabilized handheld camera, but Anderson demanded the perfect fluidity of a dolly track.[491]

Camera operator Sanjay Sami, while working on the director's 2016 H&M Christmas ad, titled *Come Together*, had custom-built switch tracks that mimicked a children's toy train set. Named the Mangalore rig, after the Indian port city he was in when the idea came to him, it was used as a basis for his creation for *The French Dispatch*, which featured three 90-degree direction changes.[492]

The French Dispatch began production in late 2018, with the editing completed in early 2020.[493] It was originally scheduled to premiere at that year's Cannes Film Festival, but the COVID-19 pandemic pushed it back by more than 12 months. When it finally debuted, in July 2021, the critics were immediately enamoured by how much pleasure Anderson took in the art of invention and manipulation. His usual detractors stood firm.

The New Yorker's Richard Brody, even if there was a touch of bias, called it "perhaps Anderson's best film to date. It is certainly his most accomplished",[494] while *The Guardian*'s Wendy Ide declared it "among the most punchable films I have ever seen" in an otherwise measured review.[495] In the director's career-long search to define the Andersonian, he had achieved a new milestone of specialization.

Cadazio, at one point, asks Rosenthaler to draw him a sparrow as proof of his genius. "He can make it look perfectly realistic," he says of the artist. "He could paint this beautifully if he wanted, but he thinks this is better." Anderson, too, could easily do the same with his work. But, as *The French Dispatch* argues, he thinks this is better.

OPPOSITE The city of Angoulême plays the role of Ennui-sur-Blasé.
NEXT SPREAD Zeffirelli (Timothée Chalamet) and Juliette (Lyna Khoudri) lean against the jukebox in the café Le Sans Blague, its exterior walls pulled away like a theatrical set.

TEAUX
AIGUISAGE
LIBRAIRIE

MASCULIN · FEMININ
COIFFEUR
FLOP QUARTER
AMBRE
APERITIF

RAIL ROAD
CROSSING
RAIL ROAD
CROSSING

11
LAST TRAIN TO SAN FERNANDO

On *Asteroid City*

Wes Anderson had begun to ruminate on death. All people must do, at some point in their lives. The thought had hardly crossed his path before. He wasn't someone who anxiously counted down the years. Yet, he'd reached his fifties now, and had a daughter who was not yet ten, and loss had started to colour the edges of his life.[496]

"A thing that happens over the years is that all of the dead people begin to pile up," he reflected. "I've always kind of felt like there's so much that gets dealt with by saying, 'Okay, let's do another one. Let's go to the next movie.'"[497] Cinema, his self-professed "lifesaver", once again came to his rescue. His next movie, *Asteroid City*, would deal with the infinite, with what exists beyond flesh, and how art can reach out towards the cosmic.

By looking backwards, Anderson could look forward. When he and Owen Wilson were on the cusp of adulthood, they dreamed of the Actors Studio, a New York City collective of actors, directors and playwrights, founded in 1947 by Elia Kazan, Cheryl Crawford and Robert Lewis.[498]

Alongside Lee Strasberg, who served as its director from 1952 until his death in 1982, they refined Konstantin Stanislavsky's teachings on acting into what we now know of as the Method. It, in turn, shaped the careers of many of its most famous members, among them Marlon Brando, James Dean and Montgomery Clift.

Anderson, for many years after, had wanted to set a movie within the Actors Studio or an environment like it. *Asteroid City* would satisfy that desire. Set at some point in the '50s, it's presented to us as a black-and-white television special about the production of a stage play about an alien visitation to the American Southwest.

An unnamed narrator, played by Bryan Cranston, first introduces the drama, informing us that the said stage play, itself called *Asteroid City*, "does not exist. It is an imaginary drama created expressly for this broadcast.

The outskirts of Asteroid City. Population 87, plus one roadrunner, a handmade puppet created for the film.

The characters are fictional, the text hypothetical, the events an apocryphal fabrication – but together they present an authentic account of the inner-workings of a modern theatrical production."

We then move to the next layer, also in monochrome, in which Conrad Earp (Edward Norton) workshops his script for *Asteroid City* with an Actors Studio-like unit, whose luminaries include Jones Hall (Jason Schwartzman), his head often buried inside his turtleneck sweater in reference to a famous Phil Stern photograph of James Dean, and the Bette Davis-like Mercedes Ford (Scarlett Johansson).[499]

At the very centre of Anderson's story is the stage play itself, presented in vivid colour. It begins as a set of parents and children descend on the titular Asteroid City, barely a town, somewhere in the south-west. It's host to the annual Junior Stargazer Space Cadet convention, which commemorates the day, in 3007 BCE, that a meteorite made impact with Earth.

Hall (and, thus, Schwartzman) plays Augie Steenbeck, a war photojournalist who is yet to tell his children – Woodrow (Jake Ryan) and triplets Andromeda (Ella Faris), Pandora (Gracie Faris) and Cassiopeia (Willan Faris) – that their mother passed three weeks earlier. Ford (and, thus, Johansson) plays Midge Campbell, an actress preparing for a role, and mother to Dinah (Grace Edwards).

Asteroid City's screenplay, which Anderson wrote with the help of Roman Coppola in the early days of the COVID-19 pandemic,[500] shifts between these worlds. They even, on occasion, bleed into each other. While Midge talks to another parent, Cranston's narrator steps into frame. "Am I not in this?" he enquires. He politely steps back out.

"In real life, I feel like the actor often puts much of himself or herself into the role," Anderson explained. "What I intended is that the people telling the story are a part of the story, and they're taking everything from their lives that they do and don't understand and trying to make something out of it and find answers – or at least explore the right questions."[501]

In fact, there was more of Schwartzman in Augie than Anderson had even realized. When he first reached out to his old friend, alluding vaguely to a character he wanted him to play, he told the actor to think of Kazan. Schwartzman sent him a picture of the book on his bedside table. It was about Kazan. Anderson, later, changed his mind. He should actually think about Stanley Kubrick. Schwartzman sent him another photo, of another book he had near him. It was about Kubrick. He'd recently seen *2001: A Space Odyssey* at the cinema, and had promptly begun to devour interviews and documentaries on the man.[502]

Stranger still, Schwartzman's grandfather had waited a month after his wife's death to break the news to their son, and only after they'd crossed from one side of the country to the other, from Brooklyn to Los Angeles. "So when I read that part, it was eerie, like my dad was a part of the scene," the actor said. "It was very emotional."[503]

Anderson had wanted to build a movie around Schwartzman,[504] who he'd had the privilege of seeing grow up in his movies, from *Rushmore* to

At the very centre of Anderson's story is the stage play itself, presented in vivid colour. It begins as a set of parents and children descend on the titular Asteroid City, barely a town, somewhere in the south-west.

OPPOSITE (ABOVE) The Junior Stargazers (Ethan Josh Lee, Jake Ryan, Grace Edwards, Sophia Lillis, and Aristou Meehan).
OPPOSITE (BELOW) An unnamed narrator, played by Bryan Cranston, welcomes us.

JUNIOR STARGAZER
"BRAINIAC"

ROTTERDAM
THEATRE
NARCISSIST
TONIGHT 10 PM BUGLE BOY BLOWS THE BLUES
SALTZBURG KEITEL THEATRE
VARIETY

Photojournalist Augie Steenbeck (Jason Schwartzman), whose weary expressions and slightly dishevelled beard were inspired by director Stanley Kubrick.

The Darjeeling Limited to *Moonrise Kingdom*. The actor, like Augie, had become a father of three.[505] Ryan, his onscreen son, was now the same age he was in *Rushmore*.[506]

At first, Schwartzman hesitated, faced with such a heavy and expansive role, but his friend trusted him implicitly to do right by it. "When you know someone for so long, there's really no hiding," Schwartzman said. "Reading the script, it was definitely like: I don't know how to do this. I felt like what he was saying by giving this to me was: 'I think you have this in you.'"[507]

At first, the pair worked on breaking down what had attracted Anderson to the idea of Kubrick. His weary expressions and slightly dishevelled beard could be easily replicated. Harder was the director's voice, a little stiff but still rhythmic. It reminded Schwartzman of his father's, so he went to work unearthing his family's old videos and cassettes.[508] He also sought out dialect coach Tanera Marshall, who he'd met while filming the FX series *Fargo*. She pointed out that Kubrick never moved his face very much. Schwartzman did the opposite.

He tried several exercises. They didn't quite do the job. One day, his wife had on a clay facial mask and mentioned she wouldn't be able to talk much when it hardened. Schwartzman slapped one on. It worked like a miracle. He brought the idea to *Asteroid City*'s make-up department, who, in return, came up with a dental prosthetic that clipped onto the back of his molars and locked his jaw. Marshall also helped him lower his voice from around a B-flat to a G.[509]

Schwartzman then devised an intricate ritual in order to get into his character's voice and demeanour. Anderson hadn't realized, and one day

Wes Anderson directs Jason Schwartzman and Tom Hanks, who on screen play aggrieved son and father-in-law.

called on him to film an impromptu scene. The actor said he couldn't. He needed an hour to prepare. It hit the director, then and there, how much Schwartzman had changed since he'd first met him, "this person who was a teenager and now has command of his craft and his medium in a way that I wasn't even aware of".[510]

Asteroid City's story within its story, about the Junior Stargazers and their alien out in the desert, nods to the Hollywood landscape that lay outside the confines of the Actors Studio – the Cinemascope epic and its widescreen horizons.[511] Scorsese had given Anderson a list of desert-set movies to watch: *Bottom of the Bottle* (1956), *Colorado Territory* (1949), *Inferno* (1953) and *The Petrified Forest* (1936). In return, he was thanked in the movie's credits.[512]

Yet, Anderson no longer called America home. He'd become, in a way, an outsider to his own country. So, he looked to the work of the German-born Wim Wenders and the California-raised, New York transplant Sam Shepard, who directed and wrote the 1984 neo-Western *Paris, Texas*, in which Harry Dean Stanton searches for his wife across a luminous, mythic South.

This is America as a delicate curiosity, porcelain-crafted. By setting his story in the '50s, Anderson could play with the post-war period's internal tensions. Families devastated by the trauma of war were told to plaster on a salesman's smile and welcome in the decade's economic fortunes. "I remember reading Sam Shepard talking about his father and talking about this generation of American men who were suffering some kind of post-traumatic stress from the war," the director noted. "And how they brought that home to their families and shared it with them without speaking of it, instead by creating some kind of tumult and conflict."[513]

Augie has the pain of his work written into his skin, into the back of his eyes. It's drained him. He's half a man. His children seem to sense it. One of them asks, after he finally breaks the news of their mother's death, whether that makes them orphans now. "No," he replies, a little incredulously, "because I'm still alive."

The Junior Stargazer Space Cadet convention has been sponsored by the US military and the LARKINGS Foundation, a fictitious weapons-and-aeronautics company. It's overseen by General Grif Gibson (Jeffrey Wright), who delivers a speech under a banner which reads, "for a powerful America".

Many of the children's inventions have an implied military use, including a jetpack and an electromagnetic death-ray. Woodrow's machine can project an image onto the moon's surface which, he stresses, "may have applications in the development of interstellar advertising." For much of the movie, General Gibson and the LARKINGS representative argue over ownership of the patents.

Into that concoction of the traumatic, industrious, the material and the certain, Anderson throws in the unexplainable: in the middle of the convention's gathering to watch the Astronomical Ellipses, a rare event in which the lights of three neighbouring star systems align, a spaceship descends above the crater. An alien hops out, picks up the meteorite and departs.

This eclectic, outsider's portrait of America is fused together by its soundtrack, compiled by Anderson and music supervisor Randall Poster. It's busy with Western ditties performed mostly by British bands. Tracks like Johnny Duncan & His Bluegrass Boys' "Last Train to San Fernando" and the Chas McDevitt Skiffle Group's "Freight Train", part of a folk music revival in the UK in the '50s, sit side by side with an original score by Alexandre Desplat, a Frenchman.

The movie's in-house band, headed up by singing cowboy Montana (Rupert Friend, an Englishman), also features Jarvis Cocker, another Englishman, the Brazilian Seu Jorge, the French Jean-Yves Lozac'h and the Spanish Perè Mallén. Cocker and his one-time Pulp bandmate Richard Hawley even recorded an original song, with lyrics by Anderson, titled "Dear Alien (Who Art In Heaven)".

Furthermore, Anderson's movie wasn't shot in Nevada or Arizona, but outside Madrid, Spain, between the towns of Chinchón and Colmenar de Oreja, in a 60-hectare patch of land owned by 140 different farmers.[514] Usually, they grow chickpeas and watermelons.

"It's great to be out there in the middle of the desert in America, but if you need to put people up or you need a piece of wood or a new prop, you don't want to be driving 200 miles in either direction," noted producer Jeremy Dawson. "So, our goal was to find a flat piece of land, with the big skies and the horizons, that was also near enough to a place where we could live together and where we could get the resources and things we needed."[515]

Asteroid City's luncheonette, the subject of production designer Adam Stockhausen's first sketch for the movie.

EAKFAST
LUNCHEON
HOT SUP
FRIED CHICKEN
SODA FOUNTAIN
COLD DRINKS
HOME MADE
EGGS
BACON
HOTCAKES 50¢
CHILI B
LK SHAKES
HAMBURGERS 65¢
HOT SANDWICH
TOASTED CHEESE 50¢

Production designer Adam Stockhausen's first sketch for *Asteroid City* depicted the town's luncheonette, a lonely set of walls promising spare ribs and hot cakes, embedded into the vast desert. He'd coloured the surrounding dirt brown. Anderson corrected him: "No, the desert is red, almost Mars red."[516] In the end, they used pulverized rock from a nearby quarry.[517] The landscape behind, with its towering mesas, was created using large, foam miniatures, paired with both real and fake cactuses,[518] and telegraph poles in a shrinking line to achieve a sense of forced perspective.[519]

On that land, Stockhausen and his team built a functional '50s town, with its own electrical supply, plumbing system and gas station complete with gasoline. It was first planned out as a digital 3D model, in order to work out where individual structures should be placed, so that Anderson could achieve his desired shots.[520]

He'd wanted to avoid, too, anything that looked too stereotypically Western, so the cabins where visiting families stay were given the look of upstate New York or Maine holiday retreats, with simple white, wooden boards.[521] It never really had to look like a real place because it wasn't – this is, after all, merely the theatrical set for Conrad Earp's play.[522]

The director wanted to shoot the town in natural light so his audience could feel the heat of the sun's rays on his characters.[523] Practical lights, like scattered lanterns, helped spread a little magic in the dusk scenes, while the buildings included open roofs, with silks used to soften and diffuse the daylight. It was a trick borrowed from the early days of cinema.[524]

ABOVE After Augie's (Jason Schwartzman) car breaks down while in Asteroid City, he takes it to a mechanic (Matt Dillon) for repairs. **OPPOSITE (ABOVE)** The alien poses for a photograph with his newly acquired meteorite. **OPPOSITE (BELOW)** All three generations of discontent: Stanley (Tom Hanks), Augie and Woodrow (Jake Ryan).

Augie Steenbeck (Jason Schwartzman) and Midge Campbell (Scarlett Johansson) converse out of the windows of their respective rooms. The cabins were given the look of upstate New York or Maine holiday retreats.

As Stockhausen explained, "In a weird way, you're taking a place that is entirely a trick, but then you're shooting it with no tricks in some sense. It plays with reality in a very interesting way."[525]

A garlic warehouse was used to build the cabin home where Conrad Earp first meets Jones Hall[526] and the two become lovers – it's decorated with egg-tempera paintings of homoerotic cowboys by New Mexico-based figurative painter Michael Berg[527] – and the train compartment where a hesitant Ford is confronted by the understudy for Woodrow's role (Ryan). "I love garlic so it was fine by me," Schwartzman joked. "I'm Mr Garlic! When they said we're shooting in a garlic place . . . perfect!"[528] Stage play scenes were shot in old, 99-seat theatres, some of them in Chinchón,[529] with the lights arranged to mimic those in a theatrical production.[530]

Cast and crew lodged at the Parador de Chinchón, a former Augustinian monastery at the edge of town, converted into a luxury hotel.[531] Schwartzman and Johansson, plus fellow regulars Norton, Wright, Friend, Cranston, Adrien Brody, Tilda Swinton, Liev Schreiber, Stephen Park, Willem Dafoe, Fisher Stevens, Tony Revolori and Bob Balaban, were joined by newcomers Hope Davis, Maya Hawke, Matt Dillon and Hong Chau.

Tom Hanks was cast as Stanley Zak, Augie's disapproving father-in-law, who comes to the rescue when their car breaks down. "It's a great thing," Anderson reflected, "when someone who has done every version of making a movie, says, 'I'm totally open. I'm on board for everything you're doing, and I'm happy.' That's what we had with Tom Hanks."[532]

Anderson thought it was funny that, out of his entire cast, it was the man in the alien costume who seemed to most understand his movie.

The actor's wife, Rita Wilson, joined the production in a small role, as parent to a child who never quite made it to the convention. Margot Robbie, who'd reached out to Anderson with an interest in future collaboration,[533] also briefly appears as the actress cast as Augie's deceased wife in Earp's play, who meets Hall out on the theatre balcony between scenes and recites her cut lines.

Anderson had, of course, set a part aside for Bill Murray – that of the motel's enterprising manager, whose fleet of vending machines includes one that sells tiny parcels of land. But the actor contracted COVID four days before he was scheduled to start shooting, while in Ireland on a family vacation. Steve Carell jumped in at the last minute. Murray eventually came to Spain, once his full quarantine had ended, and Anderson rushed to try to find a spot to squeeze him into the movie.[534]

He came up with the dual characters of Jock Larkings, head of the LARKINGS Foundation, and Tab Whitney, the actor playing him. But there was no scene for Jock or Whitney. So, he found his own solution: Murray would star as Whitney in an in-universe promotional trailer for *Asteroid City*. He and Anderson then hopped in a car and drove to France. It was their way to celebrate a job well done.[535]

The mood on set seemed especially serene. Hawke joked that the closest Anderson ever came to raising his voice was when he called her over to whisper, "Maya, how do I get everyone to stop using their phones on the set?" She added, "I was like, 'Oh, you're furious, and that's what furious looks like on you!' His temperature doesn't rise."[536] After the traditional nightly dinners, the cowboy band would pick up their instruments and perform.[537]

As Schwartzman observed, something subtle in the director's demeanour had changed. He waited now, just a little longer, before he called "cut" on a take. "I can't articulate what that means other than a kind of waiting," the actor said. "There was just like a . . . happy in the moment."[538]

In the role of the alien is Jeff Goldblum, present for a single scene, as he potters towards the camera on stilts in a skin-tight suit and with enormous eyeballs.[539] The character is otherwise depicted in stop-motion, as shot by cinematographer Tristan Oliver, and using a three-foot (0.9 metres) alien puppet made by Andy Gent and animated by Kim Keukeleire, who made the creature move as she imagined Goldblum would move.[540]

Anderson thought it was funny that, out of his entire cast, it was the man in the alien costume who seemed to most understand his movie. He'd overhear him explain, to the others, that "you're an actor playing an actor, but you're actually an actor playing an actor, playing an actor playing . . ." and so on.[541] *Asteroid City* cares as much about Anderson's actors, telling his story, as it does the actors inside his movie, telling Earp's.

Critics, for the most part, seemed to understand this. When it debuted at the Cannes Film Festival, on 23 May 2023, it received an almost identical reception to *The French Dispatch*. Grand statements were made. *Asteroid City* was either Anderson at his best or at his worst.

IndieWire's David Ehrlich declared it "by far the director's best effort since *The Grand Budapest Hotel*, and in some respects the most poignant thing he's ever made",[542] but the BBC's Nicholas Barber thought that "this perplexing pile of postmodernism seems intended to test the patience of the director's fans – to see how far he can venture away from human emotion and into arch, self-congratulatory whimsy before they give up on him."[543]

What could be agreed on, however, was that something deeply personal lived here. *Asteroid City* is not autobiographical, nor does it illuminate much about the director's personal history, but it does tell us a startling amount about his relationship with his own art. A fear of mortality can't be cured, but it can be soothed through stories about the unkillable, the heavens and the movies.

Earp, keen to break through his writer's block, gathers the members of his own Actors Studio, as they begin to chant a simple phrase: "You can't wake up if you don't fall asleep." Can we really see our world with clarity unless we've tested its boundaries with dreams and imagination?

Everywhere in *Asteroid City*, there are people turning to fiction in order to seek out the truth. After the alien's first visit, Hawke's character, a teacher named June Douglas, attempts to reimpose order by focusing on what she knows is real and factual about the universe.

She starts to lecture about the planets in the solar system, only to be interrupted by her students. Their impulse is to create art – to draw their interstellar visitor, or write for him a catchy tune. June eventually relents and asks her timorous sweetheart Montana for a dance.

Hall, throughout the movie, becomes fixated on why Augie, right after he tells Midge that the alien looked at them all like they were doomed, intentionally burns his hand on the sandwich grill. "Why?" she asks him. "It's not clear," he replies. Hall can't wrap his head around it. He interrupts the climax of the play to ask about the grill again, before storming off stage to track down Brody's director, Schubert Green. "I still don't understand the play," he confesses. "I feel like my heart is getting broken. My own, personal heart. Every night."

At this point, it's as if Anderson himself turns to both his critics and fans, to any person who looks at his movies as if they were mere puzzles to be solved – deemed worthless if their emotions don't provide answers, and instead remain obscure or mysterious. A movie can be an open question, because there's as much pleasure and profundity to be found in how a story is told. Anderson's movies prove that. "Doesn't matter," Green tells his actor. "Just keep telling the story."

OPPOSITE Lucretia Shaver (Maya Hawke), the actress who plays the role of schoolteacher June Douglas in the play *Asteroid City*.
NEXT SPREAD Augie Steenbeck (Jason Schwartzman) and Stanley Zak (Tom Hanks) on either end of a telephone conversation.

12 PLAY FOR TODAY

On *The Wonderful Story of Henry Sugar*

As children, Wes Anderson and his brothers would try to replicate a trick they read about in a book.[544] Roald Dahl's *The Wonderful Story of Henry Sugar*, a short story published in 1977, introduces us to a man who claims he can see without using his eyes. His name is Imhrat Khan. He's a circus performer, who studied under the Yogi Hardawar in India and can now correctly name the number and suit of a playing card turned away from his face.

A doctor writes a report on the phenomenon, and it falls into the hands of Henry Sugar, who is wealthy but largely amoral. As Dahl writes, "Men like Henry Sugar are to be found drifting like seaweed all over the world. They are not particularly bad men. But they are not good men either."

Henry is a keen gambler. He teaches himself the man's strange ability, mastering it within three years. He then promptly takes himself to the casino and wins a fortune at blackjack. Yet, he's unnerved by how empty a guaranteed victory feels. The next morning, Henry tosses his winnings off his apartment balcony, and sets about using his newfound skills for the greater good.

The little Anderson boys did believe, somewhere in their hearts, that if they remained persistent, they, too, could perhaps see without eyes. Khan, Sugar and the Yogi Hardawar are all fictional characters, but Dahl had based his story on a real person, the subject of an article he wrote in 1952. His name was Kuda Bux, born in Akhnur, Kashmir, in 1905, and he claimed he could read a book with his eyes closed.[545]

Anderson, in adulthood, would become friends with Dahl's widow, Felicity, having stayed at the author's English home, the famous Gipsy House, while writing *Fantastic Mr. Fox* (2009). He'd asked if she might put aside the rights to *The Wonderful Story of Henry Sugar* for him. She

Ben Kingsley and Richard Ayoade, two members of *The Wonderful Story of Henry Sugar*'s core acting troupe, here in the roles of Imdad Khan and The Great Yogi.

obliged.[546] And even as Felicity handed control of the copyright, managed by the Roald Dahl Story Company, over to her grandson Luke Kelly, that promise was kept.[547]

Yet, the director could never find a satisfactory way to tell Dahl's story. Eventually, Kelly had to present him with an ultimatum: commit, or allow one of the other interested filmmakers their turn.

After Anderson completed his script for *Asteroid City* early in the 2020 COVID-19 lockdown, he copied the story's complete text into a Microsoft Word document and began to pull out the pieces he liked best – only to realize that, in truth, he wanted every word of it. "Without his language, I was not really as interested," he said.[548] Instead, his characters would speak Dahl's prose directly, sometimes to camera, with even the "I said"s dutifully preserved.

It wouldn't be a feature film but a short, like the 1994 version of *Bottle Rocket*, where Anderson's cinematic dreams had first begun. He'd made other shorts over the years, largely as accompaniments to his features: *Hotel Chevalier*, the prologue to *The Darjeeling Limited*, alongside two for *Moonrise Kingdom* and one for *Asteroid City*.

By the time Anderson formally decided to embark on his adaptation of *The Wonderful Story of Henry Sugar*, Kelly had sold the rights to his grandfather's entire body of work to the streaming company Netflix. This suited Anderson fine. What he was making was "not really a movie", and since there was no tradition of theatrical distribution for shorts, he was happy in this instance for it to be released directly on the digital platform.[549]

In fact, he'd imagined *The Wonderful Story of Henry Sugar* to be something like an old episode of the BBC's *Play for Today*,[550] a British anthology series of the '70s and '80s that adapted new or pre-existing work, but kept the running time of each episode to between fifty and a hundred minutes. Ian McEwan, Sir David Hare and Alan Bleasdale were among its contributing writers, while Stephen Frears, Ken Loach and Mike Leigh all directed episodes.

After Anderson delivered *The Wonderful Story of Henry Sugar* to Netflix under budget, he asked if he might adapt three more stories.[551] The company agreed. *The Swan* concerns a small boy's stoicism in the face of his bullies' torments. In *The Ratcatcher*, an exterminator's pride and pleasure in his execution of rodents first beguiles, then perturbs the locals.

Poison, lastly, sees an Indian doctor called in to tend to a white man, after a venomous snake slithers under his bedcovers and curls up on his stomach to sleep. It's eventually revealed there was no snake, and realizing he has no more use of the doctor, the white man begins to hurl racist insults.

Anderson eventually compiled the shorts together into an anthology, which opens with the title card: "The following series of telefilms were produced and photographed entirely in the United Kingdom for Channel

ABOVE The poster for *The Wonderful Story of Henry Sugar*.

OPPOSITE (ABOVE) Henry Sugar (Benedict Cumberbatch) and a policeman (Ralph Fiennes).

OPPOSITE (BELOW) Imdad Khan (Ben Kingsley), the man who can see without using his eyes.

He'd imagined *The Wonderful Story of Henry Sugar* to be something like an old episode of the BBC's *Play for Today*

Imdad Khan (Ben Kingsley) visits the The Great Yogi (Richard Ayoade) in order to learn his methods of meditation.

7 between 1978 and 1981. They have not been aired since the time of their original broadcast."

His idea was to create "something between theater and cinema",[552] with sets by Adam Stockhausen that slide apart like the walls of Le Sans Blague in *The French Dispatch*. Anderson's characters are aware of their audience. If one says of another, "his whole face was rigid with shocked disbelief," the other will oblige by turning to look directly down the camera's lens to demonstrate. Stop-motion and miniatures are deployed when appropriate.

There's no illusion to be maintained here. Stagehands are often visible, assisting in the movement of false walls, the transfer of props and the changing of actors' costumes. When Henry Sugar drives his car, Anderson uses the old cinematic trick of rear projection. Pre-recorded footage plays behind him, yet, this time, we can see the edges of the screen. Film by film, Anderson had allowed the craft behind his stories to emerge out of the shadows, to be honoured and celebrated.

All four shorts were shot on 16 mm,[553] at Maidstone Studios in Kent, England.[554] Two stages were used. While filming took place on one, the next set would be constructed on the other.[555] Anderson's fastidiousness when it came to cultural detail – costume designer Walicka Maimone looked deeply into the design of doctors' uniforms in 1930s India[556] – flourished next to his wild imagination. For the jungle featured in *The Wonderful Story of Henry Sugar*, Stockhausen drew heavily from the illustrative, fanciful exoticisms of post-impressionist artist Henri Rousseau.

Henry Sugar (Benedict Cumberbatch), after three years of practice, learns to see through the backs of playing cards in order to cheat at the casino.

Anderson also had the idea to rustle up for himself a real theatre troupe, a small circle of English actors who could play multiple roles, often within the same short: Ralph Fiennes, Ben Kingsley, Benedict Cumberbatch, Dev Patel, Rupert Friend and Richard Ayoade. Cumberbatch, for example, plays Henry Sugar, his make-up artist and the man threatened by a snake in *Poison*; Friend is both the older version of the bullied boy in *The Swan*, who tells us of his childhood woe, and a villager in *The Ratcatcher*. The actor was obsessed with Dahl as a boy. He had his obituary pinned to his bedroom door.[557]

Anderson owned a house near the movie's set, where Fiennes, Cumberbatch and Friend all lived as guests. Ayoade lived less than an hour away, while Kingsley, who respectfully did not want to live in his director's home, stayed in separate accommodation alongside Patel. The latter, however, was often around for dinner. Cumberbatch caught COVID-19 on the last day of production, which meant his stay was extended by a week. He communicated via walkie-talkie and, being entirely asymptomatic, spent his idle hours stretched out in the sun.[558]

With Dahl's voice so prominent, it made sense that the author himself should appear as a character. He's played by Fiennes, who addresses the viewer directly from his writing hut at Gipsy House – already built in miniature in *Fantastic Mr. Fox*, but here meticulously recreated in life-size, filled with objects Stockhausen either borrowed directly or had perfectly replicated.[559]

While setting up a shot, Anderson could hear Fiennes muttering something. He enquired about it, only to learn that the actor had read

Henry Sugar (Benedict Cumberbatch) tosses his blackjack winnings over the balcony of his apartment, determined instead to put his skills to better use.

up on the author's pre-writing rituals, and was rehearsing them in order to get into character. "Start over, start over! We'll film this!" the director exclaimed.[560] And so Fiennes improvised *The Wonderful Story of Henry Sugar*'s opening scene, in which Dahl gathers his cigarettes, coffee, chocolates and six sharpened pencils. "And then, finally, one starts," he concludes.

When the first short, *The Wonderful Story of Henry Sugar*, debuted at the Venice Film Festival on 1 September 2023 – it would receive a limited run in cinemas – Anderson had quite the advantage over his critics. At only 37 minutes, there simply wasn't time for anyone to grow weary of his quirks. As *The Hollywood Reporter*'s Leslie Felperin wrote, "even Anderson-phobes will perhaps find in *The Wonderful Story of Henry Sugar* a perfectly well-balanced reduction. It's got most of Anderson's signature flavor notes but in healthy, clarified stock."[561]

It also won Anderson his first Academy Award, for Best Live Action Short, after a run of seven nominations. Almost all agreed it was long overdue, yet the director couldn't be present to collect his trophy.

He had already moved on to the next project, titled *The Phoenician Scheme*, shot at Studio Babelsberg and starring Benicio del Toro, Michael Cera and Bill Murray, with a story co-developed by Anderson and Roman Coppola.[562]

It would be his first live-action project without Robert Yeoman as a cinematographer – the role instead filled by Bruno Delbonnel, who Anderson had worked with on the 2016 ad *Come Together: A Fashion Picture in Motion*, for the fashion brand H&M.

Ralph Fiennes as Roald Dahl.

Anderson, now in a place of total creative security, confident in his ability to secure a budget and an A-list cast, chose not to rest on his laurels. Henry Sugar discovers there's far more pleasure to be found in the process, in the discipline of training and meditation, than in the rewards reaped once those skills are mastered.

He did, however, leave the Academy one reminder, in a note sent out after his win: "If I had not met Owen Wilson in a corridor at the University of Texas between classes when I was eighteen years old, I would certainly not be receiving this award tonight."[563]

13 GULF OF METHUSELAH

On *The Phoenician Scheme*

Not long before he died, Lebanese engineer Fouad Malouf took his daughter Juman aside and produced from his closet a collection of shoeboxes, accumulated over decades of work.[564] One by one, he opened them and explained their contents. Such a scene could have easily been plucked from any film belonging to Juman's partner, Wes Anderson, in which possessions function as a skeleton key to a person's psyche.

In fact, the director not only borrowed the image for *The Phoenician Scheme*, but added a closing dedication to Fouad. The film, at its centre, is a story of father and daughter, and the expanse that can sometimes stretch between them. Inside his shoeboxes, Zsa-zsa Korda (Benicio del Toro) – one of the richest men in Europe, the survivor of six plane crashes and father to nine sons and one nun, Liesl (Mia Threapleton) – has laid out plans for what he believes will be his greatest work yet: an infrastructure scheme in the (fictional) Middle Eastern nation of Modern Greater Independent Phoenicia.

Korda has summoned Liesl not only to inspect said plans, but to endorse them as his new heir. She agrees, reluctantly, and purely on a trial basis. Fouad, according to Anderson, was formidable but wise. The director loved him very much.[565] Yet, Korda is a brute. He is capitalism made flesh, a man who sees slavery and induced famine as nothing more than business tactics, who blends characteristics from some of history's most notorious dealmakers, from shipping magnate Aristotle Onassis to British-Armenian oil man Calouste Gulbenkian.[566] "I don't live anywhere," Korda declares. "I'm not a citizen at all. I don't need my human rights." Liesl may be a bride of Christ, trying to steer er father back onto the path of humanity, but her green tights, a nod by costume designer Milena Canonero to the sex worker played by Shirley MacLaine in Billy Wilder's *Irma la Douce* (1963),[567] suggests she may not be entirely free of her father's consumerist influence.

Zsa-zsa Korda (Benicio del Toro), one of the richest men in Europe, recovers from his latest plane crash.

Threapleton, daughter of Oscar-winner Kate Winslet, would come across an old diary entry in which she'd written, "Watching Moonrise Kingdom again, bloody love this film. Would love to work with Wes Anderson one day."[568]

Other newcomers included Riz Ahmed and Michael Cera, the latter in the role of a Norwegian tutor called Bjørn Lund. Meanwhile, the regulars assembled: Benedict Cumberbatch, Rupert Friend, Richard Ayoade, Mathieu Amalric, Tom Hanks, Scarlett Johansson, Bryan Cranston and Jeffrey Wright. Those around Korda ask incessant questions about his childhood, as if he might suddenly let slip the trauma that emptied his heart. Audiences have grown equally curious when it comes to Anderson, though on far more affectionate terms. People want to know what kind of life incubates a wondrous imagination like his.

When *The Phoenician Scheme* first debuted at the 2025 Cannes Film Festival, reviews both positive and negative had a certain probing quality to them. Salon's Coleman Spilde theorized that the director was reckoning "with being seen as a brand instead of a storyteller".[569] Alissa Wilkinson, in *The New York Times*, proposed that "this is a rather soul-obsessed movie, the kind you often see from artists who have been pondering the meaning of life lately."[570]

Even Anderson himself seemed to have grown increasingly frank of late. In an interview with Mashable, he said of his tendency towards insufficient father figures: "I love my father, but it's probably – he moved out of the house at a certain point. And I'm sure that if we really trace it back to, why do I get drawn to that? What's my personal investment in this kind of story? I guess it must start there. It's something about when he got in his car and moved to another place."[571]

This seems a very different man to the one who once expressed regret for sharing that he'd found a pamphlet titled "How to Cope with the Very Troubled Child" on top of his parent's refrigerator. We might think we know Wes Anderson. But, really, we've only begun to scratch the surface.

OPPOSITE Sister Liesl (Mia Threapleton) and her Norwegian tutor, Bjørn Lund (Michael Cera).

FEATURE FILMS

W E S A N D E R S O N

BOTTLE ROCKET

(Columbia Pictures, Gracie Films)
91 minutes
Writers: Wes Anderson, Owen Wilson, based on Bottle Rocket by Wes Anderson, Owen Wilson
Director of Photography: Robert Yeoman
Cast: Owen Wilson (Dignan), Luke Wilson (Anthony Adams), Robert Musgrave (Bob Mapplethorpe), Andrew Wilson (Future Man), Lumi Cavazos (Inez), and James Caan (Mr Henry).
Release date: 21 February 1996

RUSHMORE

(Touchstone Pictures)
93 minutes
Writers: Wes Anderson, Owen Wilson
Director of Photography: Robert Yeoman
Cast: Jason Schwartzman (Max Fischer), Olivia Williams (Rosemary Cross), Bill Murray (Herman Blume), Brian Cox (Dr Nelson Guggenheim), Seymour Cassel (Bert Fischer), Sara Tanaka (Margaret Yang), and Mason Gamble (Dirk Calloway).
Release date: 19 February 1999

THE ROYAL TENENBAUMS

(Touchstone Pictures, American Empirical Pictures)
110 minutes
Writers: Wes Anderson, Owen Wilson
Director of Photography: Robert Yeoman
Cast: Gene Hackman (Royal Tenenbaum), Anjelica Huston (Etheline Tenenbaum), Bill Murray (Raleigh St Clair), Danny Glover (Henry Sherman), Gwyneth Paltrow (Margot Tenenbaum), Ben Stiller (Chas Tenenbaum), Luke Wilson (Richie Tenenbaum), and Owen Wilson (Eli Cash).
Release date: 4 January 2002

THE LIFE AQUATIC WITH STEVE ZISSOU

(Touchstone Pictures, American Empirical Pictures)
119 minutes
Writers: Wes Anderson, Noah Baumbach
Director of Photography: Robert Yeoman
Cast: Bill Murray (Steve Zissou), Owen Wilson (Ned Plimpton), Cate Blanchett (Jane Winslett-Richardson), Anjelica Huston (Eleanor Zissou), Willem Dafoe (Klaus Daimler), Jeff Goldblum (Alistair Hennessey), Michael Gambon (Oseary Drakoulias), and Bud Cort (Bill Ubell).
Release date: 25 December 2004

THE DARJEELING LIMITED

(Collage Cinemagraphique, American Empirical Pictures, Dune Entertainment, Cine Mosaic, Indian Paintbrush, Scott Rudin Productions)
91 minutes
Writers: Wes Anderson, Roman Coppola, Jason Schwartzman
Director of Photography: Robert Yeoman
Cast: Owen Wilson (Francis), Adrien Brody (Peter), Jason Schwartzman (Jack), Amara Karan (Rita), Wally Wolodarsky (Brendan), Waris Ahluwalia (The Chief Steward), and Irrfan Khan (The Father).
Release date: 26 October 2007

FANTASTIC MR. FOX

(Indian Paintbrush, Regency Enterprises, American Empirical Pictures)
87 minutes
Writers: Wes Anderson, Noah Baumbach
Director of Photography: Tristan Oliver
Cast: George Clooney (Mr Fox), Meryl Streep (Mrs Fox), Jason Schwartzman (Ash), Bill Murray (Badger), Willem Dafoe (Rat), and Owen Wilson (Coach Skip).
Release date: 25 November 2009

FILMOGRAPHY

MOONRISE KINGDOM

(Indian Paintbrush, American Empirical Pictures)
94 minutes
Writers: Wes Anderson,c
Director of Photography: Robert Yeoman
Cast: Bruce Willis (Captain Sharp), Edward Norton (Scout Master Ward), Bill Murray (Mr Bishop), Frances McDormand (Mrs Bishop), Tilda Swinton (Social Services), Jason Schwartzman (Cousin Ben), Bob Balaban (The Narrator), Jared Gilman (Sam), and Kara Hayward (Suzy).
Release date: 29 June 2012

THE GRAND BUDAPEST HOTEL

(Fox Searchlight Pictures, TSG Entertainment, Indian Paintbrush, Studio Babelsberg, American Empirical Pictures)
99 minutes
Writer: Wes Anderson
Director of Photography: Robert Yeoman
Cast: Ralph Fiennes (M Gustave), F. Murray Abraham (Mr Moustafa), Mathieu Amalric (Serge X), Adrien Brody (Dmitri), Willem Dafoe (Jopling), Jeff Goldblum (Deputy Kovacs), Harvey Keitel (Ludwig), Jude Law (Young Writer), and Tony Revolori (Zero).
Release date: 28 March 2014

ISLE OF DOGS

(Studio Babelsberg, Indian Paintbrush, American Empirical Pictures)
101 minutes
Writer: Wes Anderson
Director of Photography: Tristan Oliver
Cast: Bryan Cranston, Koyu Rankin (Atari), Edward Norton (Rex), Liev Schreiber (Spots), Bill Murray (Boss), Bob Balaban (King), Jeff Goldblum (Duke), Scarlett Johansson (Nutmeg), Kunichi Nomura (Mayor Kobayashi), Tilda Swinton (Oracle), Ken Watanabe (Head Surgeon), Akira Ito (Professor Watanabe), and Greta Gerwig (Tracy Walker).
Release date: 13 April 2018

THE FRENCH DISPATCH

(Indian Paintbrush, American Empirical Pictures)
107 minutes
Writer: Wes Anderson
Director of Photography: Robert Yeoman
Cast: Owen Wilson (Herbsaint Sazerac), Benicio del Toro (Moses Rosenthaler), Adrien Brody (Julian Cadazio), Tilda Swinton (JKL Berensen), Léa Seydoux (Simone), Frances McDormand (Lucinda Krementz), Timothée Chalamet (Zeffirelli), Lyna Khoudri (Juliette), Jeffrey Wright (Roebuck Wright), Liev Schreiber (Talk Show Host), Mathieu Amalric (The Commissaire), and Stephen Park (Nescaffier).
Release date: 22 October 2021

ASTEROID CITY

(Indian Paintbrush, American Empirical Pictures)
105 minutes
Writer: Wes Anderson
Director of Photography: Robert Yeoman
Cast: Jason Schwartzman (Augie Steenbeck), Scarlett Johansson (Midge Campbell), Tom Hanks (Stanley Zak), Jeffrey Wright (General Gibson), Tilda Swinton (Dr Hickenlooper), Bryan Cranston (Host), Edward Norton (Conrad Earp), Adrien Brody (Schubert Green), Liev Schreiber (J J Kellogg), Hope Davis (Sandy Borden), Stephen Park (Roger Cho), Rupert Friend (Montana), and Maya Hawke (June).
Release date: 23 June 2023

THE WONDERFUL STORY OF HENRY SUGAR AND THREE MORE

(Indian Paintbrush, American Empirical Pictures)
88 minutes
Writer: Wes Anderson
Director of Photography: Robert Yeoman, Roman Coppola
Cast: Ralph Fiennes (Roald Dahl / The Policeman / Rat Man), Benedict Cumberbatch (Henry Sugar / Max Engelman / Harry), Dev Patel (Dr Chatterjee / John Winston / Woods), Ben Kingsley (Imdad Khan / The Dealer / Dr Ganderbai), Richard Ayoade (Dr Marshall / The Great Yogi / Editor / Reporter), and Rupert Friend (Narrator / Claude).
Release date: 15 March 2024

THE PHOENICIAN SCHEME

(Indian Paintbrush, American Empirical Pictures, Focus Features)
101 minutes
Writers: Wes Anderson, Roman Coppola
Director of Photography: Robert Yeoman, Roman Coppola
Cast: Benicio Del Toro (Zsa-zsa Korda), Mia Threapleton (Liesl), Michael Cera (Bjørn), Wilem Dafoe (Knave), Rupert Friend (Excalibur), Tom Hanks (Leland), Bryan Cranston (Reagan), Scarlett Johansson (Cousin Hilda), Bill Murray (God), Benedict Cumberbatch (Uncle Nubar).
Release date: 23 May 2025

SHORT FILMS & COMMERCIALS

BOTTLE ROCKET

13 minutes
Writers: Wes Anderson, Owen Wilson
Directors of Photography: Barry Braverman, Bert Guthrie
Cast: Luke Wilson (Anthony), Owen Wilson (Dignan), and Robert Musgrave (Bob Hanson).
1993

AMERICAN EXPRESS: MY LIFE. MY CARD.

2 minutes
Writer: Wes Anderson
Director of Photography: Robert Yeoman
Cast: Waris Ahluwalia, Wes Anderson, Roman Coppola, Barry Mendel, Jason Schwartzman, Wally Wolodarsky, and Robert Yeoman.
2006

HOTEL CHEVALIER

13 minutes
Writer: Wes Anderson
Director of Photography: Robert Yeoman
Cast: Jason Schwartzman (Jack Whitman), Natalie Portman (Jack's Girlfriend), Waris Ahluwalia (Security), and Michel Castejon (Waiter).
2007

SOFTBANK COMMERCIAL

1 minute
Cast: Brad Pitt
2008

STELLA ARTOIS LE APARTOMATIC COMMERCIAL

1 minute
2010

MOONRISE KINGDOM: ANIMATED BOOK SHORT

5 minutes
Writer: Wes Anderson
Cast: Bob Balaban (The Narrator) and Kara Hayward (Suzy).
2012

COUSIN BEN TROOP SCREENING WITH JASON SCHWARTZMAN

2 minutes
Writers: Wes Anderson, Roman Coppola
Cast: Jason Schwartzman (Cousin Ben), Jake Ryan (Khaki Scout), and Gabriel Rush (Khaki Scout).
2012

PRADA: CANDY

3 minutes
Director of Photography: Darius Khondji
Cast: Peter Gadiot (Gene), Rodolphe Pauly (Julius), and Léa Seydoux (Candy).
2013

CASTELLO CAVALCANTI

8 minutes
Writer: Wes Anderson
Director of Photography: Darius Khondji
Cast: Jason Schwartzman (Jed Cavalcanti), Giada Colagrande (Bartender), and Francesco Zippel (Paparazzo).
2013

COME TOGETHER: A FASHION PICTURE IN MOTION

4 minutes
Writer: Wes Anderson
Director of Photography: Bruno Delbonnel
Cast: Yasmin Kaur Barn (Passenger), Adrien Brody (Ralph), Leo Hatton (Passenger), and Garth Jennings (Fritz).
2016

TIP-TOP: ALINE

4 minutes
Writer: Christophe
2021

ASTEROID CITY LOCATION FEATURETTE

3 minutes
Writer: Wes Anderson
Cast: Bill Murray (Tab Whitney) and Jason Schwartzman (Jones Hall).
2023

THE WONDERFUL STORY OF HENRY SUGAR

40 minutes
Writer: Wes Anderson
Director of Photography: Robert Yeoman
Cast: Ralph Fiennes (Roald Dahl / Policeman), Benedict Cumberbatch (Henry Sugar / Make-Up Artist), Dev Patel (Dr Chatterjee / John Winston), Ben Kingsley (Imdad Khan / Croupier), and Richard Ayoade (Dr Marshall / Yogi).
2023

THE SWAN

17 minutes
Writer: Wes Anderson
Director of Photography: Roman Coppola
Cast: Rupert Friend (Narrator) and Ralph Fiennes (Roald Dahl).
2023

THE RAT CATCHER

17 minutes
Writer: Wes Anderson
Director of Photography: Robert Yeoman
Cast: Richard Ayoade (Editor), Ralph Fiennes (Rat Man / Roald Dahl), and Rupert Friend (Claude).
2023

POISON

17 minutes
Writer: Wes Anderson
Director of Photography: Robert Yeoman
Cast: Dev Patel (Timber Woods), Benedict Cumberbatch (Harry Pope), Ralph Fiennes (Roald Dahl), and Ben Kingsley (Dr Ganderbai).
2023

MONTBLANC: 100 YEARS OF MEISTERSTÜCK

3 minutes
Director of Photography: Linus Sandgren
Cast: Wes Anderson, Rupert Friend, and Jason Schwartzman.
2024

MUSIC DEPARTMENT

FANTASTIC MR. FOX (WRITER)

"Petey's Song"

ASTEROID CITY (WRITER)

"Dear Alien (Who Art in Heaven)"

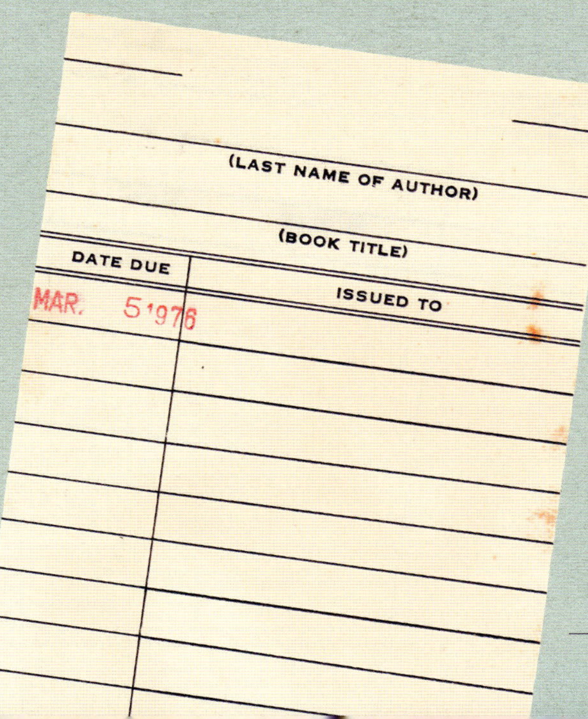
(LAST NAME OF AUTHOR)

(BOOK TITLE)

DATE DUE	ISSUED TO
MAR. 5 1976	

SOURCES & NOTES

PROLOGUE

SOURCES

- "Audio commentary with Wes Anderson", Criterion Collection, 2016
- Maher, Kevin, "Wes Anderson: 'Please do not send me memes of people doing me'", The Times, 2023
- "Interview with Wes Anderson", Charlie Rose, 2007
- Brooks, James L., Forward to "Rushmore: A Screenplay", Faber and Faber, 1999
- Allen, Holly, Kirk, Chris, and Wickman, Forrest, "Wes Anderson Bingo!", Slate, 2012
- "The Life Aquatic With Steve Zissou press conference", Berlin International Film Festival, 2005
- Brody, Richard, "Wild, Wild Wes", The New Yorker, 2009
- Hines, Nico, "The Cast of 'The Grand Budapest Hotel' Says Wes Anderson Is a Genius Hardass", Daily Beast, 2014
- Buchanan, Kyle, "Wes Anderson Finally Found a Way Into His New Roald Dahl Film", The New York Times, 2023

NOTES

1 "Audio commentary with Wes Anderson", Criterion Collection
2 Maher, "Wes Anderson: 'Please do not send me memes of people doing me'"
3 Buchanan, "Wes Anderson Finally Found a Way Into His New Roald Dahl Film"
4 "Interview with Wes Anderson", *Charlie Rose*
5 Brooks, Foreword to *Rushmore: A Screenplay*
6 "*The Life Aquatic With Steve Zissou* press conference", Berlin International Film Festival
7 Brody, "Wild, Wild Wes"

BOTTLE ROCKET

SOURCES

- Seitz, Matt Zoller, "The Wes Anderson Collection", Abrams, 2013
- Feinberg, Scott, "Wes Anderson on His Life, Career and Biggest Success Yet, Moonrise Kingdom", The Hollywood Reporter, 2012
- Mackenzie, Suzie, "Into the deep", The Guardian, 2005
- Seitz, Matt Zoller, "Slouching toward Hollywood", Dallas Observer, 1995
- "Bottle Rocket movie – interviews 1996", Irving Community Television Network, 1996
- "Audio Commentary with Wes Anderson and Owen Wilson", Criterion Collection, 2017
- Silverman, Jeff, "Their Feet in Texas, Their Heads in the Clouds", The New York Times, 1996
- "Interview with Owen Wilson, Bottle Rocket", Late Night with Conan O'Brien, 1996
- Brooks, James L., Forward to "Rushmore: A Screenplay", Faber and Faber, 1999
- "Jason Reitman Talks With Luke Wilson About Bottle Rocket", The Ultimate Rabbit, 2011
- "The Making of Bottle Rocket", Criterion Collection, 2017
- Kaines, Rachael, "Interview with Robert Yeoman, Bottle Rocket", Flickering Myth, 2018
- "Press Notes, Bottle Rocket", Sony Pictures, 1996
- "Wes Anderson & Noah Baumbach", LIVE from the NYPL, 2007
- The Numbers (the–numbers.com)
- Turan, Kenneth, "The Gang That Couldn't Shoot, or Think, Straight", Los Angeles Times, 1996
- Walters, Barry, "Bottle Rocket fails to explode", SFGate, 1996
- "Ebert & Scorsese: Best Films of the 1990s", At the Movies, Buena Vista Television, 2000
- Scorsese, Martin, "Wes Anderson", Esquire, 2000

NOTES

8 Seitz, *The Wes Anderson Collection*, 37
9 Feinberg, "Wes Anderson on His Life, Career and Biggest Success Yet, *Moonrise Kingdom*"
10 Seitz, *The Wes Anderson Collection*, 40
11 Mackenzie, "Into the deep"
12 Seitz, "Slouching toward Hollywood"
13 "*Bottle Rocket* movie – interviews 1996", Irving Community Television Network
14 Seitz, *The Wes Anderson Collection*, 41
15 "Audio Commentary with Wes Anderson and Owen Wilson", Criterion Collection
16 Seitz, "Slouching toward Hollywood"
17 "*Bottle Rocket* movie – interviews 1996", Irving Community Television Network
18 Seitz, "Slouching toward Hollywood"
19 Seitz, *The Wes Anderson Collection*, 45
20 Seitz, "Slouching toward Hollywood"
21 Silverman, "Their Feet in Texas, Their Heads in the Clouds"
22 "Owen Wilson Once Strangled James Caan", *Late Night with Conan O'Brien*
23 Brooks, "*Bottle Rocket*"
24 "Jason Reitman Talks With Luke Wilson About *Bottle Rocket*", The Ultimate Rabbit
25 Brooks, *Bottle Rocket*
26 Braverman, "*The Making of Bottle Rocket*"
27 Silverman, *Their Feet in Texas, Their Heads in the Clouds*
28 Brooks, *Bottle Rocket*
29 Kaines, "Cinematographer Robert Yeoman talks about *Bottle Rocket* and his longterm collaboration with Wes Anderson"
30 "Press Notes, *Bottle Rocket*"
31 Seitz, "Slouching toward Hollywood"
32 "Wes Anderson & Noah Baumbach", LIVE from the NYPL
33 "Jason Reitman Talks With Luke Wilson About *Bottle Rocket*", The Ultimate Rabbit

34 "Wes Anderson & Noah Baumbach", LIVE from the NYPL
35 "Audio Commentary with Wes Anderson and Owen Wilson", Criterion Collection
36 "Audio Commentary with Wes Anderson and Owen Wilson", Criterion Collection
37 The Numbers
38 Brooks, *Bottle Rocket*
39 Turan, "The Gang That Couldn't Shoot, or Think, Straight"
40 Walters, "*Bottle Rocket* fails to explode"
41 Ebert, "Ebert & Scorsese: Best Films of the 1990s"
42 Scorsese, "Wes Anderson"

RUSHMORE

SOURCES

- Stein, Ruth, "Shaping Rushmore In His Own Image", SFGate, 1999
- "Audio commentary with Wes Anderson, Owen Wilson, and Jason Schwartzman", Criterion Collection, 2018
- Bergeron, Michael, "Interview with Wes Anderson", Public News, 1997
- The Numbers (the–numbers.com)
- "Interview with Wes Anderson", Charlie Rose, 1999
- Seitz, Matt Zoller, "The Wes Anderson Collection", Abrams, 2013
- Dansby, Andrew, "The untold story behind Wes Anderson's Rushmore", Houston Chronicle, 2023
- "Interview with Jason Schwartzman", Overheard with Evan Smith, Austin PBS, 2014
- Taylor, Trey, "The secret history of Wes Anderson's Rushmore", Dazed, 2015
- "Interview with Jason Schwartzman", Later with Judd Nelson, 1998
- Bland, Simon, "'It was the best time of my life' – Jason Schwartzman on Rushmore at 20", Little White Lies, 2018
- Anderson, Wes, "New Again: Bill Murray", Interview, 2014
- "Interview with Bill Murray", Charlie Rose, 1999
- "Interview with Bill Murray", Fresh Air with Terry Gross, NPR, 1999
- Mottram, James, "Caught in the eye of the Murricane", The Independent, 2014
- Medley, Alison, "Remembering Houston's iconic film 'Rushmore' as it turns 21 years old", Houston Chronicle, 2019
- Bergeron, Michael, "Interview with Wes Anderson", Houston's Other, 1998
- Westbrook, Caroline, "Rushmore Review", Empire, 2000
- Anderson, Wes, "My Private Screening With Pauline Kael", The New York Times, 1999

NOTES

43 Stein, "Shaping *Rushmore* In His Own Image"
44 "Audio commentary with Wes Anderson, Owen Wilson, and Jason Schwartzman", Criterion Collection
45 Stein, "Shaping *Rushmore* In His Own Image"
46 Bergeron, "Interview with Wes Anderson"
47 Stein, "Shaping *Rushmore* In His Own Image"
48 The Numbers
49 "Interview with Wes Anderson", *Charlie Rose*
50 Ibid.
51 Bergeron, "Interview with Wes Anderson"
52 Seitz, *The Wes Anderson Collection*, 76
53 Dansby, "The untold story behind Wes Anderson's *Rushmore*"
54 "Audio commentary with Wes Anderson, Owen Wilson, and Jason Schwartzman", Criterion Collection
55 Seitz, *The Wes Anderson Collection*, 80
56 "Interview with Wes Anderson", *Charlie Rose*
57 "Interview with Jason Schwartzman", Overheard with Evan Smith
58 Taylor, "The secret history of Wes Anderson's *Rushmore*"
59 "Interview with Jason Schwartzman", Later with Judd Nelson
60 Bland, "'It was the best time of my life' – Jason Schwartzman on *Rushmore* at 20"
61 Taylor, "The secret history of Wes Anderson's *Rushmore*"
62 "Audio commentary with Wes Anderson, Owen Wilson, and Jason Schwartzman", Criterion Collection
63 Seitz, *The Wes Anderson Collection*, 80
64 Anderson, "New Again: Bill Murray"
65 "Interview with Bill Murray", *Charlie Rose*
66 Anderson, "New Again: Bill Murray"
67 "Interview with Wes Anderson", *Charlie Rose*
68 Seitz, *The Wes Anderson Collection*, 83
69 "Interview with Wes Anderson", *Charlie Rose*
70 "Audio commentary with Wes Anderson, Owen Wilson, and Jason Schwartzman", Criterion Collection
71 Bland, "'It was the best time of my life' – Jason Schwartzman on *Rushmore* at 20"
72 Anderson, "New Again: Bill Murray"
73 "Interview with Jason Schwartzman", *Later with Judd Nelson*
74 "Interview with Jason Schwartzman", *Later with Judd Nelson*
75 Seitz, *The Wes Anderson Collection*, 83
76 Medley, "Remembering Houston's iconic film *Rushmore* as it turns 21 years old"
77 "Interview with Wes Anderson", *Charlie Rose*
78 Bland, "'It was the best time of my life' – Jason Schwartzman on *Rushmore* at 20"
79 "Audio commentary with Wes Anderson, Owen Wilson, and Jason Schwartzman", Criterion Collection
80 "Audio commentary with Wes Anderson, Owen Wilson, and Jason Schwartzman", Criterion Collection

81 Dansby, "The untold story behind Wes Anderson's *Rushmore*"
82 Stein, "Shaping *Rushmore* In His Own Image"
83 Anderson, "My Private Screening With Pauline Kael"
84 "Audio commentary with Wes Anderson, Owen Wilson, and Jason Schwartzman", Criterion Collection

THE ROYAL TENENBAUMS

SOURCES

◇ "Audio commentary with Wes Anderson", Criterion Collection, 2016
◇ "Meet the Filmmaker: Wes Anderson", Apple Inc, 2011
◇ Holub, Christian, "Everything we learned from the Royal Tenenbaums reunion at Tribeca", Entertainment Weekly, 2021
◇ Tenenbaum, Margot, "The Real Tenenbaums", Observer, 2001
◇ Seitz, Matt Zoller, "The Wes Anderson Collection", Abrams, 2013
◇ "Press Notes, The Royal Tenenbaums", Touchstone Pictures, 2001
◇ Bailey, Jason, "The Royal Tenenbaums at 20: When Wes Anderson Imagined New York", The New York Times, 2021
◇ "The Royal Tenenbaums's 10th Anniversary panel", New York Film Festival, 2011
◇ Salamon, Julie, "Looking Back at The Royal Tenenbaums, Wes Anderson's Unique Take on NYC", Avenue, 2021
◇ "Royal Tenenbaums with Gwyneth Paltrow – Script to Screen", University of California Television, 2018
◇ Aftab, Kaleem, "Owen Wilson: "You just go with it", The Talks
◇ "Intimacy, Miguel Calderon, Tom Waits", Studio 360, 2001
◇ Sollosi, Mary, "The Royal Tenenbaums costume designer looks back on dressing 'a family in decline'", Entertainment Weekly, 2021
◇ "Interview with Angelica Huston", Criterion Collection, 2016
◇ "Interview with Irina Gorovaia", Mirá a Quién Encontré, 2020
◇ Hewitt, Chris, "Gene Hackman Interview: On His Retirement, Acting, And Writing Westerns", Empire, 2020
◇ "Interview with Gene Hackman", Criterion Collection, 2016
◇ "Owen Wilson Interview", Jimmy Kimmel Live, 2023
◇ Scott, A.O., "Brought Up to Be Prodigies, Three Siblings Share a Melancholy Oddness", The New York Times, 2001
◇ Robey, Tim, "Genius on a budget: how Wes Anderson designed The Royal Tenenbaums", The Telegraph, 2018
◇ Perez, Rodrigo, "Interview with Wes Anderson", The Playlist, 2014
◇ Sheck, Frank, "The Royal Tenenbaums Review" , The Hollywood Reporter, 2001
◇ Ebert, Roger, "The Royal Tenenbaums Review", Chicago Sun-Times, 2001
◇ Turan, Kenneth, "Their Particular Brand of Dysfunction, Los Angeles Times, 2001

NOTES

85 "Audio commentary with Wes Anderson", Criterion Collection
86 "Meet the Filmmaker: Wes Anderson", Apple Inc.
87 Holub, "Everything we learned from *The Royal Tenenbaums* reunion at Tribeca"
88 "Audio commentary with Wes Anderson", Criterion Collection
89 Holub, "Everything we learned from *The Royal Tenenbaums* reunion at Tribeca"
90 "Meet the Filmmaker: Wes Anderson", Apple Inc.
91 Seitz, *The Wes Anderson Collection*, 123
92 Seitz, *The Wes Anderson Collection*, 120
93 Bailey, "*The Royal Tenenbaums* at 20: When Wes Anderson Imagined New York"
94 "*The Royal Tenenbaums*'s 10th Anniversary panel", New York Film Festival
95 "Press Notes, *The Royal Tenenbaums*", Touchstone Pictures
96 Salamon, "Looking Back at *The Royal Tenenbaums*, Wes Anderson's Unique Take on NYC"
97 "Audio commentary with Wes Anderson", Criterion Collection
98 "Press Notes, *The Royal Tenenbaums*", Touchstone Pictures
99 Seitz, *The Wes Anderson Collection*, 142
100 "Press Notes, *The Royal Tenenbaums*", Touchstone Pictures
101 "Audio commentary with Wes Anderson", Criterion Collection
102 "*The Royal Tenenbaums*'s 10th Anniversary panel", New York Film Festival
103 "Press Notes, *The Royal Tenenbaums*", Touchstone Pictures
104 "*The Royal Tenenbaums* with Gwyneth Paltrow – Script to Screen", University of California Television
105 "Audio commentary with Wes Anderson", Criterion Collection
106 Aftab, "Owen Wilson: 'You just go with it'", The Talks
107 "Audio commentary with Wes Anderson", Criterion Collection
108 Seitz, *The Wes Anderson Collection*, 138
109 "Intimacy, Miguel Calderon, Tom Waits", Studio 360
110 Seitz, *The Wes Anderson Collection*, 141
111 "Interview with Angelica Huston", Criterion Collection
112 "Press Notes, *The Royal Tenenbaums*", Touchstone Pictures
113 "*The Royal Tenenbaums* with Gwyneth Paltrow – Script to Screen", University of California Television
114 "Interview with Irina Gorovaia", Mirá a Quién Encontré
115 "Press Notes, *The Royal Tenenbaums*", Touchstone Pictures
116 Seitz, *The Wes Anderson Collection*, 130
117 Hewitt, "Gene Hackman Interview: On His Retirement, Acting, And Writing Westerns"
118 "Meet the Filmmaker: Wes Anderson", Apple Inc.

119 "Interview with Gene Hackman", Criterion Collection

120 "Meet the Filmmaker: Wes Anderson", Apple Inc.

121 "Owen Wilson Interview", *Jimmy Kimmel Live!*

122 "*The Royal Tenenbaums*'s 10th Anniversary panel", New York Film Festival

123 Ibid.

124 "*The Royal Tenenbaums*'s 10th Anniversary panel", New York Film Festival

125 Hewitt, "Gene Hackman Interview: On His Retirement, Acting, And Writing Westerns"

126 Scott, "Brought Up to Be Prodigies, Three Siblings Share a Melancholy Oddness", *The New York Times*

127 Robey, "Genius on a budget: how Wes Anderson designed *The Royal Tenenbaums*"

128 Perez, "Interview with Wes Anderson", The Playlist

129 "*The Royal Tenenbaums* with Gwyneth Paltrow – Script to Screen", University of California Television

130 Perez, "Interview with Wes Anderson", The Playlist

131 "Audio commentary with Wes Anderson", Criterion Collection

132 Sheck, "*The Royal Tenenbaums* Review", *The Hollywood Reporter*

133 Ebert, "*The Royal Tenenbaums* Review", *Chicago Sun-Times*

134 Turan, "Their Particular Brand of Dysfunction", *Los Angeles Times*

135 "Owen Wilson Interview", *Jimmy Kimmel Live!*

THE LIFE AQUATIC WITH STEVE ZISSOU

SOURCES

◇ "The Life Aquatic With Steve Zissou press conference", Berlin International Film Festival, 2005

◇ Mackenzie, Suzie, "Into the deep", The Guardian, 2005

◇ Papamichael, Stella, "Interview with Wes Anderson, BBC, 2005

◇ "Audio commentary with Wes Anderson and Noah Baumbach", Criterion Collection, 2018

◇ Seitz, Matt Zoller, "The Wes Anderson Collection", Abrams, 2013

◇ "Wes Anderson & Noah Baumbach", LIVE from the NYPL, 2007

◇ "Interview with Wes Anderson", Charlie Rose, 2004

◇ Hesse, Neils, "Interview with Wes Anderson and Anjelica Huston", Phase9 Entertainment

◇ Goldman, Andrew, "In Conversation: Anjelica Huston", Vulture, 2019

◇ "Starz on Set", Criterion Collection, 2018

◇ Scott, Kevin Conroy, "Lesser Spotted Fish And Other Stories…", Sight & Sound, 2005

◇ "Interview with Owen Wilson", Criterion Collection, 2018

◇ "Interview with Cate Blanchett", Criterion Collection, 2018

◇ Tribbey, Chris, "Interview with Bud Cort", DVDTalk

◇ "Intern video journal by actor Matthew Gray Gubler", Criterion Collection, 2018

◇ "Interview with Mark Friedberg", Criterion Collection, 2018

◇ Jessen, Taylor, "Interview with Henry Selick", Animation World Network, 2004

◇ "Interview with Mark Mothersbaugh", Criterion Collection, 2018

◇ The Numbers (the–numbers.com)

◇ "This is an Adventure", Criterion Collection, 2018

◇ Rosen, Christopher, "Wes Anderson On The 'Life Aquatic' Scene That Made You Cry", Huffington Post, 2014

◇ "Bittersweet Reminiscences of The Life Aquatic", Criterion Collection, 2014

◇ Tucker, Ken, "The Life Examined with Wes Anderson", New York Magazine, 2004

◇ Ebert, Roger, "Whimsy leaves viewer at sea", Chicago Sun-Times, 2004

◇ Koehler, Robert, "The Life Aquatic With Steve Zissou Review", Variety, 2004

◇ Zacharek, Stephanie, "The Life Aquatic With Steve Zissou Review", Salon, 2004

◇ "Interview with Nina Jacobson", Without Fail, 2018

◇ Aquilina, Tyler, "The Life Aquatic cinematographer on staging one of Wes Anderson's most emotional scenes", Entertainment Weekly, 2021

NOTES

136 "*The Life Aquatic With Steve Zissou* press conference", Berlin International Film Festival

137 Mackenzie, "Into the deep"

138 Papamichael, "Interview with Wes Anderson", BBC

139 "Audio commentary with Wes Anderson and Noah Baumbach", Criterion Collection

140 Seitz, *The Wes Anderson Collection*, 164

141 "Wes Anderson & Noah Baumbach", LIVE from the NYPL

142 "Audio commentary with Wes Anderson and Noah Baumbach", Criterion Collection

143 "Audio commentary with Wes Anderson and Noah Baumbach", Criterion Collection

144 "Audio commentary with Wes Anderson and Noah Baumbach", Criterion Collection

145 "Interview with Wes Anderson and Anjelica Huston", Phase9 Entertainment

146 Goldman, "In Conversation: Anjelica Huston"

147 "Starz on Set", Criterion Collection

148 "*The Life Aquatic With Steve Zissou* press conference", Berlin International Film Festival

149 "Interview with Wes Anderson", *Charlie Rose*

150 "Interview with Cate Blanchett", Criterion Collection

151 Hesse, "Interview with Wes Anderson and Anjelica Huston"
152 "*The Life Aquatic With Steve Zissou* press conference", Berlin International Film Festival
153 Tribbey, "Interview with Bud Cort"
154 Seitz, *The Wes Anderson Collection*, 146
155 Scott, *Lesser Spotted Fish And Other Stories...*
156 "Interview with Mark Friedberg", Criterion Collection
157 Seitz, *The Wes Anderson Collection*, 182
158 Scott, *Lesser Spotted Fish And Other Stories...*
159 "Audio commentary with Wes Anderson and Noah Baumbach", Criterion Collection
160 Jessen, "Interview with Henry Selick"
161 "*The Life Aquatic With Steve Zissou* press conference", Berlin International Film Festival
162 Tribbey, "Interview with Bud Cort"
163 Rosen, "Wes Anderson On The *Life Aquatic* Scene That Made You Cry"
164 "Bittersweet Reminiscences of *The Life Aquatic*", Criterion
165 "Audio commentary with Wes Anderson and Noah Baumbach", Criterion Collection
166 "Bittersweet Reminiscences of *The Life Aquatic*", Criterion
167 Tucker, "The Life Examined with Wes Anderson"
168 The Numbers
169 Ebert, "Whimsy leaves viewer at sea"
170 Koehler, "*The Life Aquatic With Steve Zissou* Review"
171 Zacharek, "*The Life Aquatic With Steve Zissou* Review"
172 "Audio commentary with Wes Anderson and Noah Baumbach", Criterion Collection
173 Aquilina, "*The Life Aquatic* cinematographer on staging one of Wes Anderson's most emotional scenes"
174 Seitz, *The Wes Anderson Collection*, 187

THE DARJEELING LIMITED

SOURCES

◇ Brody, Richard, "Wild, Wild Wes", The New Yorker, 2009
◇ Fielder, Miles, "Interview with Jason Schwartzman", The List, 2007
◇ Brody, Richard, "The Darjeeling Limited: Voyage to India", Criterion Collection, 2010
◇ "Interview with Wes Anderson", Charlie Rose, 2007
◇ Weintraub, Steven, "Interview with Wes Anderson & Roman Coppola", Collider, 2007
◇ Seitz, Matt Zoller, "The Wes Anderson Collection", Abrams, 2013
◇ Guillén, Michael, "Interview With Wes Anderson, Jason Schwartzman & Roman Coppola", ScreenAnarchy, 2007
◇ Carnevale, Rob, "Interview with Randall Poster", indieLONDON
◇ "Audio commentary with Wes Anderson, Jason Schwartzman, and Roman Coppola", Criterion Collection, 2021
◇ "Interview with Jason Schwartzman and Wes Anderson", Ain't It Cool News, 2007
◇ "Press Notes, The Darjeeling Limited", Fox Searchlight, 2007
◇ "Interview with Adrien Brody", Tribute, 2007
◇ Banks, Ruth, "Interview with Amara Karan", Cherwell, 2008
◇ "Interview with The Darjeeling Limited Cast & Crew", IGN, 2007
◇ Gritten, David, "The Darjeeling Limited: Who needs a film set in LA when you have a speeding train in India?", The Telegraph, 2007
◇ Pandey, Swati, "White man's accessory", Los Angeles Times, 2007
◇ Box Office Mojo (boxofficemojo.com)
◇ Foxley, David, "Welcome to Wes World", Observer, 2007
◇ Bayer, "Interview with Wes Anderson & Jason Schwartzman", The Scorecard Review, 2007
◇ "Interview with Jason Schwartzman", MovieWeb, 2007
◇ "Shooting The Darjeeling Limited", D&CFilm, 2007
◇ Rich, Katey, "The Darjeeling Limited New York Film Festival Press Conference", CinemaBlend, 2007
◇ French, Philip, "The Darjeeling Limited Review", The Guardian, 2007
◇ Zacharek, Stephanie, "The Darjeeling Limited Review", Salon, 2007
◇ The Numbers (the–numbers.com)

NOTES

175 Brody, "Wild, Wild Wes"
176 Fielder, "Interview with Jason Schwartzman"
177 Ibid.
178 Brody, "*The Darjeeling Limited*: Voyage to India"
179 Weintraub, "Interview with Wes Anderson and Roman Coppola"
180 Seitz, *The Wes Anderson Collection*, 203
181 Guillén, "Interview With Wes Anderson, Jason Schwartzman and Roman Coppola"
182 Carnevale, "Interview with Randall Poster"
183 Weintraub, "Interview with Wes Anderson and Roman Coppola"
184 "Interview with Jason Schwartzman and Wes Anderson", Ain't It Cool News
185 "Audio commentary with Wes Anderson, Jason Schwartzman, and Roman Coppola", Criterion Collection
186 Guillén, "Interview With Wes Anderson, Jason Schwartzman and Roman Coppola"
187 "Press Notes, *The Darjeeling Limited*", Fox Searchlight
188 "Audio commentary with Wes Anderson, Jason Schwartzman, and Roman Coppola", Criterion Collection

189 Weintraub, "Interview with Wes Anderson and Roman Coppola"
190 "Interview with Adrien Brody", *Tribute*
191 "Audio commentary with Wes Anderson, Jason Schwartzman, and Roman Coppola", Criterion Collection
192 Brody, "*The Darjeeling Limited*: Voyage to India"
193 Gritten, "*The Darjeeling Limited*: Who needs a film set in LA when you have a speeding train in India?"
194 "Audio commentary with Wes Anderson, Jason Schwartzman, and Roman Coppola", Criterion Collection
195 "Interview with Jason Schwartzman and Wes Anderson", Ain't It Cool News
196 Pandey, "White man's accessory"
197 Box Office Mojo
198 Brody, "*The Darjeeling Limited*: Voyage to India"
199 "Press Notes, *The Darjeeling Limited*", Fox Searchlight
200 Seitz, *The Wes Anderson Collection*, 229
201 Foxley, "Welcome to Wes World"
202 Brody, "*The Darjeeling Limited*: Voyage to India"
203 Foxley, "Welcome to Wes World"
204 Bayer, "Interview with Wes Anderson and Jason Schwartzman"
205 "Press Notes, *The Darjeeling Limited*", Fox Searchlight
206 "Audio commentary with Wes Anderson, Jason Schwartzman, and Roman Coppola", Criterion Collection
207 "Shooting *The Darjeeling Limited*", D&CFilm
208 "Audio commentary with Wes Anderson, Jason Schwartzman, and Roman Coppola", Criterion Collection
209 Ibid.
210 Rich, "*The Darjeeling Limited* New York Film Festival Press Conference"
211 "Shooting *The Darjeeling Limited*", D&CFilm
212 "Audio commentary with Wes Anderson, Jason Schwartzman, and Roman Coppola", Criterion Collection
213 Seitz, *The Wes Anderson Collection*, 152
214 The Numbers
215 French, "*The Darjeeling Limited* Review"
216 Zacharek, "*The Darjeeling Limited* Review"
217 "Interview with Jason Schwartzman and Wes Anderson", Ain't It Cool News

FANTASTIC MR. FOX

SOURCES

◇ Mclean, Craig, "Wes Anderson interview for Fantastic Mr Fox", The Telegraph, 2009
◇ "Interview with Wes Anderson & Felicity Dahl", Star Movies VIP Access, 2010
◇ Anderson, Wes, "Welcome to the Dahl House", The New York Times, 2002
◇ "Wes Anderson Covers New Ground With Mr. Fox", Fresh Air with Terry Gross, 2009
◇ "Behind The Scenes of The Fantastic Mr Fox", Searchlight Pictures, 2009
◇ "Interview with Felicity Dahl & Wes Anderson", Associated Press, 2009
◇ Weintraub, Steven, "Interview with Wes Anderson", Collider, 2009
◇ "The World of Roald Dahl", Searchlight Pictures, 2009
◇ Leader, Michael, "George Clooney, Bill Murray & Wes Anderson talk Fantastic Mr. Fox", Den of Geek, 2009
◇ Seitz, Matt Zoller, "The Wes Anderson Collection", Abrams, 2013
◇ "Interview with Wes Anderson", Ain't It Cool News, 2009
◇ "Audio commentary with Wes Anderson", Criterion Collection, 2021
◇ Carter, Lance, "Jason Schwartzman on 'The Fantastic Mr. Fox': 'It's the best movie I've ever been a part of'", Daily Actor, 2009
◇ "'Toon Time: A Q&A with Wes Anderson", Criterion Collection, 2009
◇ Karger, Dave, "Talking with the stars of Fantastic Mr. Fox", Entertainment Weekly, 2009
◇ Desowitz, Bill, "A Fantastic Opportunity with Mr. Fox" Animation World Network, 2009
◇ "Interview with Ian McKinnon, Andy Biddle and Andy Ghent", Pure Movies, 2010
◇ Sancton, Julian, "How the Puppets from Fantastic Mr. Fox Were Made", Vanity Fair, 2009
◇ "Achieving the Look of Fantastic Mr. Fox", ComingSoon.Net, 2009
◇ Brody, Richard, "Wild, Wild Wes", The New Yorker, 2009
◇ Utichi, Joe, "Interview with Wes Anderson", Rotten Tomatoes, 2009
◇ The Numbers (the–numbers.com)
◇ "A Visit to the Studio", The Criterion Collection, 2021
◇ Lee, Chris, "Fur flies on Mr. Fox", Los Angeles Times, 2009
◇ "Fantastic Mr. Fox: A Cutting-Edge Fox", Searchlight Pictures, 2009
◇ "OCD like a Fox", San Antonio Current, 2009
◇ "Fantastic Mr Fox Q&A with cinematographer Tristan Oliver", The Garden Cinema, 2024
◇ "Wes Anderson on his 'Fox' cinematographer: 'I could work with him again'", Los Angeles Times, 2009
◇ Huff, Lauren, "Fantastic Mr. Fox composer Alexandre Desplat on joys of working with 'mischievous' Wes Anderson", Entertainment Weekly, 2021
◇ "How Wes Anderson Soundtracks His Movies", Fresh Air with Terry Gross, 2012
◇ "Wes Anderson on Fantastic Mr Fox: Film4 Interview Special", Film4, 2014
◇ Reichert, Jeff, "Fantastic Mr Fox Review", Reverse Shot, 2009
◇ Scott, A.O., "Don't Count Your Chickens", The New York Times, 2009

NOTES

218 Mclean, "Wes Anderson interview for *Fantastic Mr Fox*"
219 "Interview with Wes Anderson & Felicity Dahl", Star Movies VIP Access
220 Anderson, "Welcome to the Dahl House"

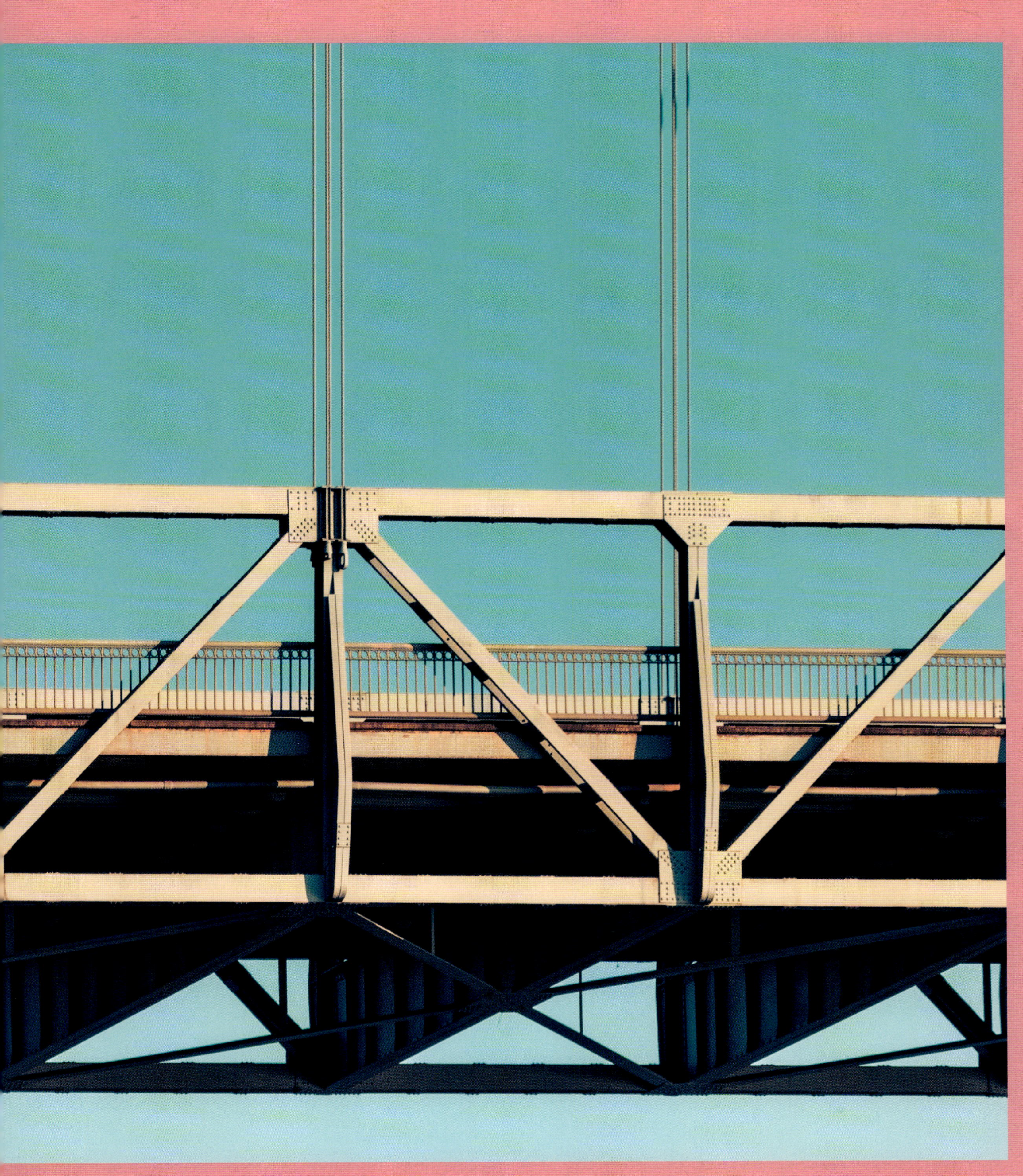

221 Mclean, "Wes Anderson interview for *Fantastic Mr Fox*"
222 "Wes Anderson Covers New Ground With Mr Fox", *Fresh Air* with Terry Gross
223 "Wes Anderson Covers New Ground With Mr Fox", *Fresh Air* with Terry Gross
224 Anderson, "Welcome to the Dahl House"
225 "Behind The Scenes of *The Fantastic Mr Fox*", 20th Century Fox
226 "Interview with Felicity Dahl & Wes Anderson", Associated Press
227 Mclean, "Wes Anderson interview for *Fantastic Mr Fox*"
228 "The World of Roald Dahl", Searchlight Pictures
229 Weintraub, "Interview with Wes Anderson"
230 Leader, "George Clooney, Bill Murray and Wes Anderson talk Fantastic Mr Fox"
231 Seitz, *The Wes Anderson Collection*, 257
232 "Interview with Wes Anderson", Ain't It Cool News
233 "Audio commentary with Wes Anderson", Criterion Collection
234 "Wes Anderson Covers New Ground With Mr Fox", *Fresh Air* with Terry Gross
235 "Behind The Scenes of *The Fantastic Mr Fox*", 20th Century Fox
236 "Audio commentary with Wes Anderson", Criterion Collection
237 Weintraub, "Interview with Wes Anderson"
238 "Interview with Wes Anderson", Ain't It Cool News
239 Carter, "Jason Schwartzman on *The Fantastic Mr Fox*: 'It's the best movie I've ever been a part of'"
240 "'Toon Time: A Q&A with Wes Anderson", Criterion Collection
241 Carter, "Jason Schwartzman on *The Fantastic Mr Fox*: 'It's the best movie I've ever been a part of'"
242 Karger, "Talking with the stars of *Fantastic Mr Fox*"
243 "'Toon Time: A Q&A with Wes Anderson", Criterion Collection
244 "Interview with Ian McKinnon, Andy Biddle and Andy Ghent", Pure Movies
245 "Wes Anderson Covers New Ground With Mr Fox", *Fresh Air* with Terry Gross
246 Mclean, "Wes Anderson interview for *Fantastic Mr Fox*"
247 Sancton, "How the Puppets from Fantastic Mr Fox Were Made"
248 "Achieving the Look of *Fantastic Mr Fox*", ComingSoon.Net
249 "Interview with Ian McKinnon, Andy Biddle and Andy Ghent", Pure Movies
250 Mclean, "Wes Anderson interview for *Fantastic Mr Fox*"
251 Sancton, "How the Puppets from Fantastic Mr Fox Were Made"
252 Brody, "Wild, Wild Wes"
253 "Achieving the Look of Fantastic Mr Fox", ComingSoon.Net
254 Utichi, "Interview with Wes Anderson"
255 Brody, "Wild, Wild Wes"
256 Mclean, "Wes Anderson interview for *Fantastic Mr Fox*"
257 The Numbers
258 "A Visit to the Studio", Criterion Collection
259 Leader, "George Clooney, Bill Murray & Wes Anderson talk Fantastic Mr Fox"
260 Lee, "Fur flies on Mr Fox"
261 "OCD like a Fox", *San Antonio Current*
262 "Fantastic Mr Fox: A Cutting-Edge Fox", Searchlight Pictures
263 Brody, "Wild, Wild Wes"
264 Lee, "Fur flies on Mr Fox"
265 Sancton, "How the Puppets from Fantastic Mr Fox Were Made"
266 Lee, "Fur flies on Mr Fox"
267 "*Fantastic Mr Fox* Q&A with cinematographer Tristan Oliver", The Garden Cinema
268 "Wes Anderson on his *Fox* cinematographer: 'I could work with him again'"
269 "Wes Anderson Covers New Ground With Mr Fox", *Fresh Air* with Terry Gross
270 Huff, "*Fantastic Mr Fox* composer Alexandre Desplat on joys of working with 'mischievous' Wes Anderson"
271 Utichi, "Interview with Wes Anderson"
272 "How Wes Anderson Soundtracks His Movies", *Fresh Air* with Terry Gross
273 "Wes Anderson on *Fantastic Mr Fox*: Film4 Interview Special", Film4
274 The Numbers
275 Reichert, "*Fantastic Mr Fox* Review"
276 Mclean, "Wes Anderson interview for *Fantastic Mr Fox*"
277 Scott, "Don't Count Your Chickens"

MOONRISE KINGDOM
SOURCES

◇ Seitz, Matt Zoller, "The Wes Anderson Collection", Abrams, 2013
◇ Moonrise Kingdom Press Conference, Festival de Cannes, 2012
◇ O'Hehir, Andrew, "Wes Anderson on Moonrise Kingdom: I'm trying to make something unfamiliar", Salon, 2012
◇ Geoghegan, Kev, "Wes Anderson returns with Moonrise Kingdom", BBC, 2012
◇ Weisberg, Jacob, "The World According to Wes", Slate, 2012
◇ Smith, Nigel M., "Honor Roll 2012: Wes Anderson On the Success of 'Moonrise Kingdom' and What Separates Him From Robert Zemeckis", IndieWire, 2012
◇ Goodsell, Luke, "Interview with Kara Hayward", Rotten Tomatoes, 2012
◇ Buchanan, Kyle, "Wes Anderson on Moonrise Kingdom, Halloween Costumes, and Summer Movie Surprises", Vulture, 2012
◇ Waxman, Sharon, "Wes Anderson on Moonrise Kingdom: 'It's a Memory of a Fantasy'". TheWrap, 2012
◇ Chew-Bose, Durga, "Roman Coppola is Young at Heart", Interview, 2012
◇ Audio commentary with Wes Anderson, Bill Murray, Edward Norton, Jason Schwartzman, and Roman Coppola, Criterion Collection, 2019
◇ Miller, Julie, "Wes Anderson on Moonrise Kingdom, First Loves, and Cohabitating with Bill Murray", Vanity Fair, 2012

- Kilday, Gregg, "Cannes 2012: Wes Anderson on Making Moonrise Kingdom and His Cannes Debut (Q&A)", The Hollywood Reporter, 2012
- Nemiroff, Perri, "Interview with Kara Hayward", Shockya News, 2012
- Brillantes, Mariam, "'Moonrise Kingdom' Star Kara Hayward Takes Questions From Tweens", The Wall Street Journal, 2012
- "Next Factor Q&A: 'Moonrise Kingdom' Star Jared Gilman", MTV, 2012
- Bland, Simon, "'There were certain dance moves that were all me' – Jared Gilman on Moonrise Kingdom at 10", Little White Lies, 2022
- Hornaday, Anne, "Wes Anderson talks about Moonrise Kingdom and his Cannes debut", The Washington Post, 2012
- Lyttelton, Oliver, "The Playlist Interview From Cannes: Wes Anderson Discusses The Nostalgia, Music, & Making Of Moonrise Kingdom", The Playlist, 2012
- Dombal, Ryan, "Interview with Wes Anderson", Pitchfork, 2012
- Fleming Jr, Mike, "Fleming Q&A's Moonrise Kingdom Director Wes Anderson", Deadline, 2012
- "Wes Anderson, Creating A Singular Kingdom", Fresh Air with Terry Gross, 2013
- Raab, Scott, "Bill Murray: The ESQ+A", Esquire, 2012
- Donohue, Walter, "Love on the Run: Wes Anderson on Moonrise Kingdom", Filmmaker Magazine, 2012
- "Norton's home movies from the set", Criterion Collection, 2019
- The Numbers (the–numbers.com)
- Stevens, Dana, "Moonrise Kingdom Review", Slate, 2012
- Edelstein, David, "Formalist Goes to Camp", New York Magazine, 2012
- Vishnevetsky, Ignatiy, "Moonrise Kingdom Review", MUBI Notebook, 2012
- Brody, Richard, "Loving Moonrise Kingdom For the Right Reasons", The New Yorker, 2012

NOTES

278 Seitz, *The Wes Anderson Collection*, 284
279 *Moonrise Kingdom* Press Conference, Festival de Cannes
280 Seitz, *The Wes Anderson Collection*, 280
281 O'Hehir, "Wes Anderson on *Moonrise Kingdom*: I'm trying to make something unfamiliar"
282 Geoghegan, "Wes Anderson returns with *Moonrise Kingdom*"
283 Weisberg, "The World According to Wes"
284 Smith, "Honor Roll 2012: Wes Anderson On the Success of '*Moonrise Kingdom*' and What Separates Him From Robert Zemeckis"
285 Goodsell, "Interview with Kara Hayward"
286 *Moonrise Kingdom* Press Conference, Festival de Cannes
287 Chew-Bose, "Roman Coppola is Young at Heart"
288 Buchanan, "Wes Anderson on *Moonrise Kingdom*, Halloween Costumes, and Summer Movie Surprises"
289 Waxman, "Wes Anderson on *Moonrise Kingdom*: 'It's a Memory of a Fantasy'"
290 Chew-Bose, "Roman Coppola is Young at Heart"
291 "Audio commentary with Wes Anderson, Bill Murray, Edward Norton, Jason Schwartzman and Roman Coppola", Criterion Collection
292 Miller, "Wes Anderson on *Moonrise Kingdom*, First Loves and Cohabitating with Bill Murray"
293 Geoghegan, "Wes Anderson returns with *Moonrise Kingdom*"
294 Kilday, "Cannes 2012: Wes Anderson on Making *Moonrise Kingdom* and His Cannes Debut (Q&A)"
295 Nemiroff, "Interview with Kara Hayward"
296 Miller, "Wes Anderson on *Moonrise Kingdom*, First Loves, and Cohabitating with Bill Murray"
297 Brillantes, "*Moonrise Kingdom* Star Kara Hayward Takes Questions From Tweens"
298 "Next Factor Q&A: *Moonrise Kingdom* Star Jared Gilman"
299 Weisberg, "The World According to Wes"
300 Bland, "'There were certain dance moves that were all me' – Jared Gilman on *Moonrise Kingdom* at 10"
301 Hornaday, "Wes Anderson talks about *Moonrise Kingdom* and his Cannes debut"
302 Lyttelton, "The Playlist Interview From Cannes: Wes Anderson Discusses The Nostalgia, Music, & Making Of *Moonrise Kingdom*"
303 Dombal, "Interview with Wes Anderson"
304 "Audio commentary with Wes Anderson, Bill Murray, Edward Norton, Jason Schwartzman, and Roman Coppola", Criterion Collection
305 Fleming, "Fleming Q&A's *Moonrise Kingdom* Director Wes Anderson"
306 "Wes Anderson, Creating A Singular Kingdom", *Fresh Air* with Terry Gross
307 Raab, "Bill Murray: The ESQ+A"
308 *Moonrise Kingdom* Press Conference, Festival de Cannes
309 "Wes Anderson, Creating A Singular Kingdom", *Fresh Air* with Terry Gross
310 "Audio commentary with Wes Anderson, Bill Murray, Edward Norton, Jason Schwartzman, and Roman Coppola", Criterion Collection
311 Geoghegan, "Wes Anderson returns with *Moonrise Kingdom*"
312 Hornaday, "Wes Anderson talks about *Moonrise Kingdom* and his Cannes debut"
313 "Audio commentary with Wes Anderson, Bill Murray, Edward Norton, Jason Schwartzman, and Roman Coppola", Criterion Collection

314 "Audio commentary with Wes Anderson, Bill Murray, Edward Norton, Jason Schwartzman, and Roman Coppola", Criterion Collection
315 Geoghegan, "Wes Anderson returns with *Moonrise Kingdom*"
316 Seitz, *The Wes Anderson Collection*, 299
317 Donohue, "Love on the Run: Wes Anderson on *Moonrise Kingdom*"
318 Seitz, *The Wes Anderson Collection*, 300
319 Kilday, "Cannes 2012: Wes Anderson on Making *Moonrise Kingdom* and His Cannes Debut (Q&A)"
320 Seitz, *The Wes Anderson Collection*, 300
321 Ibid, 304
322 Miller, "Wes Anderson on *Moonrise Kingdom*, First Loves, and Cohabitating with Bill Murray"
323 "Norton's home movies from the set", Criterion Collection
324 *Moonrise Kingdom* Press Conference, Festival de Cannes
325 Lyttelton, "The Playlist Interview From Cannes: Wes Anderson Discusses The Nostalgia, Music and Making Of *Moonrise Kingdom*"
326 The Numbers
327 Stevens, "*Moonrise Kingdom* Review"
328 Vishnevetsky, "*Moonrise Kingdom* Review"
329 Brody, "Loving *Moonrise Kingdom* For the Right Reasons"
330 The Numbers
331 Bland, "'There were certain dance moves that were all me' – Jared Gilman on *Moonrise Kingdom* at 10"

THE GRAND BUDAPEST HOTEL
SOURCES

- Collin, Robbie, "Interview with Wes Anderson", The Telegraph, 2014
- Prochnik, George, "'I stole from Stefan Zweig': Wes Anderson on the author who inspired his latest movie", The Telegraph, 2014
- Foundas, Scott, "Wes Anderson Talks About His Grand Influences", Variety, 2014
- "Rooms With A View: Wes Anderson", Harper's Bazaar, 2014
- "Wes Anderson: 'We Made A Pastiche' Of Eastern Europe's Greatest Hits'", Fresh Air with Terry Gross, 2014
- Sartin, Hank, "Stories within Stories: Wes Anderson Talks About The Grand Budapest Hotel", RogerEbert.com, 2014
- Audio commentary with Wes Anderson, Roman Coppola, Kent Jones, and Jeff Goldblum, Criterion Collection, 2020
- Rothman, Lily, "Wes Anderson on The Grand Budapest Hotel, Nostalgia and Standing-Still Tennis", Time, 2014
- Crow, David, "Wes Anderson Interview Looks Inside The Grand Budapest Hotel", Den of Geek, 2014
- Cohane, Ondine, "Finding a Setting That Captures a Scene", The New York Times, 2014
- Vineyard, Jennifer, "Wes Anderson on The Grand Budapest Hotel, Reimagined Nazis, and His Sock Drawer", Vulture, 2014
- Seitz, Matt Zoller, "The Wes Anderson Collection: The Grand Budapest Hotel", Abrams, 2015
- "Editing The Grand Budapest Hotel", American Cinema Editors, 2014
- "Academy Conversations: The Grand Budapest Hotel", Academy of Motion Picture Arts and Sciences, 2014
- White, Adam, "How to make a Wes Anderson movie, by his trusted cinematographer Robert Yeoman", The Telegraph, 2018
- Olson, Mike, "The Grand Budapest Hotel Production Designer Adam Stockhausen Goes Handmade", Motion Picture Association, 2014
- Billington, Alex, "Interview with Wes Anderson & Jeremy Dawson", FirstShowing.net, 2014
- Wilford, Lauren, "The Wes Anderson Collection: Isle of Dogs", Abrams, 2018
- The Numbers (the–numbers.com)
- "Wes Anderson's Production Design", Cooke Optics, 2018
- Meslow, Scott, "The untold story behind The Grand Budapest Hotel's Boy with Apple", The Week, 2015
- Woodward, Adam, "The story behind The Grand Budapest Hotel's Boy with Apple painting", Little White Lies, 2021
- Quito, Anne, "The graphic designer behind Wes Anderson's The Grand Budapest Hotel", Quartz, 2015
- "Vogue Archive: A Quirk Of Art", Vogue, 2015
- Barlow, Helen, "Interview with Wes Anderson", SBS, 2014
- "Extended Q&A with Wes Anderson", SXSW, 2014
- "Interview with Wes Anderson", Charlie Rose, 2014
- Rich, Katey, "Wes Anderson Still Likes a Great Hotel, But He Doesn't Want to Live In One Anymore", Vanity Fair, 2014
- Geoghegan, Kev, "Wes Anderson's Grand Budapest Hotel reunion", BBC, 2014
- "A Psychological Game Of Casting For The Grand Budapest Hotel", NPR, 2014
- Dawes, Amy, "The Envelope: Ralph Fiennes on nostalgia, heart in Wes Anderson's Grand Budapest Hotel", Los Angeles Times, 2014
- Osenlund, R. Kurt, "Wes Anderson Interview", Slant, 2014
- Seymour, Tom, "The Grand Budapest Hotel: the kid stays in the picture", The Guardian, 2014
- Yotka, Steff, "The Insider: Tony Revolori", Nylon, 2014
- "Interview with Wes Anderson, Ralph Fiennes & Tony Revolori", Star Sessions, 2014
- "Interview with F. Murray Abraham", Rotten Tomatoes, 2014
- "Tour of Grand Budapest Hotel", Criterion Collection, 2020

PASSENGER'S CHECK
To identify accommodations purchased.
From
To
Accommodation
Steamer Sailing
$4.00
FORM 4-409
The Company reserves the right, without any liability, to delay or cancel the scheduled sailing of any steamer.
Accommodation and service specified hereon must be cancelled four hours before schedule departure of Steamer to make this ticket valid for refund.
Property taken into room will be entirely at owner's risk. Pass. Traf. Mgr.

SOUTH STATION Parcel Room
B 81
3-17-48

- Crouch, Ian, "Does Wes Anderson Hate Dogs?", The New Yorker, 2012
- "Anderson & Fiennes: Inventing a Hotel", The New York Times, 2014
- Hines, Nico, "The Cast of 'The Grand Budapest Hotel' Says Wes Anderson Is a Genius Hardass", Daily Beast, 2014
- Lamont, Tom, "Wes Anderson: in a world of his own", The Guardian, 2014
- Casey, Dan, "Checking in to The Grand Budapest Hotel with Tony Revolori", Nerdist, 2014
- Brody, Richard, "The Grand Budapest Hotel: Wes Anderson's Artistic Manifesto", The New Yorker, 2014
- "Film of the week: The Grand Budapest Hotel", Sight & Sound, 2014
- Travers, Peter, "The Grand Budapest Hotel Review", Rolling Stone, 2014
- Beaumont-Thomas, Ben, "The Grand Budapest Hotel becomes Wes Anderson's highest-grossing film", The Guardian, 2014

NOTES

332 Prochnik, "'I stole from Stefan Zweig': Wes Anderson on the author who inspired his latest movie"
333 Collin, "Interview with Wes Anderson"
334 Foundas, "Wes Anderson Talks About His Grand Influences"
335 "Rooms With A View: Wes Anderson", *Harper's Bazaar*
336 "Wes Anderson: 'We Made A Pastiche Of Eastern Europe's Greatest Hits'", *Fresh Air* with Terry Gross
337 Collin, "Interview with Wes Anderson"
338 Sartin, "Stories within Stories: Wes Anderson Talks About *The Grand Budapest Hotel*"
339 "Audio commentary with Wes Anderson, Roman Coppola, Kent Jones, and Jeff Goldblum", Criterion Collection
340 Rothman, "Wes Anderson on *The Grand Budapest Hotel*, Nostalgia and Standing-Still Tennis"
341 Crow, "Wes Anderson Interview Looks Inside *The Grand Budapest Hotel*"
342 Cohane, "Finding a Setting That Captures a Scene"
343 Prochnik, "'I stole from Stefan Zweig': Wes Anderson on the author who inspired his latest movie"
344 Vineyard, "Wes Anderson on *The Grand Budapest Hotel*, Reimagined Nazis, and His Sock Drawer"
345 Cohane, "Finding a Setting That Captures a Scene"
346 Seitz, "*The Wes Anderson Collection: The Grand Budapest Hotel*", 105
347 "Editing *The Grand Budapest Hotel*", American Cinema Editors
348 "Wes Anderson: 'We Made A Pastiche Of Eastern Europe's Greatest Hits'", *Fresh Air* with Terry Gross
349 Cohane, "Finding a Setting That Captures a Scene"
350 "Rooms With A View: Wes Anderson", *Harper's Bazaar*
351 "Academy Conversations: *The Grand Budapest Hotel*", Academy of Motion Picture Arts and Sciences
352 Cohane, "Finding a Setting That Captures a Scene"
353 White, "How to make a Wes Anderson movie, by his trusted cinematographer Robert Yeoman"
354 Olson, "*The Grand Budapest Hotel* Production Designer Adam Stockhausen Goes Handmade"
355 Wilford, *The Wes Anderson Collection: Isle of Dogs*, 69
356 Billington, "Interview with Wes Anderson and Jeremy Dawson"
357 The Numbers
358 Olson, "*The Grand Budapest Hotel* Production Designer Adam Stockhausen Goes Handmade"
359 "Wes Anderson's Production Design", Cooke Optics
360 Seitz, *The Wes Anderson Collection: The Grand Budapest Hotel*, 105
361 Meslow, "The untold story behind *The Grand Budapest Hotel*'s Boy with Apple"
362 Woodward, "The story behind *The Grand Budapest Hotel*'s Boy with Apple painting"
363 Vineyard, "Wes Anderson on *The Grand Budapest Hotel*, Reimagined Nazis, and His Sock Drawer"
364 Quito, "The graphic designer behind Wes Anderson's *The Grand Budapest Hotel*"
365 Crow, "Wes Anderson Interview Looks Inside *The Grand Budapest Hotel*"
366 Seitz, *The Wes Anderson Collection: The Grand Budapest Hotel*, 136
367 "Vogue Archive: A Quirk Of Art", *Vogue*
368 Collin, "Interview with Wes Anderson"
369 "Vogue Archive: A Quirk Of Art", *Vogue*
370 Foundas, "Wes Anderson Talks About His Grand Influences"
371 Barlow, "Interview with Wes Anderson"
372 "Interview with Wes Anderson", *Charlie Rose*
373 "Extended Q&A with Wes Anderson", SXSW
374 Sartin, "Stories within Stories: Wes Anderson Talks About *The Grand Budapest Hotel*"
375 "A Psychological Game Of Casting For *The Grand Budapest Hotel*", NPR
376 Dawes, "The Envelope: Ralph Fiennes on nostalgia, heart in Wes Anderson's *Grand Budapest Hotel*"
377 Osenlund, "Wes Anderson Interview"
378 Billington, "Interview with Wes Anderson and Jeremy Dawson"
379 Seymour, "*The Grand Budapest Hotel*: the kid stays in the picture"
380 Yotka, "The Insider: Tony Revolori"
381 Osenlund, "Wes Anderson Interview"
382 Yotka, "The Insider: Tony Revolori"
383 "Interview with F. Murray Abraham", Rotten Tomatoes
384 Seitz, "*The Wes Anderson Collection: The Grand Budapest Hotel*", 163
385 Ibid, 164
386 "Tour of *Grand Budapest Hotel*", Criterion Collection
387 Seitz, *The Wes Anderson Collection: The Grand Budapest Hotel*, 61

388 Seitz, *The Wes Anderson Collection: The Grand Budapest Hotel*, 48
389 Barlow, "Interview with Wes Anderson"
390 Seitz, *The Wes Anderson Collection: The Grand Budapest Hotel*, 90
391 Hines, "The Cast of *The Grand Budapest Hotel* Says Wes Anderson Is a Genius Hardass"
392 Seymour, "*The Grand Budapest Hotel*: the kid stays in the picture"
393 "Rooms With A View: Wes Anderson", *Harper's Bazaar*
394 Lamont, "Wes Anderson: in a world of his own"
395 "Wes Anderson: 'We Made A Pastiche Of Eastern Europe's Greatest Hits'", *Fresh Air* with Terry Gross
396 Hines, "The Cast of *The Grand Budapest Hotel* Says Wes Anderson Is a Genius Hardass"
397 Brody, "*The Grand Budapest Hotel*: Wes Anderson's Artistic Manifesto"
398 "Film of the week: *The Grand Budapest Hotel*", *Sight & Sound*
399 Travers, "*The Grand Budapest Hotel* Review"
400 The Numbers
401 Beaumont-Thomas, "*The Grand Budapest Hotel* becomes Wes Anderson's highest-grossing film"

ISLE OF DOGS

SOURCES

◇ Sinha-Roy, Piya, "Wes Anderson explains why he went to Japan for Isle of Dogs", Entertainment Weekly, 2018
◇ Maher, Kevin, "The director Wes Anderson on his new movie, Isle of Dogs", The Times, 2018
◇ Kaufman, Sophie Monks, "Wes Anderson: 'I wanted language to play a role without it becoming an obstacle'", Little White Lies, 2018
◇ Fujii, Katsuro, "From Texas to Tokyo: An Interview with Wes Anderson About His New Film, Isle of Dogs", Japan Forward, 2018
◇ Wilford, Lauren, "The Wes Anderson Collection: Isle of Dogs", Abrams, 2018
◇ Chen, Nick, "The Isle of Dogs animators on the intensity of working with Wes Anderson", Dazed, 2018
◇ "Tristan Oliver on Isle Of Dogs", The British Society of Cinematographers, 2018
◇ "Interview with Tristan Oliver", The Next Best Picture Podcast, 2018
◇ Horovitz, Oliver, "Isle of Dogs Cocreators Wes Anderson and Jason Schwartzman Tell AD What Went into Creating the Film's Fictional World", Architectural Digest, 2018
◇ "Interview with Kunichi Nomura", ScreenSlam, 2018
◇ Desowitz, Bill, "Isle of Dogs: How Team Wes Anderson Created a Stop-Motion Love Letter to Japanese Cinema", IndieWire, 2018
◇ Healy, Claire Marie, "Wes Anderson, Jason Schwartzman, and Roman Coppola go deep on Isle of Dogs", Dazed, 2018
◇ Grobar, Matt, "The Art Of Craft: Isle Of Dogs Production Designer Bends Form Of Stop-Motion To Realize Vision Of An Auteur", Deadline, 2018
◇ "Unrolling the Masterful Sushi Scene in Isle of Dogs", Variety, 2018
◇ Byng, Malaika, "Inside the insane sets of Wes Anderson's Isle of Dogs", CNN, 2018
◇ Murphy, Mekado, "Making the Dogs of Isle of Dogs", The New York Times, 2018
◇ Murphy, Jackson, "Interview with Andy Gent", Animation Scoop, 2018
◇ Tartaglione, Nancy, "Isle Of Dogs Team On Realizing Wes Anderson's Vision & Bending Physics", Deadline, 2018
◇ Soo Hoo, Fawnia, "The Stop-Motion Puppets in Wes Anderson's 'Isle of Dogs' Required a Costume Designer", Fashionista, 2018
◇ Failes, Ian, "Isle of Dogs: How Every Frame Was Touched by VFX", Visual Effects Society, 2019
◇ Dean, Jonathan, "Wes Anderson's Isle of Dogs: the director gathers together a fantastic cast, including Bill Murray, Greta Gerwig, Bryan Cranston and Jeff Goldblum", The Times, 2018
◇ Eisenberg, Eric, "Anjelica Huston Has A Hilariously Mysterious Role In Isle Of Dogs", Cinemablend, 2018
◇ Jones, Emma, "Why Isle of Dogs is no shaggy dog story", BBC News, 2018
◇ Aftab, Kaleem, "'If you are offered a job, take it'. How Bryan Cranston became top dog", Square Mile, 2018
◇ "Interview with Wes Anderson", Searchlight Pictures, 2018
◇ Grobar, Matt, "Composer Alexandre Desplat On The Booming Taiko Drums & Barking Saxophones Of Isle Of Dogs", Deadline, 2019
◇ "Isle of Dogs Red Carpet and Q & A", SXSW, 2018
◇ Yoshida, Emily, "What It's Like to Watch Isle of Dogs As a Japanese Speaker", Vulture, 2018
◇ Fujii, Moeko, "What Isle of Dogs Gets Right About Japan", The New Yorker, 2018
◇ Chang, Justin, "Wes Anderson's Isle of Dogs is often captivating, but cultural sensitivity gets lost in translation", Los Angeles Times, 2018
◇ Robey, Tim, "Isle of Dogs review: if you're looking for cute, cuddly Wes Anderson you're barking up the wrong tree", The Telegraph, 2018

NOTES

402 Sinha-Roy, "Wes Anderson explains why he went to Japan for *Isle of Dogs*"
403 Maher, "The director Wes Anderson on his new movie, *Isle of Dogs*"
404 Kaufman, "Wes Anderson: 'I wanted language to play a role without it becoming an obstacle'"
405 Fujii, "From Texas to Tokyo: An Interview with Wes Anderson About His New Film, *Isle of Dogs*"

406 Wilford, *The Wes Anderson Collection: Isle of Dogs*, 22
407 Chen, "The *Isle of Dogs* animators on the intensity of working with Wes Anderson"
408 "Tristan Oliver on *Isle of Dogs*", The British Society of Cinematographers
409 Horovitz, "*Isle of Dogs* Cocreators Wes Anderson and Jason Schwartzman Tell AD What Went into Creating the Film's Fictional World"
410 Wilford, *The Wes Anderson Collection: Isle of Dogs*, 49
411 Kaufman, "Wes Anderson: 'I wanted language to play a role without it becoming an obstacle'"
412 "Interview with Kunichi Nomura", ScreenSlam
413 Maher, "The director Wes Anderson on his new movie, *Isle of Dogs*"
414 Desowitz, "*Isle of Dogs*: How Team Wes Anderson Created a Stop-Motion Love Letter to Japanese Cinema"
415 Wilford, *The Wes Anderson Collection: Isle of Dogs*, 49
416 Desowitz, "*Isle of Dogs*: How Team Wes Anderson Created a Stop-Motion Love Letter to Japanese Cinema"
417 Healy, "Wes Anderson, Jason Schwartzman, and Roman Coppola go deep on *Isle of Dogs*"
418 Sinha-Roy, "Wes Anderson explains why he went to Japan for *Isle of Dogs*"
419 Grobar, "The Art Of Craft: *Isle of Dogs* Production Designer Bends Form Of Stop-Motion To Realize Vision Of An Auteur"
420 Horovitz, "*Isle of Dogs* Cocreators Wes Anderson and Jason Schwartzman Tell AD What Went into Creating the Film's Fictional World"
421 Sinha-Roy, "Wes Anderson explains why he went to Japan for *Isle of Dogs*"
422 Chen, "The *Isle of Dogs* animators on the intensity of working with Wes Anderson"
423 "Unrolling the Masterful Sushi Scene in *Isle of Dogs*", *Variety*
424 Wilford, *The Wes Anderson Collection: Isle of Dogs*, 25
425 Fujii, "From Texas to Tokyo: An Interview with Wes Anderson About His New Film, *Isle of Dogs*"
426 Horovitz, "*Isle of Dogs* Cocreators Wes Anderson and Jason Schwartzman Tell AD What Went into Creating the Film's Fictional World"
427 Maher, "The director Wes Anderson on his new movie, *Isle of Dogs*"
428 Murphy, "Making the Dogs of *Isle of Dogs*"
429 Murphy, "Interview with Andy Gent"
430 Murphy, "Making the Dogs of *Isle of Dogs*"
431 Tartaglione, "*Isle of Dogs* Team On Realizing Wes Anderson's Vision & Bending Physics"
432 Murphy, "Making the Dogs of *Isle of Dogs*"
433 Desowitz, "*Isle of Dogs*: How Team Wes Anderson Created a Stop-Motion Love Letter to Japanese Cinema"
434 Grobar, "The Art Of Craft: *Isle of Dogs* Production Designer Bends Form Of Stop-Motion To Realize Vision Of An Auteur"
435 Desowitz, "*Isle of Dogs*: How Team Wes Anderson Created a Stop-Motion Love Letter to Japanese Cinema"
436 Chen, "The *Isle of Dogs* animators on the intensity of working with Wes Anderson"
437 Soo Hoo, "The Stop-Motion Puppets in Wes Anderson's '*Isle of Dogs*' Required a Costume Designer"
438 Failes, "*Isle of Dogs*: How Every Frame Was Touched by VFX"
439 Dean, "Wes Anderson's *Isle of Dogs*: the director gathers together a fantastic cast, including Bill Murray, Greta Gerwig, Bryan Cranston and Jeff Goldblum"
440 Eisenberg, "Anjelica Huston Has A Hilariously Mysterious Role In *Isle of Dogs*"
441 Jones, "Why *Isle of Dogs* is no shaggy dog story"
442 Aftab, "'If you are offered a job, take it'. How Bryan Cranston became top dog"
443 "Interview with Wes Anderson", Searchlight Pictures
444 Grobar, "Composer Alexandre Desplat On The Booming Taiko Drums & Barking Saxophones Of *Isle of Dogs*"
445 Wilford, "*The Wes Anderson Collection: Isle of Dogs*", 227
446 Sinha-Roy, "Wes Anderson explains why he went to Japan for *Isle of Dogs*"
447 Healy, "Wes Anderson, Jason Schwartzman, and Roman Coppola go deep on *Isle of Dogs*"
448 Wilford, "*The Wes Anderson Collection: Isle of Dogs*", 25
449 Yoshida, "What It's Like to Watch *Isle of Dogs* As a Japanese Speaker"
450 Wilford, *The Wes Anderson Collection: Isle of Dogs*, 146
451 Fujii, "What *Isle of Dogs* Gets Right About Japan"
452 Chang, "Wes Anderson's *Isle of Dogs* is often captivating, but cultural sensitivity gets lost in translation"
453 Dean, "Wes Anderson's *Isle of Dogs*: the director gathers together a fantastic cast, including Bill Murray, Greta Gerwig, Bryan Cranston and Jeff Goldblum"
454 Wilford, *The Wes Anderson Collection: Isle of Dogs*, 29

THE FRENCH DISPATCH

SOURCES

- Collin, Robbie, "Interview with Wes Anderson", The Telegraph, 2014
- Weisberg, Jacob, "The World According to Wes", Slate, 2012
- Morrison, Susan, "How Wes Anderson Turned The New Yorker Into The French Dispatch", The New Yorker, 2021
- Seitz, Matt Zoller, "The Wes Anderson Collection: The French Dispatch", Abrams, 2023
- Chalabi, Mona, "In the Company of Wes Anderson", The New York Times, 2021

- Apiou, Virginie, "Lyna Khoudri is Wes Anderson's Newest Star", L'Officiel, 2020
- Ford, Rebecca, "From Westworld to Wes's World: Jeffrey Wright on The French Dispatch", Vanity Fair, 2021
- Wallace, Rachel, "Go Behind the Scenes of Wes Anderson's New Film, The French Dispatch", Architectural Digest, 2021
- James, Daron, "French Dispatch uses color, frame and miniatures for an alluring production design", Los Angeles Times, 2022
- Basu, Ritupriya, "How Wes Anderson's Creative Team Designed The French Dispatch Magazine for His Latest Film", 2021
- Cascone, Sarah, "The Real-Life Artists Behind The French Dispatch Share What It Was Like to Paint for Exacting Auteur Wes Anderson", Artnet, 2021
- Mutter, Zoe, "A Love Letter to Literature", British Cinematographer, 2021
- McGowan, Chris, "The French Dispatch: Tracking all the Visual Nuances and Moving Part for Several Films in One", VFXV, 2022
- Larki, Shadan, "Alexandre Desplat Explains Why He Wanted to Create a 'Musically Unpredictable' Score for The French Dispatch", AwardsDaily, 2022
- "Interview with Robert Yeoman", Next Best Picture Podcast, 2021
- Giroux, Jack, "The French Dispatch Editor Andrew Weisblum On Crafting Wes Anderson's Films", SlashFilm, 2021
- "Interview with Timothée Chalamet", Coup de Main, 2021
- Seitz, Matt Zoller, "'You Just Have to Accept That Wes Is Right' The French Dispatch crew explains how it pulled off the movie's quietly impossible tracking shot", Vulture, 2021
- Hullfish, Steve, "Art of the Cut: Wes Anderson's Latest Tableau, The French Dispatch", Frame.io Insider, 2021
- Brody, Richard, "The French Dispatch, Reviewed: Wes Anderson's Most Freewheeling Film", The New Yorker, 2021
- Ide, Wendy, "The French Dispatch review – exasperating Wes Anderson portmanteau picture", The Guardian, 2021

NOTES

456 Collin, "Interview with Wes Anderson"
457 Weisberg, "The World According to Wes"
458 Morrison, "How Wes Anderson Turned *The New Yorker* Into *The French Dispatch*"
459 Ibid.
460 Seitz, *The Wes Anderson Collection*: *The French Dispatch* 18
461 Morrison, "How Wes Anderson Turned *The New Yorker* Into *The French Dispatch*"
462 Ibid.
463 Morrison, "How Wes Anderson Turned *The New Yorker* Into *The French Dispatch*"
464 Morrison, "How Wes Anderson Turned The New Yorker Into *The French Dispatch*"
465 Ibid.
466 Seitz, *The Wes Anderson Collection*: *The French Dispatch*, 45
467 Seitz, *The Wes Anderson Collection*: *The French Dispatch*, 101
468 Morrison, "How Wes Anderson Turned *The New Yorker* Into *The French Dispatch*"
469 Ibid.
470 Chalabi, "In the Company of Wes Anderson"
471 Apiou, "Lyna Khoudri is Wes Anderson's Newest Star"
472 Seitz, *The Wes Anderson Collection*: *The French Dispatch*, 121
473 Morrison, "How Wes Anderson Turned *The New Yorker* Into *The French Dispatch*"
474 Chalabi, "In the Company of Wes Anderson"
475 Ford, "From Westworld to Wes's World: Jeffrey Wright on *The French Dispatch*"
476 Seitz, *The Wes Anderson Collection*: *The French Dispatch*, 23
477 Seitz, *The Wes Anderson Collection*: *The French Dispatch*, 75
478 James, "French Dispatch uses color, frame and miniatures for an alluring production design"
479 Seitz, *The Wes Anderson Collection*: *The French Dispatch*, 72
480 Seitz, *The Wes Anderson Collection*: *The French Dispatch*, 83
481 Basu, "How Wes Anderson's Creative Team Designed *The French Dispatch* Magazine for His Latest Film"
482 Seitz, *The Wes Anderson Collection*: *The French Dispatch*, 92
483 Cascone, "The Real-Life Artists Behind *The French Dispatch* Share What It Was Like to Paint for Exacting Auteur Wes Anderson"
484 Wallace, "Go Behind the Scenes of Wes Anderson's New Film, *The French Dispatch*"
485 Cascone, "The Real-Life Artists Behind *The French Dispatch* Share What It Was Like to Paint for Exacting Auteur Wes Anderson"
486 Mutter, "A Love Letter to Literature"
487 McGowan, "*The French Dispatch*: Tracking all the Visual Nuances and Moving Part for Several Films in One"
488 Larki, "Alexandre Desplat Explains Why He Wanted to Create a 'Musically Unpredictable' Score for *The French Dispatch*"
489 Mutter, "A Love Letter to Literature"
490 "Interview with Timothée Chalamet", Coup de Main
491 Seitz, "'You Just Have to Accept That Wes Is Right' *The French Dispatch* crew explains how it pulled off the movie's quietly impossible tracking shot"
492 Seitz, *The Wes Anderson Collection*: *The French Dispatch*, 165

493 Hullfish, "Art of the Cut: Wes Anderson's Latest Tableau, *The French Dispatch*"
494 Brody, "*The French Dispatch*, Reviewed: Wes Anderson's Most Freewheeling Film"
495 Ide, "*The French Dispatch* review – exasperating Wes Anderson portmanteau picture"

ASTEROID CITY

SOURCES

◇ Maher, Kevin, "Wes Anderson: 'Please do not send me memes of people doing me'", The Times, 2023
◇ Mitchell, Elvis, "Director Wes Anderson on building Asteroid City", KCRW, 2023
◇ Kohn, Eric, "Wes Anderson on Asteroid City: Mental Health, Marilyn Monroe, and Sending Emails to Tom Hanks", IndieWire, 2023
◇ Holub, Christian, "Scarlett Johansson teases her Bette Davis-esque character in Wes Anderson's Asteroid City", Entertainment Weekly, 2023
◇ Ungano, Julian, "Wes Anderson's Guide to his Galaxy", Sight & Sound, 2023
◇ Holub, Christian, "Here's what you need to know about Asteroid City, courtesy of Wes Anderson", Entertainment Weekly, 2023
◇ Schwartzman, Jason, "Jason Schwartzman: How Wes Anderson's Asteroid City Helped Me Revisit the Grief in My Life", IndieWire, 2023
◇ Schager, Nick, "Wes Anderson Knows About the Memes and Has Thoughts", Daily Beast, 2023
◇ Gilchrist, Todd, "Wes Anderson on How Asteroid City Star Jason Schwartzman Helped Inspire His Latest Film", Variety, 2023
◇ Strong, Hannah, "Jason Schwartzman: 'Working with Wes so long, it really has become like we're brothers'", Little White Lies, 2023
◇ Coyle, Jake, "What it's like to get a Wes Anderson education, from Rushmore to Asteroid City", Associated Press, 2023
◇ Ebiri, Bilge, "Jason Schwartzman and Wes Anderson Forever", Vulture, 2023
◇ Kemp, Ella, "Stellar Storyteller: Wes Anderson on Star Wars, Satyajit Ray and staging Asteroid City", Letterboxd, 2023
◇ Hobbs, Charlie, "On Location: The Bright Red Desert and Big Blue Sky of Asteroid City", Condé Nast Traveler, 2023
◇ Peacock, Amy, "'We built the entire town and landscape' says Asteroid City production designer", Dezeen, 2023
◇ Strauss, Bob, "Inside the deceptively spare look of Wes Anderson's Asteroid City", Los Angeles Times, 2024
◇ Mottram, James, "Asteroid City cast talk Wes Anderson, taco nights, and working in a fully functional mini-town", Total Film, 2023
◇ Coates, Tyler, "Asteroid City Production Designer Created a Love Letter to the 1950s American Southwest", The Hollywood Reporter, 2023
◇ Canfield, David, "How Asteroid City Became Wes Anderson's Most Visually Ambitious Movie Yet", Vanity Fair, 2023
◇ Mutter, Zoe, "Cosmic Creation", British Cinematographer, 2023
◇ Friedtanzer, Abe, "Asteroid City Editor Barney Pilling on Cutting the Wild World of Wes Anderson", Below the Line, 2023
◇ Mottram, James, "Wes Anderson took a cast of stars to the Spanish desert and made his best film in years", The Independent, 2023
◇ Schulman, Michael, "The Missing Bill Murray Part from Asteroid City", The New Yorker, 2023
◇ Kohn, Eric, "Interview with Wes Anderson", IndieWire, 2023
◇ Jones, Tamera, "Asteroid City's Maya Hawke & Rupert Friend on the Way Wes Anderson Directs and Doing One More Take 'For the Pleasure'", Collider, 2023
◇ Sim, Jonathan, "Hope Davis & Stephen Park Interview", ComingSoon.Net, 2023
◇ "Jason Schwartzman, Jake Ryan, Hope Davis & Stephen Park Interview", Film4, 2023
◇ Bedard, Mike, "Asteroid City: Scarlett Johansson And Jason Schwartzman Enjoy The Small Things About Wes Anderson", Looper, 2023
◇ Ehrlich, David, "Asteroid City Review: Wes Anderson's Cosmic Grief Comedy Is One of His Very Best Movies Yet", IndieWire, 2023
◇ Barber, Nicholas, "Asteroid City review: Even Wes Anderson fans may be irritated by this 'empty' and 'cartoonish' film", BBC, 2023

NOTES

496 Maher, "Wes Anderson: 'Please do not send me memes of people doing me'"
497 Mitchell, "Director Wes Anderson on building *Asteroid City*", KCRW
498 Kohn, "Wes Anderson on *Asteroid City*: Mental Health, Marilyn Monroe, and Sending Emails to Tom Hanks"
499 Holub, "Scarlett Johansson teases her Bette Davis-esque character in Wes Anderson's *Asteroid City*"
500 Ungano, "Wes Anderson's Guide to his Galaxy"
501 Holub, "Here's what you need to know about *Asteroid City*, courtesy of Wes Anderson"
502 Schwartzman, "Jason Schwartzman: How Wes Anderson's *Asteroid City* Helped Me Revisit the Grief in My Life"
503 Schwartzman, "Jason Schwartzman: How Wes Anderson's *Asteroid City* Helped Me Revisit the Grief in My Life"
504 Gilchrist, "Wes Anderson on How *Asteroid City* Star Jason Schwartzman Helped Inspire His Latest Film"
505 Schager, "Wes Anderson Knows About the Memes and Has Thoughts"

506 Strong, "Jason Schwartzman: 'Working with Wes so long, it really has become like we're brothers'"
507 Coyle, "What it's like to get a Wes Anderson education, from *Rushmore* to *Asteroid City*"
508 Strong, "Jason Schwartzman: 'Working with Wes so long, it really has become like we're brothers'"
509 Schwartzman, "Jason Schwartzman: How Wes Anderson's *Asteroid City* Helped Me Revisit the Grief in My Life"
510 Ebiri, "Jason Schwartzman and Wes Anderson Forever"
511 Kohn, "Wes Anderson on *Asteroid City*: Mental Health, Marilyn Monroe, and Sending Emails to Tom Hanks"
512 Ungano, "Wes Anderson's Guide to his Galaxy"
513 Ibid.
514 Ungano, "Wes Anderson's Guide to his Galaxy"
515 Hobbs, "On Location: The Bright Red Desert and Big Blue Sky of *Asteroid City*"
516 Peacock, "'We built the entire town and landscape' says *Asteroid City* production designer"
517 Hobbs, "On Location: The Bright Red Desert and Big Blue Sky of *Asteroid City*"
518 Strauss, "Inside the deceptively spare look of Wes Anderson's *Asteroid City*"
519 Mottram, "*Asteroid City* cast talk Wes Anderson, taco nights, and working in a fully functional mini-town"
520 Peacock, "'We built the entire town and landscape' says *Asteroid City* production designer"
521 Coates, "*Asteroid City* Production Designer Created a Love Letter to the 1950s American Southwest"
522 Peacock, "'We built the entire town and landscape' says *Asteroid City* production designer"
523 Canfield, "How *Asteroid City* Became Wes Anderson's Most Visually Ambitious Movie Yet"
524 Mutter, "Cosmic Creation"
525 Strauss, "Inside the deceptively spare look of Wes Anderson's *Asteroid City*"
526 Ibid.
527 Ungano, "Wes Anderson's Guide to his Galaxy"
528 Mottram, "*Asteroid City* cast talk Wes Anderson, taco nights, and working in a fully functional mini-town"
529 Strauss, "Inside the deceptively spare look of Wes Anderson's *Asteroid City*"
530 Canfield, "How *Asteroid City* Became Wes Anderson's Most Visually Ambitious Movie Yet"
531 Mottram, "*Asteroid City* cast talk Wes Anderson, taco nights, and working in a fully functional mini-town"
532 Kemp, "Stellar Storyteller: Wes Anderson on Star Wars, Satyajit Ray and staging *Asteroid City*"
533 Mottram, "Wes Anderson took a cast of stars to the Spanish desert and made his best film in years"
534 Schulman, "The Missing Bill Murray Part from *Asteroid City*"
535 Kohn, "Interview with Wes Anderson", IndieWire
536 Jones, "*Asteroid City*'s Maya Hawke & Rupert Friend on the Way Wes Anderson Directs and Doing One More Take 'For the Pleasure'"
537 Sim, "Hope Davis and Stephen Park Interview", ComingSoon.Net
538 Bedard, "*Asteroid City*: Scarlett Johansson And Jason Schwartzman Enjoy The Small Things About Wes Anderson"
539 Canfield, "How *Asteroid City* Became Wes Anderson's Most Visually Ambitious Movie Yet"
540 Kemp, "Stellar Storyteller: Wes Anderson on Star Wars, Satyajit Ray and staging *Asteroid City*"
541 Ungano, "Wes Anderson's Guide to his Galaxy"
542 Ehrlich, "*Asteroid City* Review: Wes Anderson's Cosmic Grief Comedy Is One of His Very Best Movies Yet"
543 Barber, "*Asteroid City* review: Even Wes Anderson fans may be irritated by this 'empty' and 'cartoonish' film"

THE WONDERFUL STORY OF HENRY SUGAR AND THREE MORE

SOURCES

◇ "Wes Anderson, Benedict Cumberbatch & Dev Patel on The Wonderful Story of Henry Sugar", Netflix, 2023

◇ Sudarshan, Rudraa Abirami, "The Wonderful Story of Henry Sugar and the Mysterious Case of Kuda Bux", Rolling Stone India, 2023

◇ Buchanan, Kyle, "Wes Anderson Finally Found a Way Into His New Roald Dahl Film", The New York Times, 2023

◇ Zuckerman, Esther, "The Wonderful Story of Henry Sugar: Wes Anderson and Collaborators on the Cinematic Language of Roald Dahl", The Hollywood Reporter, 2024

◇ Weintraub, Steven, "Wes Anderson & Roman Coppola Interview", Collider, 2007

◇ "Interview with Jason Schwartzman and Wes Anderson", Ain't It Cool News, 2007

◇ Weisberg, Jacob, "The World According to Wes", Slate, 2012

◇ Binkley, Christina, "Montblanc asked Wes Anderson to direct its ad. He did — and designed a pen", Vogue Business, 2024

◇ Kohn, Eric, "Wes Anderson on Asteroid City: Mental Health, Marilyn Monroe, and Sending Emails to Tom Hanks", IndieWire, 2023

◇ Thompson, Anne, "Wes Anderson on Why He Loves Making Shorts: They Set Him Free", IndieWire, 2024

◇ Greenwood, Douglas, "Wes Anderson on His New Short, Screening Movies for His 'Little Club' of New York Filmmakers, and the Possibility of Directing for the Stage", Vogue, 2023

◇ "Interview with Kasia Walicka-

Maimone & Robert Yeoman", The Next Best Picture Podcast, 2024

◇ Goldstein, Gregg, "Asteroid City's Rupert Friend: 'Maybe I've Got the Scars and the Bruises Now' to Play James Bond", Variety, 2023

◇ Wise, Damon, "Wes Anderson Talks About Roald Dahl's The Wonderful Story Of Henry Sugar, Teases His Next Movie, And Claims: 'I Don't Have An Aesthetic'", Deadline, 2023

◇ Felperin, Leslie, "The Wonderful Story of Henry Sugar Review: Benedict Cumberbatch in Wes Anderson's Mini-Marvel of a Roald Dahl Adaptation", The Hollywood Reporter, 2023

◇ Calnan, Ellie, "Wes Anderson starts shooting The Phoenician Scheme in Germany", ScreenDaily, 2024

◇ Tenreyro, Tatiana, "Wes Anderson Shares Why He Was Unable to Accept His First-Ever Oscar in Person", The Hollywood Reporter, 2024

◇ Tonet, Aureliano, 'Wes Anderson on your TikTok tributes: 'I'd be afraid to think, is this really how people see my films?", Le Monde, 2023

◇ Travis, Ben, 'Michael Cera Joins The Wonderful World Of Wes Anderson In The Phoenician Scheme', Empire, 2025

NOTES

544 "Wes Anderson, Benedict Cumberbatch and Dev Patel on *The Wonderful Story of Henry Sugar*", Netflix

545 Sudarshan, "The Wonderful Story of Henry Sugar and the Mysterious Case of Kuda Bux"

546 Buchanan, "Wes Anderson Finally Found a Way Into His New Roald Dahl Film"

547 "Wes Anderson, Benedict Cumberbatch and Dev Patel on *The Wonderful Story of Henry Sugar*", Netflix

548 Zuckerman, "*The Wonderful Story of Henry Sugar:* Wes Anderson and Collaborators on the Cinematic Language of Roald Dahl"

549 Kohn, "Wes Anderson on *Asteroid City*: Mental Health, Marilyn Monroe, and Sending Emails to Tom Hanks"

550 Ibid.

551 Thompson, "Wes Anderson on Why He Loves Making Shorts: They Set Him Free"

552 Greenwood, "Wes Anderson on His New Short, Screening Movies for His 'Little Club' of New York Filmmakers, and the Possibility of Directing for the Stage"

553 Zuckerman, "*The Wonderful Story of Henry Sugar:* Wes Anderson and Collaborators on the Cinematic Language of Roald Dahl"

554 Greenwood, "Wes Anderson on His New Short, Screening Movies for His 'Little Club' of New York Filmmakers, and the Possibility of Directing for the Stage"

555 "Interview with Kasia Walicka-Maimone and Robert Yeoman", The Next Best Picture Podcast

556 Zuckerman, "*The Wonderful Story of Henry Sugar:* Wes Anderson and Collaborators on the Cinematic Language of Roald Dahl"

557 Goldstein, "*Asteroid City*'s Rupert Friend: 'Maybe I've Got the Scars and the Bruises Now' to Play James Bond"

558 Greenwood, "Wes Anderson on His New Short, Screening Movies for His 'Little Club' of New York Filmmakers, and the Possibility of Directing for the Stage"

559 Zuckerman, "*The Wonderful Story of Henry Sugar:* Wes Anderson and Collaborators on the Cinematic Language of Roald Dahl"

560 Wise, "Wes Anderson Talks About Roald Dahl's *The Wonderful Story Of Henry Sugar*, Teases His Next Movie, And Claims: 'I Don't Have An Aesthetic'"

561 Felperin, "*The Wonderful Story of Henry Sugar* Review: Benedict Cumberbatch in Wes Anderson's Mini-Marvel of a Roald Dahl Adaptation"

562 Calnan, "Wes Anderson starts shooting *The Phoenician Scheme* in Germany"

563 Tenreyro, "Wes Anderson Shares Why He Was Unable to Accept His First-Ever Oscar in Person"

THE PHOENICIAN SCHEME

NOTES

564 Sims, David, 'Wes Anderson Lets the Real World Filter In', The Atlantic, 2025

565 Galuppo, Mia, 'Wes Anderson on *The Phoenician Scheme*,' His Cannes Party Bus and Why You Should Always See His Movies Twice, The Hollywood Reporter, 2025

566 Sims, David, 'Wes Anderson Lets the Real World Filter In',

567 Page, Thomas, 'Wes Anderson on the secrets and struggles behind his impeccably stylish men', CNN, 2025

568 Seth, Radhika, '*The Phoenician Scheme*'s Mia Threapleton On Crying During Her Standing Ovation And Mum Kate Winslet's Cannes Advice', British Vogue, 2025

569 Spilde, Coleman, 'With *The Phoenician Scheme*, Wes Anderson perfects his product to cold, shiny results', Salon, 2025

570 Wilkinson, Alissa '*The Phoenician Scheme* Review: Benicio Del Toro Plans to Save His Soul', The New York Times, 2025

571 Puchko, Kristy, 'Wes Anderson on the personal inspirations for 'The Phoenician Scheme'', Mashable, 2025

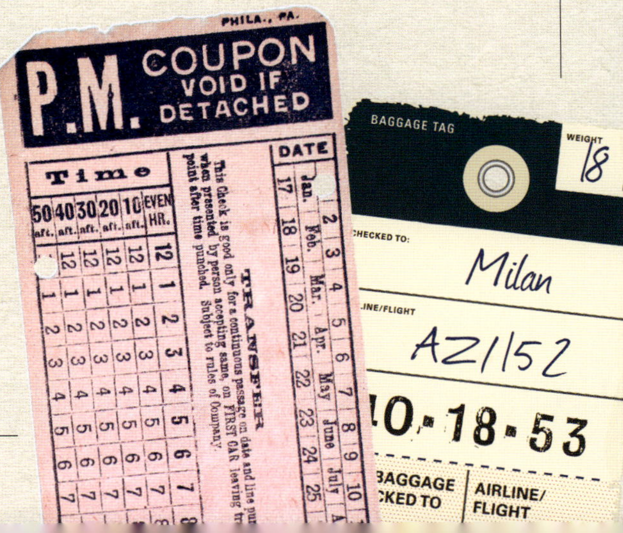

MAGAZZINI GENERA

SILOS E FRIGORIFERI

ACKNOWLEDGEMENTS

TO EVERYONE WHO HELPED ME SEE THAT THERE'S SOMETHING KIND OF FANTASTIC IN FEELING DIFFERENT.

PICTURE SOURCES

Courtesy of Alamy AJ Pics: 6–7, 14–15, 48, 50t, 59, 83b, 99, 137b; Album: 91, 114, 140b, 159, 174t, 178–179, 196–197, 200, 236-237; Associated Press: 102; BFA: 16t, 31, 65, 164; Cinematic: 19t, 26–27, 36t, 45b, 51, 112–113, 121t, 124b, 137t, 138, 140t, 143; Collection Christophel: 22t, 24–25, 35, 45t, 50b, 52, 71t, 76–77, 89, 132, 139, 142, 188–189, 202; Collection Christophel: 198–199; Entertainment Pictures: 56t, 64, 67, 72–73, 75, 80–81t, 84, 90, 101, 106t, 151, 185b, 209; Everett Collection Inc: 19b, 20, 21, 22b, 32, 37, 46t, 53, 54–55, 57, 68, 71b, 74, 78, 83t, 8–87, 93b, 96, 106b, 111b, 121b, 123, 124t, 145, 146–147, 148, 156b, 156t, 164, 171, 180–181, 185t, 187, 201b, 204; FlixPix: 201t, 206; Frank Tozier: 46–47; LANDMARK MEDIA: 128, 153, 154t; Lucy Williams: 234–235, Nathaniel Noir: 154b; Maximum Film: 9b, 16b, 36b, 62–63, 80b, 88b, 94–95, 105, 116, 117; Menno van der Haven: 214–215; Moviestore Collection Ltd: 49, 85, 150, 155, 158; PA Images: 100; Photo 12: 8, 12–13, 28–29, 30, 40–41, 56b, 69, 103t, 103b, 108, 111t, 127, 131, 135, 141, 172–173, 175, 186, 190, 192; PictureLux / The Hollywood Archive: 9t, 38–39; RGR Collection: 4, 33, 109; Rajiv Dasan: 160–161; TCD/Prod.DB: 88t, 92, 93t, 119, 122, 133, 162, 167b, 167t, 169, 170, 174b, 176–177, 182–183, 191t, 191b, 195, 203, 205; United Archives GmbH: 42–43, 60–61.
Courtesy of Getty Roberto Serra – Iguana Press / Contributor: 238–239; Pascal Le Segretain: 10–11.
Courtesy of Shutterstock Freepik2: 212, 216tl, 220tr, 221; Happie Hippie Chick: 213b, 216tr, 221, 227tl; Jim Pruitt: 210, 220tl, 227r, 228tr, 230l, 232, 233; Mosquito: 211, 218, 225, 230r, 233; Tony Prato: 222–223; revers: 213t, 217, 219, 226, 228tl, 229, 230l, 231.